PUBLICATIONS OF THE INSTITUTE OF THE

HISTORY OF MEDICINE

FIRST SERIES: MONOGRAPHS

VOLUME V

COTTON MATHER:

FIRST SIGNIFICANT FIGURE IN AMERICAN MEDICINE

COTTON MATHER
1663-1728 PELHAM(?)

COTTON MATHER

First Significant Figure in American Medicine

By

OTHO T. BEALL, JR.

AND

RICHARD H. SHRYOCK

THE JOHNS HOPKINS PRESS: BALTIMORE

Reprinted from Volume 63 of the *Proceedings
of the American Antiquarian Society*

Originally published, 1954
Second printing, 1968

PREFACE

THE first aim of this study is to present the Reverend Cotton Mather in a new dimension—as "the first significant figure in American medicine." But it is also hoped that this procedure will serve a larger purpose, that is, to provide a detailed case study of medical thought as can be observed in the English Colonies at the *beginning* of the eighteenth century. Although this pre-Enlightenment medicine was in many respects quite different from that pursued by the leading physicians of 1750 or 1800, the latter are usually viewed as the American pioneers in this field. This is analogous to the popular tendency to think of Georgian motifs in architecture as representing *the* colonial tradition, despite the record of medieval forms which characterized the preceding era.

In medicine, as well as in the arts, it is misleading to ignore in this manner the first century of national experience. No doubt, the existence of systematic medical thought prior to 1725 has been overlooked because of the scarcity and obscurity of the materials. It is for this very reason that Mather is so valuable a source; he provides an almost unique mass of evidence concerning early American medicine, with all its implications for the social and cultural history of the times.

It was originally intended to print, as an appendix, the entire text of Mather's chief medical work, "The Angel of Bethesda." Many chapters, however, such as those containing long lists of remedies, now seem meaningless. We are therefore including in the appendix only a number of chapters which are more significant in themselves or which illustrate much that is repeated in omitted sections. The text employed is that of Worthington Ford's transcript, which has been found, by comparison with the original manuscript in the American Antiquarian Society, to be entirely reliable.

We are much indebted to Dr. Clifford K. Shipton, Librarian of the American Antiquarian Society, for constant encouragement and for making available the manuscript and typescript of "The Angel." Professor Raymond P. Stearns supplied information on Mather's relations with the Royal Society; and Professor I. Bernard Cohen, Professor Thomas P. Haviland, Professor Owsei Temkin, and Miss Genevieve Miller made helpful suggestions during various stages of the work. We are further indebted to several institutions for aid and cooperation: to the American Antiquarian Society, the Massachusetts Historical Society, the Royal Society, and the British Museum. Extensive use was made of the libraries of the Johns Hopkins University and of the University of Pennsylvania. The American Philosophical Society, by extending a grant-in-aid, enabled us to collect much of the necessary material.

OTHO T. BEALL, JR.
RICHARD H. SHRYOCK

Baltimore, May, 1954.

TABLE OF CONTENTS

Chapter I

On the Rediscovery of Cotton Mather

FEW American leaders have so suffered at the hands of posterity as has the Reverend Cotton Mather. Although clearly a notable figure in his day, the Boston clergyman has long been commonly recalled—if remembered at all—as a pompous, reactionary theologian who spent his spare time in persecuting witches. Even the opinions of scholars, over much of the past hundred years, have been little less severe.

The explanation of all this is obvious enough. For several generations both Cotton Mather and his father Increase were venerated as Puritan saints,[1] but by the mid-nineteenth century the whole intellectual climate had so changed as to place the Mathers in a far less favorable perspective. In the course of the Upham-Poole controversy of the late 1860's, for example, Cotton's connection with the Salem witchcraft trials was critically re-examined, and the results were rather devastating for his reputation.[2] In due time, the Mathers became symbolic of the so-called Puritan theocracy—with its related "blue laws"—which was generally repudiated during this later era. They were also associated with outmoded beliefs in witchcraft and other occult phenomena, which implied that they were not only theocrats, but superstitious ones at that.

---

[1] Still highly laudatory was the biography of Cotton Mather by William B. O. Peabody, Boston, 1836, which was included in Jared Spark's *Library of American Biography*. Peabody's work was largely based on Samuel Mather's biography of 1729.

[2] A whole series of publications *re* the Mathers and Salem witchcraft appeared between 1866 and 1870, some of them apparently inspired by the publication of "The Mather Papers" by the Massachusetts Historical Society in 1868. See, *e.g.*, C. W. Upham, *Salem Witchcraft*, Boston, 1867; W. F. Poole, *The Mather Papers: Cotton Mather and Salem Witchcraft*, Boston, 1868, and his *Cotton Mather and Witchcraft: two Notices of Mr. Upham, his Reply*, Boston, 1870.

It happened, moreover, that Cotton Mather exhibited personal qualities which did not endear him to later readers any more than they had to certain of his contemporaries. One can hardly ignore his vanity, his instability, and his acerbity, or deny that he was at times self-seeking.[3] And it is easy to ridicule the more naïve or artificial passages in his diary. He had, on the other hand, his virtues—a discerning and versatile mind, extraordinary industry, and self-forgetfulness in the public service. Personal qualities, for better or for worse, are often beside the point in evaluations of a man's work, but in Mather's case certain weaknesses have entered into the unfavorable opinions held by latter-day historians. These can be sensed even in the adjectives applied to his name. Thus, in a scholarly work of 1930, the two Mathers are referred to as "smug ministers of God" and as "sour old men," while Cotton is declared, by the same author as late as 1946, to have been a "conscientious busybody" and "a pompous old theocrat."[4] Even the term "old" here seems to take on a certain opprobrium, although why the Mathers should be held responsible for their advanced years is not entirely clear. In view of the life-expectancy of the times, indeed, this might be viewed as something of an accomplishment.

In consequence of the general antipathy for Mather and all that he represented, a number of critics attacked certain aspects of his work well before the end of the nineteenth century. Moses Coit Tyler, in his pioneer *History of American Literature* (1878), elaborated on Mather's literary as well as his personal failings; while Oliver Wendell Holmes found his medicine absurd and spread this opinion in his widely circulated *Medical Essays* (1883).[5] Many of the professional

[3] Kenneth Murdock, "Cotton Mather," *Dict. of Amer. Biog.*, XII, 388.

[4] Herbert W. Schneider, *The Puritan Mind*, New York, 1930, pp. 92, 94; and *A History of American Philosophy*, New York, 1946, p. 37.

[5] Holmes' views will be discussed in Chapter V.

historians of the next generation held views which were no more favorable. Such able scholars as Jernegan, J. T. Adams, and Parrington envisaged Mather as a reactionary who defended the theocracy against a liberal, *truly*-American majority. And in due time such opinions, expressed chiefly in writings of the 1920's, seeped here and there into the college texts.[6] Thus Mather became what was then termed a "stereotype."

This devastating trend overlapped, however, with more favorable treatments. Mather had not been without defenders during the controversies of the late 1860's. In 1891 Barrett Wendell's biography gave a generally fair-minded account of his life and works; and in 1926 Kenneth Murdock called attention once more to Mather's religious, literary, and scientific achievements. Far from merely "ossifying" Calvinist theology, Mather had been among the first American thinkers to transcend it. Even his faults, Murdock suggested, were human in their way.[7] Within another decade, Perry Miller provided interpretations of Mather's place in New England theology;[8] while Germanic scholars made clear the influence exerted by German pietism on his religious outlook.[9] The growing scholarly interest in the man was well served, finally, by the appearance in 1940 of Thomas J. Holmes' thorough, three-volume *Bibliography* of Mather's writings.[10]

[6] See the citations in Clifford K. Shipton, "A Plea for Puritanism," *Amer. Hist. Rev.*, XL (April, 1935), 460 ff; and "The New England Clergy," Colonial Soc. Mass., *Publications*, XXXII (December, 1933), 24–54.

[7] *Selections from Cotton Mather*, New York, 1926, Introduction.

[8] See his *New England Mind*, New York, 1939; and "Note on the *Manuductio ad Ministerium*" in T. J. Holmes, *Cotton Mather: A Bibliography*, II, (Cambridge, Mass., 1940), 630 ff.

[9] Notably Kuno Francke, during the 1890's, and more recently Harold S. Jantz. See *e.g.*, Francke, "Further Documents Concerning Cotton Mather and August Hermann Francke," *Americana Germanica*, No. 4 (1897), I, 31–6.

[10] As cited above.

Meantime, in 1933, Clifford K. Shipton examined the unfavorable tradition concerning Mather's religious and political activities and found that this was contradicted at many points by the actual evidence. The clergyman had indeed tried to maintain much of the traditional religious outlook in provincial Massachusetts—though by no means all of it—and both he and his father had lamented what they viewed as a decline in public morals. But they had also called for religious toleration and had supported the new provincial charter of 1691 which is supposed to have wiped out the theocracy. Believing in witchcraft, as did most good people in their day, they had supported the Salem trials in principle. Cotton Mather had even written vividly on the dangers of the invisible world at large. But far from heading the persecutions, Cotton had urged moderation at the trials—cautiously, it is true, but at a time when most men feared to express any opposition whatever. And Increase led the clergy in formulating the protest which finally brought an end to the proceedings.[11]

It is ironic that leaders who upheld toleration have been recalled as intolerant and that those who urged a critical caution in dealing with witchcraft have been denounced as inciters of a popular mania against it.[12] It is equally ironic that men who represented the most advanced scientific interests in the English Colonies should still be recalled as superstitious or reactionary. Easily ignored or underestimated are such aspects of the Mather record as Increase's organization of the first scientific society in the Colonies and the rare honor accorded Cotton by membership in the Royal Society.

[11] Shipton, *op. cit.*

[12] Despite Shipton's analysis of 1933, some studies published more than a decade later continued to interpret the Mathers primarily as defenders of an obsolete and intolerant theocracy. See, *e.g.*, Schneider, *op cit.*; and R. E. Spiller and H. Blodgett, *The Roots of National Culture*, New York, 1949, p. 5.

Appreciation of the latter's scientific interests was doubt-less minimized by indifference to the history of science as such, as well as by antipathy to the man himself. Wendell, although not unsympathetic, made only a passing reference in a single footnote to Mather's chief medical work. During the last two decades, however, a growing concern with the history of science happens to have coincided with the revived awareness of Mather's merits in general. As a result of this "angelic conjunction"—as he himself might have put it—the Puritan leader's scientific activities have been recog-nized by a number of able scholars. I. B. Cohen, Horn-berger, Kilgour, Kittredge, Kraus, Morison, Murdock, Stearns, and Zirkle have made valuable contributions in this connection, especially in relation to astronomy and genetics, or in reference to the influence exerted by Mather's science upon his theology.[13]

Little attention, on the other hand, has been accorded to Mather's medicine since it was ridiculed by Holmes nearly a century ago. One biographer did answer Holmes by de-manding (1892) an historical perspective on the medical writings, but this seems to have made little impression at the time.[14] Most critics have mentioned Mather's part in the inoculation controversy as creditable but view this as an isolated episode rather than being related to his wide interests in medicine as a whole.[15] Such treatment is understandable in view of the circumstances. The man is thought of pri-

---

[13] See, among others, Theodore Hornberger, "The Date, the Source, and the Significance of Cotton Mather's Interest in Science," *Amer. Lit.*, VI (January, 1935), 413 ff; Conway Zirkle, *The Beginnings of Plant Hybridization*, Philadelphia, 1935, pp. 103 ff; Samuel E. Morison, *The Puritan Pronaos*, New York, 1936, pp. 246 ff; and Michael Kraus, *The Atlantic Civilization*, Ithaca, N. Y., 1949, *passim*.

[14] See Chapter V below.

[15] Thus Kraus, who gives an unusually careful analysis of this story, makes no mention of Mather in his general review of Colonial medicine, *op. cit.*, pp. 192 ff. The latter is like-wise omitted in the account of such medicine in Max Savelle, *Seeds of Liberty*, New York, 1948, pp. 118 ff.

marily as a clergyman; his medical observations are scattered widely through many works, and the most important one— "The Angel of Bethesda"—has never been published.

About a generation ago, Worthington C. Ford prepared a careful transcript of "The Angel," and he may have intended to edit and publish it. But the few others who examined this or the other medical writings seem to have found them dull or obscure at best. Some of the materials are indeed just that. But others are clear enough and display insight as well as learning. In any case, one could as well say of the contemporary theological writings that they are difficult for present readers. Yet we must go to these for an understanding of trends in religious thinking. By the same token, an examination of Mather's medical writing is pertinent to any comprehension of the medical thought of his time and place. This is all the more true because, in Mather, we have the only instance of systematic medical writing in this country prior to the national period.[16]

A study of Mather's medicine is also significant for an understanding of the man. Not that it reveals any hitherto unsuspected traits or attitudes. But now that his rôle as an amateur scientist has received some recognition, it should be made clear that his major concern in this field was always with medicine. As will be noted shortly, medicine was more than an avocation or "side line" for this clergyman. It was rather a second vocation, to which he at one time intended to devote himself primarily and to which he returned with renewed enthusiasm at various times throughout his career. "Physic" had for him, as for many others before and since, a dual attraction: it combined the intellectual lure of the natural sciences and the moral appeal of "doing good." There is no question that Mather saw in medicine an oppor-

[16] The closest parallel is probably the work of Cadwallader Colden of New York, but the authors know of no systematic writings of his which are comparable to "The Angel."

tunity—more immediate than in any other field—to apply science to the general welfare of mankind.

Critics who view Mather's public activities merely as those of "a conscientious busybody" should ponder, notably, the effectiveness with which he labored on behalf of the public health of Boston.[17] His efforts in this cause were not only courageous, but they actually ushered in the beginnings of modern preventive medicine. In this setting, he takes on a more heroic stature than do most of those medical men who are still subjects of professional veneration. Of this, more anon.

It seems best, in treating of Mather's medicine, to begin on a biographical note. Familiarity with the general story of his life will be assumed. But whence came his initial interest in this subject, what was the nature of medicine in his day, in what measure was he prepared to deal with it, and what means did he find for expressing his knowledge and his concern? Against the background implied in these questions, it will then be possible to proceed to an analysis and interpretation of his actual work in the field.

[17] Vernon L. Parrington recognized his courage in the inoculation episode, but proceeded nevertheless to condemn him generally for "intolerable meddlesomeness;" writing in *The Cambridge History of American Literature*, I (New York, 1933), 51.

Chapter II

MATHER'S APPROACH TO MEDICINE

Mather's earliest scientific interests seem to have been directed toward medicine. Writing in his autobiography "Paterna," in reference to the years when he was between the ages of eleven and fourteen, he declared that: "I composed Systems both of Logick, and Physick, in Catechisms of my own, which have since been used by many others."[1] That the study of medicine during his precocious youth was no passing enthusiasm is borne out by further remarks in "Paterna" concerning this same period. "I fell under the Power of Melancholy," he continues, "to such a Degree, that I exceedingly wonder it had no worse Effects upon me, and *studying Physick at the time*, I was unhappily led away with Fancies, that I was myself troubled, with almost every Distemper that I read of, in my Studies; which caused me to use Medicines upon myself, that I might cure my Imaginary maladies."[2]

This picture of hypochondria is what might be expected in an imaginative adolescent who had found access to medical literature. But more than curiosity and introspection were involved; a professional motivation also appeared. Although Mather had at first hoped to become a clergyman, he feared that an impediment of speech would unfit him for preaching, and his thoughts turned to the practice of medicine. As his son Samuel wrote many years later, Cotton "almost, for some Time, laid aside the tho'ts of being a Minister, and had with great application studied Physick."[3]

[1] "Paterna," (manuscript autobiography), p. 5.

[2] *Ibid.*, pp. 7, 8. Italics not in original.

[3] Samuel Mather, *The Life of the Very Reverend and Learned Cotton Mather*, Boston, 1729, p. 26.

All this occurred while he was a student at Harvard, 1674–78, as is made clear in "The Angel of Bethesda."[4] In some way, then, Mather prepared while in college both for the ministry and for medicine—a not inconsiderable achievement for a youth who graduated at the tender age of fourteen.

There is little likelihood that any of the formal instruction received at Harvard pertained to medicine. Physics, the basic scientific subject given, served as an introduction to "natural philosophy" in general,[5] but not until 1687 was there any substantial instruction in the subject, and only in 1727 did the teaching of Newtonian science triumph.[6] Mathematics likewise seems to have been neglected during Mather's undergraduate years, and there was of course no opportunity for him to do laboratory or field work.[7] There were, indeed, no facilities for scientific training in any of the English Colonies in that period. The nature of formal instruction, therefore, would seem to explain more about Mather's limitations than about his subsequent accomplishments as a man of science.

What preparation Mather made for a possible medical career must then have consisted almost entirely of reading. While a student, as well as in later years, Mather had access to the Harvard College Library, to that of his father, and perhaps also to other private collections.[8] Just what medical works were available to the young Mather at Harvard is uncertain, since the first catalogue was not issued until

---

[4] Chapter LI: "Ephphatha, or Some Advice to Stammerers."

[5] Theodore Hornberger, *Scientific Thought in the American Colleges, 1638–1800*, Austin, Texas, 1945, pp. 16 f, 39.

[6] Samuel E. Morison, *Harvard College in the Seventeenth Century*, I (Cambridge, Mass., 1936), 236.

[7] *Ibid.*, pp. 208 ff; Hornberger, *op. cit.*, pp. 24, 35.

[8] *E.g.*, that of Dr. Hoar, whose widow gave certain volumes from it to Increase Mather, after the latter had lost some by fire; Julius H. Tuttle, "The Libraries of the Mathers," *Amer. Antiquarian Soc., Proceedings*, XX (1910).

1723, but this shows a number of classical medical works such as those of Galen, in addition to well-known sixteenth and seventeenth century publications. Among the latter were, for example, the works of Plater, a Swiss, and of Sylvius, the Dutch authority, as well as of the Englishmen Harvey, Culpeper, and Willis.[9] Presumably, some if not all of these were available during Mather's student days. Also at hand were certain medical or general scientific works in Increase Mather's library, although these cannot now be listed separately from those which Cotton subsequently added to the family collections. The latter, then, did not lack opportunities for medical instruction in so far as this could be imparted by reading in standard works. And since he was extremely precocious and studious as a lad, he doubtless made the most of this opportunity.

It is easy in our day to ridicule, as did Osler, the medical student who secures only "book learning." Yet this had been the medieval tradition of professional instruction, and it still persisted in some medical faculties of 1700. Had Mather studied physic in seventeenth-century Padua, as did Harvey, he would have been given something more than this, but had he attended Oxford or Cambridge, he would only have "read medicine" much as he did at Harvard. That he might have taken an M.D. degree in England would have made little difference in the training, save that there might have been some faculty guidance for his literary efforts.[10] What advice, if any, did he actually secure?

The answer seems to be that he was largely self-directed in medicine, even as his fellow-townsman Franklin was in physics. Yet Mather's general interest in science was

[9] *Catalogus librorum Bibliothecae Collegi Harvardini quod est Cantabrigiae in Nova Anglia,* Boston, 1723.

[10] See Phyllis Allen (Richmond), "Medical Education in 17th Century England," *Jour. of the Hist. of Med. and Allied Sciences,* I (January, 1946), 115 ff.

probably encouraged by his father's concern with the same field. The two were unusually close in all things. In 1683, Increase formed a Philosophical Society in Boston for discussions—as Cotton later described them—"upon Improvements in Philosophy [science] and Additions to the Stores of Natural History." Cotton, who was then twenty years old, noted later that he was ". . . One that had a share in the Combination."[11] Participation in the discussions, even though these continued for only a short time, must have made an impression on the younger Mather. It is also reasonable to suppose that his father exerted some influence upon his reading. Such guidance was not to be disdained when one's father had been President of Harvard College.

Indeed, the entire intellectual tradition in which the Mathers moved and had their being was not to be disdained—and least of all in respect to science. Some have held, it is true, that English Puritans took no interest in science as this is now understood. "What we call natural science," declares one scholar, "was not so much something which the Puritans were afraid of . . . as it was something entirely irrelevant to their interests and problems." They valued science only "for its incidental contributions to . . . the glorification of God."[12]

Without doubt, there is much in the writings of the Mathers and of other Puritans which lends itself to this view. But there also is much which refutes it, the truth being that they were shifting from a teleologic to a naturalistic out-

---

[11] *Parentator: Memoirs of Remarkables in the Life and the Death of the Ever-Memorable Dr. Increase Mather*, Boston, 1724, p. 86. See also Kenneth B. Murdock, *Increase Mather, the Foremost American Puritan*, Cambridge, Mass., 1926, pp. 147 f. For details regarding the Boston Philosophical Society, see Otho Beall, "Cotton Mather's Early 'Curiosa Americana' and the Boston Philosophical Society of 1683," *William and Mary Quarterly*, 3rd ser., XVIII, No. 3 (July, 1961).

[12] Herbert W. Schneider, *The Puritan Mind* New York, 1930, pp. 42 ff.

look.[13]   Moreover, this growing interest in science as such was inherent in the Puritan philosophy.   Max Weber has called attention to the dynamic rôle which Christianity played in the development of medieval and modern science, and to the especially effective service of Calvinism—of "The Protestant Ethic"—in this connection.   The fact that Puritans originally cultivated science for the glory of God is incidental; the main point is that religion and science were viewed as harmonious, and that the one therefore gave an impetus to the other.   Merton and others have shown that the record bears this out; the scientific contributions of seventeenth-century Puritans exceeded those of any other European group.[14]

The Mathers, then, were immersed in the very tradition which did the most to encourage Western science during their era.   And one can picture the young Cotton Mather as absorbing this tradition from his father and from the circle of his father's friends in the Philosophical Society.   No doubt these associations did much to determine his attitude toward science as a whole.

Whether the Philosophical Society ever discussed medicine, in particular, is not clear.   Years later, Mather recalled certain medical reports which he attempted to prepare in his youth.   (One of these involved a case history which suggested to him that the seat of the soul might lie in the head, which seems reminiscent of Descartes.)[15]   But his reference to "youth" here could relate as well to his student days as to those in which he was meeting with his father's learned

---

[13] Evidence of this, in Cotton's writings, will be discussed in later chapters.

[14] Robert K. Merton, *Social Theory and Social Structure*, Glencoe, Ill., 1949, pp. 329 ff. See also Dorothy Stimson, "Puritanism and the New Philosophy in 17th Century England," *Bull. Inst. Hist. Med.* III (1935), 327 ff; George Rosen, "Left-Wing Puritanism and Science," *ibid.*, XV (1944), 375 ff; Jean Pelseneer, "L'Origine Protestante de la Science Moderne," *Lychnos* (Stockholm), 1946, 246 ff; Bernard Barber, *Science and the Social Order*, Glencoe, Ill., 1952, pp. 57 ff.

[15] Letter of November 24, 1712, to Dr. John Woodward, Royal Society.

friends. One only knows that he was already advanced in medical reading by the latter period. Whether he gave or received suggestions on the subject within the Philosophical Society is a matter of surmise.

It was about the time of the short-lived activities of this Society that Mather made up his mind about a future profession. His first choice was clearly the Church, medicine the second, and the decision turned upon whether or not he could overcome the stammering. He gave his first sermon in 1680—blending his dual interests, as it were, in preaching on "our blessed Saviour as the glorious Physician of Souls."[16] For two years thereafter he continued to pray for deliverance from his infirmity.[17] Finally, after he had followed wise counsel to enunciate slowly, the stammering was overcome,[18] and he was ordained in May, 1685. But not until the following February did he note in his diary that he had given up the prospect of becoming a physician.[19]

Once Mather was launched on a clerical career, his medical interests in a sense took second place. But he returned to them again and again and so integrated them with religious outlooks that it is difficult to separate the two domains. This is clear throughout his writings and in his public activities. He never entirely neglected the second vocation and, if anything, became more absorbed in it in his later years.

The most human medical entries in Mather's diary are those concerned with illness and death in his immediate family. Here he had ample material, since two of his wives

[16] Samuel Mather, *op. cit.*, p. 27.

[17] Worthington Ford (ed.), "Diary of Cotton Mather," Mass. Hist. Soc. *Collections*, series 7, VII, 2 f, 50 f., hereafter referred to as Diary.

[18] The most detailed and human account of this experience is that given in "The Angel," Chapter LI. Written in the third person, the reference is transparent enough. In noting the success of his cure, Mather remarks that he was later "employed in making of Speeches on the most public Occasions . . . more than any Person that ever was in the Countrey." Transcript, p. 389.

[19] Diary, I, 115.

died during his lifetime, and only two of his fifteen children survived him. Tragic as these deaths were for the husband and father, he usually took occasion to note the nature of the illness in each case.[20] These comments seem to reflect something of the instincts of a clinician. The same attitude is implicit in the medical comments inserted in historical and other general works, as will be noted in an ensuing chapter.

The diary contains no clear statement that the clergyman ever practiced medicine in the ordinary sense. Yet there are passages which imply that he occasionally prescribed for his friends and family—to say nothing of himself. Thus, he recommended to his aged father, in 1713, the "frequent use of the *Sal Volatile*," and resolved to keep him supplied with it as long as he lived.[21] He was inclined, moreover, to make professional recommendations to the physicians regarding favorite remedies or measures to protect the public health. In 1718, for example, he became concerned about the state of "some distracted persons," and urged practitioners to employ baths in the more difficult cases—a type of therapy still employed for mental illness. Whether the "doctors" viewed such actions as helpful or officious is not always clear. In issuing an anonymous pamphlet on measles in 1713, Mather seemed aware that it might not be welcomed and went to some trouble to secure professional approval.[22] But there were implications during the smallpox controversy, five years later, that his activities were resented as those of a layman.

For his part, Mather sought to keep in touch with physicians in Boston and to correspond with those abroad.

---

[20] *E.g., re* the deaths of his wives in 1702 and 1713, respectively, Diary, I, 449; II, 255.

[21] *Ibid.*, II, 224 f.

[22] *A Letter, About a Good Management under the Distemper of the Measles*, Boston, 1713, p. 4. On this rare pamphlet, see T. J. Holmes, *Cotton Mather, a Bibliography of his Works*, II (Cambridge, 1940), 523.

The care with which he consulted them on various occasions suggests some deference to a distinct profession. Indeed, he stated that the clergy engaged in medical practice chiefly because of the absence of regular practitioners,[23] and implied that his medical pamphlets were intended only to serve "the Poor, and such as may want the help of Able Physicians."[24]

At the same time, Mather felt that there was much to be said for a combination of clerical and medical functions. This was partly because, as will be mentioned later, he believed it was in the interest of religion as such. But he also implied that the clergy, as learned men, had served well as practitioners. He was proud of their records and re-called some of them in his *Magnalia*. Certain of these worthies had served primarily as physicians at one time and as clergymen at others. The Reverend John Rogers, to cite one instance, had first been a clergyman, then a practitioner, and finally president of Harvard.[25] The two rôles were thus interchangeable, and, as Mather viewed it, this was truly an "angelic conjunction."[26]

Mather was not unaware that science in general, including medicine, might disturb clerical orthodoxy. But he was confident that this could be avoided by a farsighted inter-pretation of Nature. He warned young clergymen on this point, writing in 1726: "That you be not, like some haughty, and short-sighted, and half-witted Smatterers in Philos-ophy, seduced into the Folly of doubting the Existence or Providence of a Glorious God, by a Study, which,

---

[23] In the *Magnalia Christi Americana* of 1702, I (Hartford, 1855), 493 f.

[24] Subtitle of the measles pamphlet noted above.

[25] *Magnalia*, I, 477 ff; II, 16.

[26] Mather analyzed the relationship of clergymen to medicine in his *Essays to do Good;* see, *e.g.*, the Boston edition of 1808, pp. 84 f. Here he not only advocated pastoral practice, but urged the urban clergy to "unite your counsels" with physicians on medical problems.

if well-persued, would Compel you to come in to a Strong Faith, wherewith you would give Glory to Him, on all Occasions."[27]

Clerical physicians rarely if ever trained apprentices in the medical art in this country, but on at least one occasion Mather took upon himself the rôle of medical educator. This was in 1711, when he decided to train his daughter Katy in "Knowledge in Physic, and the Preparation, and the Dispensation of noble Medicines.[28] Parenthetically, this desire to instruct a daughter illustrates his open-mindedness concerning the education of women in medicine. Perhaps it was Katy Mather, rather than the famed Elizabeth Blackwell of 1850, who was the first American of her sex to attempt a serious study of medicine.

In his later years, Mather became more and more concerned about the medical care of the poor. In so far as he cultivated medicine as a means of doing good, he was doubtless motivated by personal inclinations as well as by Christian tradition in general. More immediately, he was influenced by early German pietism, and he has been viewed as the American pioneer in this movement which was later so ably led by Whitefield and Wesley.[29] He knew something, through correspondence, of the medical activities of the pietistic group at Halle—a center which would later inspire other clerical practitioners.[30]

Viewing himself as the shepherd of his flock, Mather was ever concerned for their welfare. His early advocacy of

---

[27] *Manuductio ad Ministerium . . . Directions for a Candidate for the Ministry*, New York, 1938, p. 51.

[28] Diary, II, 112. See "The Angel," chapter (LXI Appendix), for Mather's general defense of women in medicine.

[28] See, *e.g.*, H. S. Jantz, "German Thought and Literature in New England, 1620–1820," *Jour. of Eng. and Ger. Phil.*, XLI (1942), 1–45.

[30] Notably, in this country, Henry M. Muhlenberg of Pennsylvania, whose practice presents some parallels with that of Mather.

temperance will be recalled in this connection.[31] He was, in consequence, more social-minded than were most of the physicians. In 1716 he wrote of "getting more Medicines into the Family, to be dispensed unto the Poor, for various Maladies,"[32] and the earlier reference to training Katy in the "Dispensation" of drugs may have had significance in this same connection. The free dispensary would not appear in English-speaking cities until later in the century, but Mather evidently had something of this sort in mind. Social conscience was also evident in his efforts to warn the public against certain epidemics, as in the publication of the pamphlet on measles in 1713. Such efforts culminated in his campaign against smallpox in 1721.

Mather was especially anxious to identify, collect, and dispense useful remedies. Although his therapy was broad enough to include such other procedures as the baths just mentioned, his concept of ordinary practice was that of giving medicines. English-speaking patients, then as later, shared this view and expected their doctors to give them bottles of something for every illness. Mather, as will be noted shortly, inherited a therapeutic tradition of bleeding and purging, but he placed no emphasis upon these "heroic" treatments. He was also aware that certain drugs were dangerous and were to be avoided or used only with restraint. At the worst, therefore, the practice he recommended was not apt to do much harm of a physical sort. One could hardly have said as much for most American physicians a century later.

In all such matters, Mather was invoking the use of medical science as it was then understood. This was, to be

---

[31] His interest in temperance, which has its medical implications, has been viewed quite seriously by historians. See John A. Krout, *The Origins of Prohibition*, New York, 1925, pp. 53 f.

[32] Diary, II, 372.

sure, only one aspect of the clergyman's approach. Science and art, in his view, derived their ultimate significance from religious values. Even disease itself could be fully understood only in theological terms. Hence at times, at least, he thought of medical practice as merely supplementary to religious healing.

The religious aspect of his medicine had best be considered in connection with the writings in which it appears. But no effort will be made here to review his theology as such. We are concerned with this only in so far as it influenced his medicine, and in any case his Calvinistic background—at least in its broader outlines—is still recalled today. It is quite otherwise with the second aspect of Mather's approach—with the scientific tradition in which he also moved and had his being. The medicine of 1700—naturalistic medicine—has been largely forgotten, and some effort is needed to recapture it. Before proceeding to any analysis of Mather's work in this area, therefore, it were well to recall the medical background of his age.

Chapter III

The Medical Background

The background of the seventeenth and early eighteenth centuries, against which Mather's medical works were written, was one of spectacular discoveries. Modern science is usually dated from this era. New vistas opened in medicine, as in other fields, and when the universities failed to pursue them novel institutions were founded for this purpose. The first scientific academies were established. The Royal Society of London was an outstanding example. This body provided a clearing house for scientific interests which was taken advantage of by foreigners and colonials as well as by English leaders. All Americans who were interested in science found its *Philosophical Transactions* of great value. Until well into the eighteenth century these reports, and those of one or two other European academies, constituted the only scientific journals which were available to colonial readers.[1]

This was the era of the controversy between "the ancients" and "the moderns" when the latter vigorously questioned the older scientific authorities and sought new knowledge by emphasizing a direct observation of natural phenomena. They also employed more frequently the methods of experiment and measurement and showed an increased awareness of the need for verification. Whatever the complex social and intellectual origins of these outlooks, they had infused an optimistic spirit of discovery into science by the mid-seventeenth century.

[1] Frederick E. Brasch, *The Royal Society of London and its Influence upon Scientific Thought in the American Colonies*, pp. 3-4, reprinted from the *Scientific Monthly*, October-November, 1931, XXXIII, 336-55, 448-69; a thorough handling of the subject of scientific societies is Martha Ornstein's *The Role of Scientific Societies in the Seventeenth Century*, Chicago, 1928.

The Reverend William Turner in 1697 summed up, from a layman's point of view, the scientific achievements of the age. In discussing "Improvements in Physick, and Experimental Philosophy &c.," he listed the chemical dissolution of natural bodies, the extracting of juices and oils, the transmutation of metals, the counterfeiting of precious stones, and the invention of such devices as the thermometer, the barometer, the "pneumatic engine," and the "hygroscope." The greatest improvements in physic were the "Anatomy of the Blood," the "Spagyrical Anatomy of Urin," and the transfusing of blood. Indeed, he remarked: "Humane Wit hath arriv'd in this last Age to so high a degree of Daring, that . . . they have laid open all the Secrets of Nature, and so dissected all the Bodies they have met with, and separated their parts with so strict and Chymical Anatomy, as to unravel the whole Texture, and dissolve all natural Bodies into their first Principles; and by that means have made such excellent Discoveries, as former Ages cannot Parallel, and future Times have scarce room left to be imployed in."[2]

One of the great concerns of the seventeenth century was to interpret the bearing of scientific discoveries upon traditional Christianity. There were two groups which most desired to reconcile religion with the new science, namely, the religious scientists and the scientifically-minded clergy. Robert Boyle was in the vanguard of the first of these in preparing *Some Considerations Touching the Usefulness of Experimental Philosophy* (1663), and John Ray in *The Wisdom of God Manifested in the Works of Creation* (1691) expanded Boyle's thesis. Dr. Nehemiah Grew, Fellow of the College of Physicians and also of the Royal Society, was perhaps the best known physician who wrote upon religion.

[2] William Turner, *A Compleat History of the Most Remarkable Providences*, London, 1697, Part III, "The Curiosities of Art," pp. 6–8; in this work both Increase and Cotton Mather are quoted.

His *Cosmologia Sacra* (1701) reconciled the concept of God with scientific findings and linked the divine to medical matters through his hypothesis of a vital principle closely related to the soul.[3] All of these authors were convinced that natural phenomena demonstrated God's handiwork.

Just as the physician could write on religion, so a clergyman could write with some authority on medicine or other aspects of science. Moreover the clergy concurred in the views of scientists. The Reverend William Derham's *Physicotheology: or a Demonstration of the Being and Attributes of God from His Works of Creation* (1701) was one of the first clerical productions in English which welcomed novel scientific discoveries as manifestations of the divine. Cotton Mather and others soon produced works of a similar nature.[4]

Clerical writers on science rarely focused particularly on medicine, except when—as in the case of Mather, and later of Wesley—local circumstances seemed to call especially for clerical attention. When a clergyman did write on medicine, he was naturally apt to follow a religious approach. But it should be emphasized that such an approach was also employed by some outstanding physicians of the sixteenth and seventeenth centuries. It is a truism that religion and medicine had been closely interwoven in many if not all early cultures and that the same associations had been maintained in the Jewish-Christian tradition. In this latter context, illness as well as other misfortunes had been viewed as punishment—either for original sin, or for the particular sins of individuals or groups. In some cases, likewise, illness was believed to result from the operation of Satan or his minions.[5]

---

[3] *Cosmologia Sacra: or a Discourse of the Universe As it is the Creature and Kingdom of God*, London, 1701.

[4] Max Savelle views this harmonizing of science and religion as a "naïve Puritan" procedure on Mather's part; *Seeds of Liberty*, New York, 1948, p. 90. *Cf.* comments on Puritanism and science in preceding chapter of this study.

[5] Wolf von Siebenthal, *Krankheit als Folger der Sünde*, Hannover, 1950, pp. 42 ff.

Although religious principles might at times conflict with secular approaches to medicine,[6] what often happened was that the two were maintained simultaneously—just as in some primitive societies, the "medicine man" may employ both magical and naturalistic remedies.[7] It is therefore not surprising to find that the English physician Robert Fludd (1574–1637) held that disease resulted from original sin and that it was visited directly upon mankind by the fallen angels.[8]

Of more interest here was van Helmont of Brussels (1577–1644), an outstanding medical authority who was also distinguished as a chemist. Van Helmont had originally been a friar, and he apparently carried over—much as Mather did later—religious outlooks into the medical field. On the relation of disease to sin, the Belgian physician declared rather bluntly that: "*Alle Übel und Krankheiten dieser Welt rühren . . . in letzter Instanz . . . vom Apfelbiss und Evas Fall.*"[9] All this was part of Mather's medical, as well as of his religious background.

The seventeenth century, by its own standards, was an age of reason; yet from the present viewpoint it was still a credulous period. These two attitudes, as we now conceive them, seemed in no wise incompatible, since no clear distinctions between the natural, the supernatural, and the occult had yet been devised. Joseph Glanville, a devotee of natural philosophy, prepared a work on witchcraft; while no less a scientific figure than Robert Boyle believed in the intervention of good and bad angels in man's destiny.

---

[6] This conflict still occurs in special cases; see R. H. Shryock, "Freedom and Interference in Medicine," *Annals of the Amer. Acad. Polit. and Soc. Science*, CC (November, 1938), 32 ff.

[7] *Cf.* Bernard Barber, *Science and the Social Order*, Glencoe, Ill., 1952, p. 10.

[8] Siebenthal, *op. cit.*, pp. 57 f.

[9] *Ibid.*, p. 58; and Walter Pagel, *Jo. Bapt. van Helmont*, Berlin, 1930, p. 101.

This juxtaposition of medieval and modern outlooks was natural enough in an era of transition. It permeated medical as well as other phases of scientific thought. The supernatural or the occult still held a respectable position in medicine during the later seventeenth century, as is evidenced by the publication of serious works on medical astrology in the 1680's. Later historians, emphasizing only the "forward-looking" aspects of the science of the times, have distorted the picture. We are rarely reminded, for example, that William Harvey—having demonstrated the circulation of the blood in a quite modern manner—thereupon concluded that the origin of the heart's motion lay "in innate heat, which was ascribed to the soul or spirit of the blood; and this in turn was described as 'identical with the essence of the stars.' "[10]

It remains true, nevertheless, that serious efforts were made during the seventeenth century to provide medicine with what now would be termed a scientific basis. There is no need to review here the achievements in anatomy and physiology which antedated 1700. In the latter field, the same experimental and quantitative methods which were used in physics were employed effectively in the study of the human body, and for a time it seemed that medical would advance side by side with the physical sciences. Subsequently, however, medicine seemed to falter and then fall behind. Within Mather's lifetime, for example, Cadwallader Colden of New York observed that "physic" was lagging in the rear of astronomy.[11] This lag resulted from a number of circumstances—from social inhibitions on medical research as well as from the innate complexity of biological phenomena.

[10] Thomas C. Allbutt, *Science and Medieval Thought*, London, 1901, pp. 44 f.

[11] E. B. Greene and R. B. Morris, *Guide to the Principal Sources for Early American History in the City of New York*, New York, 1929, p. 323.

More particularly, the discoveries in anatomy and physiology were of potential value for future medicine but of small use to the medical practice of the times. So far as most physicians were concerned, anatomic or physiological studies represented only abstract biological research which had little bearing on "physic." The latter field, after all, pertained to the problem of illness, and most practitioners focused on this "practical" area. The English clinician Sydenham, who rather disdained laboratory studies, held that medical investigations should begin and end at the bedside, and on the nature of illness he had some illuminating things to say which will be noted shortly.

Scientific enthusiasm did inspire some physicians to attempt new syntheses in medicine. Could not this art also become a science in terms of God's (or Nature's) laws, even as had astronomy and dynamics? If so, the new science must face squarely its major problem—the nature of illness and related means for its prevention or cure. Perhaps hints could be found in the physical sciences? Chemistry suggested that the body might be made up of many compounds and that disease might result from chemical maladjustments—to be treated, then, by such chemical remedies as acids and alkalies. An opposing school, however, was more impressed by dynamics and sought to apply mechanical principles to the problems of life. This approach, inspired by Descartes and his concept of the animal machine, implied that disease was caused by the malfunctioning of the mechanical parts. Was not the heart a pump and the stomach a sort of churn? All the secrets of the body could be solved by mathematical means.[12] Mather's thought inclined to this view.

One can now see that there were valid elements in both the iatrochemical and the iatromechanical perspectives, but, at

[12] R. H. Shryock, *The Development of Modern Medicine*, New York, 1947, pp. 11 ff.

the time, neither could be verified or put to any great use. The immediate impact of the physical sciences on medicine resulted, therefore, in considerable confusion. The great majority of physicians continued, under the circumstances, to conceive disease in terms of the traditional Greek pathology. It followed that classical authorities—although sharply criticized at times—were usually still viewed with considerable respect. Illness was ascribed to imbalance or impurities in the four major fluids or humors, from which was deduced a need for ridding the body of such humors by various means. Bleeding, purging, sweating, and the like were practiced in varying degrees, and would be so practiced for more than a century after Mather's time. Such was the "rational" content of medicine as late as the 1700's.

One promising advance in medical thinking, however, had appeared by Mather's day, namely, the revival of the concept of disease specificity. From Galen's time until about 1550, nearly all medical men had thought of different patterns of illness as merely variations in "the general state of the system." It made little difference what names were given to these patterns, since the physician treated general states rather than particular diseases. He dealt with a biliousness or a fever, rather than with cases of malaria or typhoid. During the Renaissance, however, a few medical thinkers—notably Paracelsus—revived a second Greek tradition, that is, that there were distinct diseases, each with its own causes and cures. This view was advanced more effectively during the seventeenth century, as when Sydenham declared that diseases were as specific and as real as were species of plants or animals. This being so, an inviting panorama of future research opened up before medicine; the specific diseases must be identified in Nature and diagnosed in individuals, to the end that their specific causes and remedies could then also be found. Only when this basic taxonomy of medicine had been worked out could the aid of the physical sciences be effectively employed.[13]

This way proved long and hard, but it held all the promise of the future. It was by no means easy to set up and implement criteria for disease identification. Meantime, the physicians of 1700 or 1750 thought sometimes in terms of a generalized pathology, sometimes in those of particular diseases, and they strove somehow to reconcile all this with their notions of underlying, humoral conditions. Here, again, Mather was typical. He accepted the humoral pathology; but leaned at times on mechanical concepts. He was all for applying mathematics to the study of the body and its illnesses, but was actually able to do this in only one instance. Yet he sometimes displayed a vague awareness of specificity and was interested in finding remedies pertaining to each particular disease.

Traditional therapy, of course, had long involved the use of many drugs, as well as of the depletion procedures noted. Pharmacopeias had been printed by Mather's time and included a little sense in a great mass of nonsense. The supposed value of drugs was justified, in some measure, by reference to the prevailing humoral pathology; that is, some of them were supposed to purify the humors or restore their balance by unknown means. Others represented the response to the newer chemistry. But the majority of remedies had probably had an empirical origin: they reflected the age-old willingness to try anything which came to hand. The cumulative result of such efforts over the centuries, unchecked by objective tests for efficacy, was awe-inspiring but largely useless. Only two specific drugs were known in 1700, cinchona bark against malaria and mercury against syphilis, and the latter—as Mather well knew—was so dangerous as to be of dubious value.

[13] *Ibid.*, pp. 14 f.; Shryock, "The Interplay of Social and Internal Factors in the History of Modern Medicine," *Scientific Monthly*, LXXVI (April, 1953), 224 ff.

The use of certain remedies was based on a theory of repellency, which in turn implied the presence of occult factors in illness. In cases in which sickness was ascribed to the presence of a demon or other occult influences, it seems to have been assumed that drugs could drive these out just to the extent that the materials were repulsive in nature. The use of such substances as toads, vermin, and human excreta was common practice, and in this respect, as usual, Mather's recommendations were simply typical of the times. Oliver Wendell Holmes, who was later so outraged by Mather's repulsive remedies, himself traced their continued employment by the English profession well beyond the middle of the eighteenth century.[14]

Such was the nature of the medical heritage when Mather composed "The Angel" in 1724. Possessed of the background of the late seventeenth century, he inherited a zeal for scientific discoveries, and for the reconciliation of these findings with traditional religious and occult doctrines. He also inherited Greek pathology, which was to be combined somehow with the latest notions in physics and chemistry. In a time when pathological and therapeutic theories could be neither verified nor refuted, he was able to indulge a bent for speculation whenever this seemed to be in order. If this combination of circumstances now appears incongruous, it was nevertheless to be expected. Though living on the edge of an American wilderness, Mather nevertheless reflected in large measure the outlook of contemporary European medicine.

This is not to say that the American environment had no influence on the New England clergyman. So far as medicine was concerned, the first circumstance to be recalled here was the scarcity of trained physicians in America

---

[14] "Dr. Holmes on Dr. Stafford's Receipts," Mass. Hist. Soc., *Proceedings*, V, 384 ff.

until well after Mather's time. In all the English Colonies there was no professional focus for medicine. Not only was there no licensing authority, no medical school, no permanent scientific society, and no general hospital, but the printed literature of medicine remained so meager as to suggest that there was little interest in the dissemination of medical knowledge.

The low state of medical culture in the English Colonies was all the more unfortunate because of the seriousness of the disease problem. Much has been written about widespread sickness and the high death rates of the early settlements. Mather himself wrote of devastating epidemics among the Indians, which he viewed with an equanimity bordering on modern "racism,"[15] but he was less happy about the morbidity of later Colonial times. Endemic illness—the fevers, fluxes, consumptions, and scurvy—accounted for most of the high death rate and low life expectancy. But, as always, it was the epidemics that terrified and led to demands for action. The Colonies suffered from outbreaks of scarlet fever, diphtheria, influenza, and yellow fever, but it was the smallpox which was feared above all.[16]

These threats were sometimes met by the authorities in terms of such simple public health measures as were indicated by the medical theory of the era. There were quarantine and isolation measures, and also some sporadic efforts at sanitary control which reflected the classic theory

[15] As in his famous (or infamous) statement that "the woods were almost cleared of those pernicious creatures, to make room for a better growth," *Magnalia Christi Americana*, I, (Hartford, 1855, original ed. 1702), 51.

[16] Materials on the history of disease in the English American Colonies are found in several of the state medical histories; *e.g.*, in S. A. Green, *History of Medicine in Massachusetts*, Boston, 1881; as well as in the writings of Carl Bridenbaugh and of Francis R. Packard. Especially careful studies of epidemics have been made by Ernest Caulfield, as in his "Pursuit of a Pestilence," Amer. Antiquarian Soc. *Proceedings*, LX (April, 1950), 21 ff. A general history of Colonial epidemics by John Duffy has been published by the Louisiana State University Press, 1953.

of "airs and waters."[17] But the main resource of society against the terrifying specter of disease was the medical profession.

In the absence of medical schools, most Colonial physicians were trained simply by apprenticeship. Interest in improving the standards of the profession was beginning to appear by 1720, but at that time only one of the Boston guild had completed formal training abroad.[18] Hence the distinction between those who were generally viewed as physicians and others who cared to practice medicine was still a rather subtle one. Actually, such practice was followed by two special groups who were often better informed than were the "doctors," that is, by prominent officials and the clergy. The Winthrop family of New England well illustrates the first of these types, and there were many clergymen who represented the second, especially those who lived in rural areas.[19]

Certain clergymen had served, at times, primarily as physicians, and this procedure may be termed clerical practice in the strict sense. It was probably more common, however, for ministers to follow a sort of "pastoral practice," that is, their medical advice was incidental to pastoral care. Such guidance was more apt to be given if no satisfactory physicians were available. That practice of this sort persisted long after Mather's time is illustrated by the career

---

[17] On early Boston regulations concerning isolation and also sanitation, see Carl Bridenbaugh, *Cities in the Wilderness*, New York, 1938, pp. 85, 238, 398 ff; John Blake, "The Medical Profession and Public Health in Colonial Boston," *Bull. of the Hist. of Med.*, XXVI (May, 1952), 218 f.

[18] See Bridenbaugh, *op. cit.*, p. 402; Blake, *op. cit.*, pp. 222 ff.

[19] On the early practitioners of the province and their training, see Henry R. Viets, *A Brief History of Medicine in Massachusetts*, Boston, 1930, pp. 42 ff; also his article on the same theme in *Isis*, XXIII (September, 1935), 390 f. On the general theme of theologians and medicine, see Paul Diepgen, "Theologie u. Heilkunde: Von theologisierenden Medizinern u. medizinierenden Theologen," *Pro Medico*, XXII (January, 1953).

of the Reverend Jared Eliot of Guilford, Connecticut, who flourished until 1763.[20]

Mather's activities, as has been implied, did not fit entirely into either of the patterns noted. Like the pastoral practitioners, he was not primarily a physician, and his advice was usually incidental to the general welfare of family or parishioners. As far as is known, he never accepted medical fees, and he often advised that physicians be consulted. On the other hand, unlike most pastors, he had acquired a really professional knowledge of medicine, and he advised his community about health problems, despite the constant presence therein of physicians of the usual type.[21] No doubt, the fact that the populace was accustomed to receiving medical care from clergymen made Mather's incursions into this field less surprising than they might otherwise have seemed.

The medical activities of Colonial ministers have been interpreted as a reversion, under similarly primitive surroundings, to the type of service rendered by priests in early medieval centuries. If so, later American medicine can be viewed as recapitulating in a short time the professional stages through which European medicine had passed over the centuries.[22] That both clerical and pastoral practice in the Colonies resulted from a lack of well-qualified physicians seems undeniable, as Mather himself pointed out. But similar conditions also obtained in parts of England in this same era, where the Reverend John Wesley would later prepare a medical manual for the use of his itinerant

[20] Indeed, the great-grandfather of one of the authors, a Congregational minister in this same town, collaborated with a physician in preparing a family medical manual as late as c. 1860.

[21] The closest analogy to Mather, in this connection, was the Reverend Henry M. Muhlenberg of Pennsylvania (1711–1787). He, like Mather, was learned in medicine, but his practice was essentially parochial in nature. See MS. study by the Reverend Wallace E. Fisher, "Henry M. Muhlenberg's Knowledge and Practice of Medicine," Gettysburg, Pa., 1949.

[22] See Henry E. Sigerist, *Amerika u. die Medizin*, Leipzig, 1933, pp. 53 f.

preachers.[23] Hence the relation of American circumstances to those of the English was in some degree one of parallelism rather than of recapitulation.

The elements which entered into actual medical care in the Colonies were probably much the same, whether the practitioners were physicians, magistrates, or clergymen. No doubt the latter two groups emphasized traditional learning, while the apprentice-trained physicians depended more generally on empirical experience. Holmes later held that the physicians escaped all the "fopperies" of medical learning by depending entirely on the direct observation of Nature, but he submitted no evidence for this.[24] As a matter of fact, the procedures employed by physicians as well as by others—such as bleeding, sweating, and the like—were derived from ancient humoral theories, whether the physicians knew it or not. And all practitioners were familiar in some degree with folk medicine and with the traditional pharmacopeia.

The extent of early Colonial knowledge of rational medicine has not been fully investigated, but the evidence suggests that contemporary European theories were known in Boston throughout the seventeenth century. The transit of culture in this respect was probably a rapid one. Medical works were included, for example, in the extensive library brought over by John Winthrop, Jr., as early as 1631. Winthrop accepted the iatrochemical theory of practice, and his pharmacopeia was largely a chemical one. His chief remedies were nitre and antimony, though he also used biologicals such as human excreta, and even the occult powers of a unicorn's horn.[25] Other early New England practitioners

[23] *Primitive Physick* (London, 1747). It has even been claimed that Wesley inaugurated a major health movement. See George Newman, *Health and Social Evolution*, London, 1931, pp. 61 f. Wesley's work was widely reprinted in America during the eighteenth century.

[24] O. W. Holmes, *Medical Essays*, Boston, 1883, pp. 358, 363.

[25] C. A. Browne, "Scientific Notes from the books and letters of John Winthrop, Jr., 1606–1676," *Isis*, XI (1928), 325.

maintained the Galenic tradition of botanical remedies, in opposition to the chemical—a contrast which reflected the European controversies of the time.[26]

The only new note in Colonial practice was the use of native remedies taken over from Indian folklore. Thus John Josselyn, in his *New Englands Rarities Discovered* (1672), recorded Indian cures accomplished by the use of bear's grease for aches and of the use of a plant called dog-stone as an emetic.[27] Winthrop the Younger and Cotton Mather himself also reported on Indian medicines. None of those observed in New England proved to have such value as did the cinchona bark which Spanish colonists encountered in Peru. But the very heed given by all colonists to Indian practices suggests the confused and ineffective nature of European medicine itself prior to about 1800.

Despite their traditional learning, the Colonials were willing to try all things on empirical grounds. This was true not only of Indian remedies but of anything else that their own ingenuity could suggest. Who could be sure that some hitherto untried drug or some unusual procedure, however bizarre, might not prove to have almost magical power?

Cotton Mather was actually more critical of such expedients than were some of the physicians, as when he declared that the swallowing of bullets to cure "the Twisting of the Guts" was altogether too dangerous a device.[28] Mather's practice, nevertheless, included a wide variety of drugs and procedures, some of which seem bizarre or repulsive today. Leaning to the iatrophysical rather than to the iatrochemical

---

[26] See, *e.g.*, "John Dunton's Letters from New-England," *Publications of the Prince Society*, IV (Boston, 1867), 96. The Galenic tradition lived on in popular American medicine to influence a major nineteenth century medical sect—the Thomsonian or "botanic system." To this day, indeed, some proprietary remedies appeal on the ground that they contain "only vegetable compounds."

[27] See W. M. Smallwood, *Natural History and the American Mind*, New York, 1941, p. 96.

[28] Mather to Dr. John Woodward, Sept. 28, 1724, Royal Society.

theory, he did not emphasize chemical drugs as much as had Winthrop, but he advised the use of some, and also recommended both botanical and biological remedies in a quite eclectic fashion.

From the date of the first medical imprint in America in 1677 down to 1724, the year of Mather's completion of the "Angel of Bethesda," published medical works by Americans were limited to a few pamphlets.[29] The earliest was Thacher's well-known *Brief Rule to Guide the Common People of New England how to Order Themselves and theirs in the Small Pocks or Measels*. This, a mere broadside, was an extract from the writings of Sydenham. Cadwallader Colden's "Account of the Climate and Diseases of New York," written about 1720 but not published until 1811, was a six-page document which gave more attention to the climate than to medicine proper.[30] The only other publication of a primarily medical nature, prior to 1721, seems to have been Mather's own pamphlet of 1713 on measles. During 1721 and 1722, Mather published in Boston and in London some seven items dealing with smallpox inoculation. Other medical titles appeared in connection with the inoculation controversy. Then in 1724 Mather completed "The Angel," the first general treatise on medicine to be prepared in the English Colonies.

Mather's position in Colonial medicine becomes clearer with a consideration both of the number and scope of his medical writings. In these terms, there was no parallel figure among American contemporaries.

---

[29] Winthrop Tilley, "The Literature of Natural and Physical Science in the American Colonies from the Beginnings to 1765," unpublished doctoral thesis, Brown University (1933). The first full-length medical treatise to be published in the Colonies appeared in 1708, a reprint of an English work, Nicholas Culpeper's *The English Physician;* see Francis R. Packard, *History of Medicine in the United States*, New York, 1931, I, 491.

[30] *American Medical and Philosophical Register*, I, 304–10.

Chapter IV

MATHER'S MEDICINE IN NON-MEDICAL WORKS

Throughout most of his life, as has been noted, Mather continued to read the European medical literature. And, being the man he was, his writing in this field was as persistent as his reading. Medical themes can be followed more consistently throughout his published works than can any other scientific interest. There were of course ups and downs in his concern for the healing art. One high point, for example, coincided with his election to the Royal Society in 1713; another was reached in 1720, when he began to compose "The Angel" and then plunged into the smallpox controversy. Apparent trends in his medical thinking can be correlated in some degree with these later periods in his career.[1]

Generally speaking, however, basic ideas and attitudes appeared early in Mather's thinking and kept reappearing thereafter.[2] Certain viewpoints were emphasized in some writings more than in others, however, so that the simplest scheme of analysis will be to consider these works in turn. In the present chapter we shall note the occasional medical materials which appeared in sermons and in such other writings as the *Magnalia*, the "Curiosa Americana," and *The Christian Philosopher*. Attention can then be focused in the next chapter on "The Angel of Bethesda" as the one full-scale medical work. This procedure involves some danger of repetition, for Mather was a repetitious person, but the attempt will be made to keep this at a minimum.

[1] One instance has been noted; *i.e.*, an apparently increasing concern about medical welfare and public health.

[2] Hornberger points this out even in relation to his nascent deism, which he traces back to the early 1690's; *op. cit.*, p. 419.

As might be expected in a man who was both a "Christian philosopher" and a medical one, Mather drew no sharp line between the two. His Christian teachings were full of medical metaphors, and his medical thought involved essentially religious elements. The figurative use of medical concepts was common in his sermons. In more than one of these, he referred to Christ as the "great" or "glorious" physician. But his figures could be more striking and specific than this. In a sermon of 1700, for example, he declared that every sinner has many diseases: "He has the Palsey of an unsteady Mind; He has the Feavour of Unchastity . . . He has the Cancer of Envy; He has the Tympany of Pride," and so on. Warming up to the theme, he informed his hearers that they were but "a Congregation of Sick Souls: Where am I preaching, Sirs, but in an Hospital?"

This same sermon presented the doctrine that disease came into the world through original sin. It derived, like other types of evil, from Adam's fall and therefore served as one of God's means for chastening a wicked people. Sickness was inflicted not only upon mankind as a whole, but for good reason upon individual sinners. Yet Mather held, for reasons to be noted later, that illness could be relieved by prayers for divine intercession and forgiveness.[3] And this being the case, who could better guide the sufferer in the proper way than his pastor?

It is difficult to judge the results which Mather secured when he attempted religious healing. One may assume that many sick parishioners as well as afflicted members of his family received such ministrations. Since the first stage of the procedure was to convince the patient of innate depravity, the clergyman may sometimes have aroused terror rather than hope in his hearers. His bedside manner was

[3] *The Great Physician, Inviting Them that are Sensible of their Internal Maladies To Repair Unto Him for His Heavenly Remedies*, Boston, 1700, pp. 9 f, 26.

probably impressive but not always encouraging. Certainly, his method was in sharp contrast to that of the modern psychiatrist, who attempts at once to put the patient at ease.

At this point, indeed, one becomes aware of what may be a serious objection to the combination of medical and clerical rôles. Mather not only employed religion as a means for healing the sick, but also consciously reversed this by utilizing sickness as a means for promoting religion.[4] Thus, in such a sermon as *Elizabeth in Her Holy Retirement*,[5] he enlarged on the terrors of childbirth in the hope of arousing the piety of the victim. If he frightened the patient by such a procedure, the results could hardly have been fortunate from the medical view. There is no doubting his sincerity in the matter, but it would now seem that he was working at cross purposes.

Yet there may have been times when Mather served his parishioners well. The latter, accepting his theological premises, were in a frame of mind which is difficult to recapture today. No statements of patients' impressions seem to be available—a lack common in most medical history, where only the doctors' words usually survive. But it should be noted that, once the patient was in the proper frame of mind, Mather sought to establish an emotional state which was conducive to recovery. Perhaps some of those whom Mather saw were left with the hope of forgiveness and of divine intercession.[6] If and when sweetness and light so replaced the sense of doom, the experience was not to be disdained even from a purely psychosomatic view-

---

[4] In the *Magnalia*, I, 493 f, he declares that the clergy can serve the souls of their people the better for having also tended their bodies.

[5] Boston, 1710.

[6] Note, *e.g.*, his sermon: *The Cure of Sorrow. An Essay Directing Persons under Sadness, what Course to take that they may be no more Sad*, Boston, 1709. Here it is noted that physicians have labored without avail to find a universal medicine, but that the author has found this in prayer!

point.[7]   It is hardly necessary to add that an appreciation of religious healing has been revived—in the Emanuel movement as well as in Christian Science—during the present century.

When one proceeds from Mather's sermons to a consideration of his historical works, the *Magnalia* of 1702 is the most significant for medical as well as for other themes.   Parrington, who viewed its author with much disdain, conceded that this work had "some vitality still," and felt that it contained much material about early Massachusetts which "we should not willingly lose."[8]

In the *Magnalia*, as in the diary, Mather frequently inserted medical comments on the last illnesses of those who crossed his pages.   Such details are given in a number of the included biographies, and these usually express the tradition of a humoral pathology.   In speaking of his brother Nathaniel, Cotton observes that he was of a weak constitution and that this fostered the "congregation" of ill humors at the point where "the *os ileon* and the *os sacrum* join." In time the humors formed a tumor, an operation failed to counteract the circulation of the "putrid juices," and the latter finally brought on a fever from which he died.[9]   Note that Mather here is thinking only in terms of a generalized pathology and, like most medical contemporaries, has no interest in seeking a diagnosis of any particular disease. Nor shall we attempt one for him.

---

[7] There are various other sermons which use medical terms figuratively, ascribe illness to original sin, and utilize sickness to inculcate piety; *e.g.*, *Warnings from the Dead. Or Solemn Admonitions Unto All People*, Boston, 1693, pp. 2–22; *Seasonable Thoughts upon Mortality*, Boston, 1712, p. 9; *A Perfect Recovery. The Voice of the Glorious God, unto Persons, whom his Mercy has Recovered from Sickness*, Boston, 1714, pp. 8, 11, etc.

[8] Writing in *The Cambridge History of American Literature*, I (New York, 1933), 51. Only comments on the style of the *Magnalia* occur in Robert E. Spiller, *et al.* (editors), *Literary History of the United States*, I (New York, 1948), 59 f.

[9] *Magnalia*, II, 175.

Occasionally, however, an effort was made to be a little more specific—even though the illness involved was not one of the few well-recognized entities like smallpox. In the biography of Nathaniel Rogers, for example, it is said that this worthy suffered from the spitting of blood and that as a young man he was also affected by the *Flatus Hypocondriacus*. (Just what this picturesque affliction was is not clear, but Mather apparently thought it real enough to deserve a name.) Although Mr. Rogers deemed himself a dying man, he survived—only to perish later as a victim of his own virtues. His final illness was that of a "flood of rheum, occasioned partly by his disuse of tobacco."[10]

In the *Magnalia*, as well as in other works, Mather elaborated upon the doctrine of divine providence, that is, of God's intervention in man's affairs, especially through such dramatic occurrences as storms, earthquakes, sickness, and outstanding deliverances.[11] Logically similar was the belief in diabolic intervention in the forms of "possessions" and witchcraft. These doctrines had always been inherent in Christian theology and do not concern us in themselves. But Mather's preoccupation with them is pertinent here in several respects.

In the first place, some of the illustrations of providence which he cites were medical in nature—instances of miraculous recoveries. Thus Abigail Eliot lost part of her brains in an accident. Those which remained swelled thereafter according to the tides! Yet, with the insertion of a silver plate in her head—an interesting surgical note—she lived happily ever after.[12] There is no reason to doubt that some such happening actually occurred. In other cases reported,

[10] *Ibid.*, I, 419 f.

[11] On the particular form of this doctrine as developed by the Mathers, see Perry Miller, *The New England Mind*, pp. 229 ff.

[12] *Magnalia*, II, 356.

however, one senses the credulity of the times and Mather's habit of accepting uncritically almost any "wonders" which were reported to him. There was, for example, the instance of Sarah Wilkinson who, having died of "a dropsy," was found to have lived for years with almost no internal organs whatever![13] If an autopsy was performed in this case, as was occasionally done, it must have fallen somewhat short of present standards.

In the second place, Mather's approach to the doctrine of providence occasionally took on a quasi-scientific character. Increase Mather—following English suggestions—had called on the clergy as early as 1681 to gather examples, and his son carried on in this program. Most of the data collected by Cotton were merely reported to him. But in the case of the bewitched Goodwin children, he recorded his own observations thoroughly and with great care. He apparently felt that he was proceeding as "scientifically" here, as when he was observing what we would call natural phenomena.[14]

Finally, the clergyman's belief in providence seems inconsistent with his growing appreciation of regularities in Nature. He himself showed little awareness of the problem. This is pointed out by several scholars who have dealt with his science, chiefly in relation to astronomy, and more will be said on the issue here in so far as it was also reflected in his medicine. Meantime, one need only observe that if Mather was inconsistent in this regard, so also were many of his scientific contemporaries. Nor should it be difficult to make allowances for such inconsistency, since—as Morison points out—it survives today in popular if not in scientific thinking.[15]

[13] *Ibid.*

[14] *Ibid.*, pp. 341; 456 f. See also his *Memorable Providences relating to witchcrafts and possessions*, Boston, 1689, pp. 1–53.

[15] *The Puritan Pronaos*, p. 262.

About 1712, a decade after he had composed the *Magnalia*, Mather completed a huge commentary on the Bible which was intended to reconcile revelation with the new science. He viewed this ambitious but unpublished work—the "Biblia Americana"—as his chief gift to posterity, and it was certainly the product of many years of effort.[16] In the course of applying scientific knowledge to the interpretation of the scriptural texts, he exhibited wide curiosity and much miscellaneous learning. He evidently enjoyed this opportunity of giving full vent, simultaneously, both to his religious and scientific interests.

The end product seems somewhat rambling to the modern reader, since many topics led into tangential excursions of one sort or another. Thus he discourses on the geography of the Near East, on the races of men, on world population, on longevity and giants, and on the history of the Jews. For good measure, on the latter theme, he throws in tables on Hebrew coins and their English equivalents. But in the process, he indicates that there are "scientific" explanations of Biblical data. Many of these are incidental, as in the identification of the great fish which swallowed Jonah as a shark. But at times science leads him to reject ordinary interpretations, as when he terms the unicorn mentioned in Job[17] a "very romance," since Bellonius[18] had shown that so-called unicorn horns were no more than the teeth of whales!

The "Biblia Americana" reveals Mather not only as applying scientific commentaries to the Scriptures, but also as reconciling—or combining—Aristotelian concepts with those of the seventeenth century. His views on the location

---

[16] In the funeral sermon for Mather, Thomas Prince declared it had taken almost fifty years to compose, but Holmes (*op. cit.*, II, 734) estimates twenty years. The six volumes of the "Biblia" are in the Massachusetts Historical Society.

[17] Job, Chapter XXXIX. The sections in "The Biblia" follow the books of the Bible.

[18] Pierre Belon, 1517 (?)—1564.

of Heaven are still essentially medieval.[19] He accepts Newtonian dynamics but still holds that there is a universal center of attraction in the universe which—despite ordinary gravitation—would bring all things tumbling together were it not for divine intercession.

There is considerable biological material in the "Biblia." Some of this is simply a sort of historical taxonomy—the identification of plants or animals mentioned in the Scriptures. But principles and problems also come into the picture. He refers to the cross-pollination of plants,[20] which he would mention again in a letter to the Royal Society in 1716. And he gives much attention to the problems of generation, in which connection he accepted the theory of the preformation of parts in the seed. The creation of Eve inspires a discussion of the anatomic growth of the embryo. So fascinating did Mather find this whole subject that one can easily picture him—in a modern setting—as a candidate for a degree in genetics.

Of strictly medical themes there is little in the "Biblia," other than some casual comments on medical history and occasional attempts to identify Scriptural diseases. He decided, for example, that Job suffered from scurvy—after examining the "clinical evidence" much as present historians do in seeking to diagnose ancient plagues. (Syphilis was ruled out, in this case, because Mather was sure it had appeared in the Old World only at the end of the fifteenth century.) In such identifications, he again indicated some awareness of the existence of disease entities. It is worthy of note, finally, that Mather—in his comments on medical history—held that the medicine of Biblical times was "horribly magical" in nature.

[19] See also his unpublished "Tri-Paradisus," American Antiquarian Society.

[20] Genesis, I.

By the time that the "Biblia" was completed, Mather had
apparently acquired some scientific reputation. He was
therefore invited by Richard Waller, one of the secretaries
of the Royal Society, to send communications to that body.
The invitation, received in 1712, elicited a prompt response.
Mather sent no less than thirteen letters during November
of that year, in one of which he suggested that he be made a
member of the Society. He was duly elected the following
year, thus becoming one of the first native Americans to be
so honored.[21]

During the ensuing twelve years, Mather sent almost a
hundred communications to the Royal Society. Most of
them remained unpublished.[22] Some of the earlier ones
incorporated materials already prepared in other connections, as for the "Biblia Americana," but the later ones were
usually new compilations. The correspondence provided
Mather with opportunities to compose relatively short
scientific reports, to seek publication of some of them, and
to extend his contacts and reputation abroad. In short, this
association afforded him the closest approximation then
available of the value which present scientists derive from
innumerable professional societies and journals.

The officers with whom Mather usually corresponded
were Waller, James Jurin, and Dr. John Woodward.[23] Some

[21] Raymond P. Stearns, "Colonial Fellows of the Royal Society, 1661–1788," *William
and Mary Quarterly*, series 3, III (April, 1946), 226. On the uncertainties about this election and its final confirmation in 1723, see G. L. Kittredge, "Cotton Mather's Election into
the Royal Society," Colonial Soc. of Mass., *Publications*, XIV (1912), 81 ff.

[22] Apart from items which appeared in the Royal Society's *Transactions*, a few of the
other letters were either printed during Mather's lifetime—some anonymously—or have
appeared in various collections since. See, *e.g., The World Alarmed*, Boston, 1721; "Account of a Great Tide and Storm," Mass. Hist. Soc., *Collections*, II (1793), p. 11 f; "An
Horrid Snow," in Murdock, *Selections* (1926), pp. 373 ff.

[23] It is to be remembered, of course, that Mather's correspondence with the Royal
Society was only a part of that which he conducted with many Europeans. He is said to
have had as many as fifty correspondents overseas at one time; Michael Kraus, *The Atlantic
Civilization: Eighteenth Century Origins*, Ithaca, N. Y., 1949, p. 163.

of the earlier letters were rather ornate, exhibiting erudition and those qualities of style which have irritated later critics. But the composition of the later ones, like that of *The Christian Philosopher*, became relatively simple, clear, and even forceful.[24] The letters were sometimes read before the Royal Society and later circulated abroad after the manner of the times. Certain of them were published by the Society,[25] and occasionally an entire meeting was given over to their discussion.[26] If the Boston clergyman was merely credulous in his attitude toward Nature, his London colleagues seem to have been sublimely unaware of it. It is true that one of his contributions—that on a merman—was ridiculed subsequently by the critic John Hill (1751), but this was only one of many items in the *Transactions* which the latter exploited in order to condemn the Royal Society as a whole.[27]

Mather's letters were patterned after those then commonly sent to the early European academies. He had access, at Harvard, to a file of the *Ephemeridum* ("Miscellanea") of the first German academy,[28] and he stated that he used this series of miscellaneous reports as a model for his communications to the Royal Society.[29] Old World savants were still excited about overseas taxonomy, as they had been since the early 1500's; and Americans continued to discuss "natural history" with their London correspondents

[24] See Murdock, *Selections*, pp. 285–362 ff.

[25] See, *e.g.*, the *Philosophical Transactions*, XXIX (1714), 62 ff.

[26] Letter of R. P. Stearns to one of the authors, Sept. 12, 1950.

[27] Dorothy Stimson, *Scientists and Amateurs: A History of the Royal Society*, New York, 1948, p. 141.

[28] Originally founded as the Gesellschaft naturforschender Aerzte, Schweinfurt, 1652, which began publishing the *Miscellanea curiosa sive Ephemeridum Medico-Physicorum Germanorum* in 1670; Garrison, *History of Medicine*, Philadelphia, 1929, p. 281.

[29] Letter of May 20, 1723 to the Royal Society; *Christian Philosopher*, p. 252. Ornstein states, however, (*Role of Scientific Societies in the Seventeenth Century*, p. 171) that the German series was itself based on the *Transactions* of the Royal Society.

throughout the eighteenth century.[30] Mather was well aware
that he was a Colonial writing to the scientific headquarters
of the Empire, and he therefore emphasized data which were
peculiarly American, or which would at least provide colonial
supplements to European findings. Hence many of his
letters related to unusual storms, earthquakes, newly-
discovered fossils, biological species unknown in Europe,
and the like.[31] Occasionally, however, he wrote on processes
as well as forms. In certain letters, for example, he returned
to the problems of genetics which had been of concern in
earlier writings. In the course of more than a decade, his
letters covered—in the manner of a seventeenth-century
virtuoso—the whole range of his scientific interests. Mathematics, astronomy, geology, meteorology, biology, and
medicine all came into the picture.

As was true of his earlier writings, most of Mather's
"Curiosa" were reported at secondhand. The limitations of
this procedure are now only too obvious, but it was common
enough in his day. For one thing, standards of scientific
evidence had not yet become so rigid as is now the case.
Other physicians, such as Benjamin Rush, still noted
similarly secondhand observations more than half a century
after Mather's time. In the second place, the reporting of
exotic, overseas phenomena had in it an element of scientific
journalism, and one could hardly expect reporters to limit
themselves to the few phenomena which happened to come
under direct observation.

[30] See Kraus, *op. cit.*, chapter VII. The Royal Society received such letters from various
Americans, besides the few who were its own members. Thus, a New England sea captain
sent in, early in the eighteenth century, the most detailed account of the natural history
of whales which the authors have had the opportunity to examine.

[31] *E.g.*, the moose, the rattlesnake, etc. Note such letters as those of November 17 to
November 28, 1712; June 6, 1714; July 4, 1716; etc. Such reports were still being forwarded in 1724. See Kittredge, "Cotton Mather's Scientific Communications to the Royal
Society," Amer. Antiq. Soc., *Proceedings*, XXVI, (April, 1916), 18 ff. The letters noted
are in the Royal Society; except that of 1716, in the British Museum.

Mather was not unaware that questions might be raised about evidence, and he made some mild efforts to indicate the authenticity of data. He frequently noted that his source was "one of my Neighbors," or, again, a person of high standing in the community. On rare occasions, he secured written statements by witnesses,[32] or even sought out objects for direct observation. Thus, in describing a large fossil tooth, he adds that he had handled and weighed the object himself.[33] More significant than such gestures was the fact that he was careful *not* to claim direct observation in most cases, and also that he usually reserved personal judgment. His general attitude is well indicated in a letter of 1724, regarding the killing of a two-headed snake. Here he laments the fact that:

my Distance from the Field of Battle, where the Lad killed this little Python, which is forty miles off, made me uncapable of such an Anatomical Proceeding upon the Animal, as would have enabled me to answer many Enquiries, which would immediately offer themselves on this Occasion.[34]

Among the various fields represented in the "Curiosa," medicine and related subjects received the greatest measure of attention. Letters on native plants and animals often included observations on their medical properties or implications. One communication on rattlesnakes, for example, mentioned a valuable drug made from their gall, while another noted an antidote for snake bites.[35] Many other remedies were reported in the letters, since Mather was interested in practice as well as in theory. No doubt he also realized that it was the practical which would most appeal to English correspondents.

[32] *E.g.*, Letter of November 26, 1712, p. 3, *re* a supposed case of "second sight," Royal Society.

[33] Letter of November 17, 1712, p. 3, Royal Society.

[34] September 21, 1724, Royal Society. Whittier later composed his "Doubled-Headed Snake of Newbury" on the basis of this episode.

[35] Letters of November 27, 1712; and of June 4, 1723; Royal Society.

A striking aspect of the medical letters was their emphasis upon Indian medicine. Now Mather was no admirer of the natives. For him, they were children of the Devil rather than the "noble red men" of more romantic generations. It may therefore seem strange that he was willing to learn from such creatures. But Mather, like most of the "moderns" of the seventeenth century, was open-minded about new facts or ideas no matter what their origin. He would later give credit to a lowly slave for imparting his first knowledge of inoculation. He was convinced that God had placed remedies in each part of the world where they were appropriate,[36] and since the Indians had dwelt long in America, they might well have been the first to find the blessings peculiar to their continent. "And I alwaies thought," he wrote in 1723, "That for our Physick, as well as for our food, Every Creature of God is good, and nothing to be refused, if it be received with Thanksgiving."[37]

In one of his earliest letters, Mather discussed unique American plants with which "our Indians do cures many times which are truly stupendous."[38] In commenting on the plant Fagiana, he later remarked that "It was first communicated unto us, by a Indian, who did very strange cures upon cancers, by a decoction of it inwardly taken." The same plant was also said to be good for fevers. From personal experience, however, Mather claimed only stimulating qualities for Fagiana tea, and from his account one gathers that it had some of the properties which are known to exist in the Peruvian Indian plant of coca. "All that I

---

[36] *Christian Philosopher*, p. 136.

[37] Letter of May 21, 1723, p. 6, on "The Case of the Small-pox inoculated further cleared," Royal Society.

[38] Letter of November 18, 1712, p. 4, Royal Society. His interest in these cures extended to the folklore associated with them—how the Indians had discovered certain ones by watching animal behavior, etc. See letter of June 4, 1723 p. 2.

yet know from my experience of my own, is that in a tea, it has a mighty invigorating and exhilirating vertue. It refreshes the spirits with an uncommon Brightnesse, It prevents and removes Lassitude when great Fatigues are to be encountered."[39]

Despite a primary concern with botanic drugs, Mather also displayed enthusiasm about certain "biologicals." Among the latter was a "very noble Cordial, in the Gall of a Rattle Snake. . . . This Liquor, We incorporate into convenient Quantities of powdered Chalk, or Indian Meal, and so be praeserved for our Use in Medicine." The remedy was said to produce sweating and was therefore good for fevers; it was also helpful in the difficulties associated with childbirth.[40] A proper dosage was fourteen grains "more or less," depending on the constitution of the patient, and this could be taken in a solid, in water, in wine, "or almost any way in the World."[41]

Many other Indian remedies were noted among the "Curiosa." There was partridge berry, recommended as a powerful diuretic which would cure dropsy, "Throat-weed" which was of amazing helpfulness in sore throat, "Cranesbill" which when brewed into a tea would heal *lues venerea* in two weeks, "Bleeding root" which could cure jaundice within six days, and so on.[42]

All this was empirical lore but it was quite acceptable to the medicine of the age. Most of these drugs were probably of little if any value, and no doubt many false hopes were

[39] Letter of July 13, 1716, British Museum. Someone in the Museum later changed the spelling to "Fagrana." We have been unable to identify the plant.

[40] Our grandparents of 1890 would have laughed at such diverse claims, but a generation familiar with sulfa drugs and the antibiotics is hardly in a position to do so.

[41] Letter of November 27, 1712, pp. 3 ff, Royal Society; see also *The Christian Philosopher*, p. 169.

[42] See, *e.g.*, letter of November 18, 1712, pp. 4 ff, Royal Society.

raised. On the other hand, it was well upon occasion that learned men exhibited such "credulity" about popular remedies. Some of the most useful drugs discovered during the seventeenth and eighteenth centuries—such as cinchona bark and digitalis—were derived from folk practice. It is even conceivable that one or two of those reported in the "Curiosa" would still be worthy of investigation.

In certain of his letters, Mather continued to write about the general biologic problems of generation—ranging here from vegetables to human beings. His interest in cross-pollination had already been expressed in the "Biblia Americana," but it was his letter of July 24, 1716, to Mr. Petiver, an English correspondent, which provided the first well-known comment on this significant phenomenon. Zirkle states that this is "The earliest account of plant hybridization yet found."[43]

In relation to animal generation, Mather was fascinated by all sorts of monstrosities and other abnormalities. Two-headed snakes, animal hybrids (including the merman previously mentioned), giants and idiots, unusually fertile women and long-lived men—all these and more were carefully noted. That this expressed more than morbid curiosity is indicated in Mather's statement that "an attentive Consideration of these Curiosities might very much assist our Enquiries into that obscure work of Nature, Generation, than which, what more mysterious?"[44]

A considerable number of the "Curiosa" describe unusual case histories—presented here in their own right, rather than

---

[43] Conway Zirkle, *The Beginnings of Plant Hybridization*, Philadelphia, 1935, pp. 104 ff; see also Frederick G. Kilgour, "The Rise of Scientific Activity in Colonial New England," *Yale Jour. of Biol. and Med.*, XXII (December, 1949), 128. The substance of this letter was printed in 1720 as part of *The Christian Philosopher*, and it was recently reprinted in Murdock's *Selections* as well as by Zirkle. The original is in the British Museum.

[44] Letter of July 3, 1716, on "A Monstrous Calf," British Museum. It is of interest that Mather considered monstrosities too horrible for God to employ them as warnings.

in connection with other themes as in the *Magnalia*. Such titles occur as "An Ear Strangely Molested," "A Prodigious Worm," "The Stone Mistaken," and "Uncommon Dentition," along with reports on smallpox and inoculation.[45] In a letter on the *"Nishmath Chajim:* The probable seat, and general cure of all disease"[46] there is a discussion of basic theory, but the great majority of medical letters were factual in tone. A few included what their author thought were occult realities, as in the reported case of a man whose brother's distant murder was revealed to him in a dream, but there was less of such matters than in earlier writings.

Mental behavior associated with illness was always of interest to Mather, and this will be noted again in connection with "The Angel." In his letters, for example, he discussed what might be termed the power of suggestion. His favorite illustration here was one which still amuses the public. There are, he notes:

Husbands who breed for their Wives; and while they for diverse Months together are puling under the most Sickly Indispositions, their Wives have the Satisfaction that they suffer not one Moments Disorder, Yea, we have known several Husbands carry the Good Humour so far, as to Travail for their Wives . . . and have the Gossips attending on them; while their Wives have brought forth the Offspring, with scarce a Groan upon it.[47]

Just as there was less of the occult in the "Curiosa" than in earlier writings, so also was there a lessened dependence upon the operations of divine providence. In the *Magnalia*, for example, remarkable cures had been ascribed to divine intercession. In posing therein the question of what wounds may be considered mortal, Mather had replied: "such as he

[45] See, *e.g.*, the letters of November 22 and 24, 1712, Royal Soc.; of July 12, 1716, British Museum; of October 10, 1717, Mass. Hist. Soc.; and of September 30, 1724, Royal Soc. That of 1716, noted here, indicates Mather's interest in smallpox, some five years before the epidemic of 1721.

[46] Published in New London, 1722, as *The Angel of Bethesda*—from which the larger work was to take its name.

[47] Letter of November 20, 1712, p. 3, Royal Society.

shall in his holy providence actually make so,"[48] but in the
"Curiosa" the same problem is declared "almost impossible
to be decided."[49] About a decade had elapsed between the
appearance of histories of such wounds in the *Magnalia* and
their reappearance in the "Curiosa," and during the interval
Mather seems to have been in mid-passage between theological and scientific explanations. Similar examples of
what were termed divine providences in 1702, and which
were reported without explanation from 1712 on, finally
were to appear in "The Angel" of 1724 within the more or
less naturalistic framework of a "vital principle."

In a letter of 1723 to the Royal Society, Mather listed
among his communications an entire work entitled *The
Christian Philosopher* which had been published in London
in 1720.[50] This book was not, like most of the "Curiosa,"
a series of separate reports on particular subjects, but was
rather another general work on science and its relation to
religion. It therefore invites comparison with the "Biblia
Americana" which had been completed about a decade
earlier.

In the "Biblia" Mather had examined the Scriptures in
terms of science, whereas in *The Christian Philosopher* he
reversed this by surveying science from a religious perspective. The underlying purpose, that of reconciliation, was
the same in both cases, but the shift of focus, from religion
in the earlier work to science in the later, seems significant.
It is to be remembered that during the interval between the
composition of the two works, Mather had not only been
reading scientific works but had also been active in collecting
data and in reporting these overseas. In *The Christian*

[48] *Magnalia*, II, 606.

[49] Letter of November 24, 1712, Royal Society.

[50] The subtitle is *Religio Philosophica* (Scientific Religion).

Philosopher he finally brought together his cumulative knowledge of science at large. This he did for the glory of God, but also—one feels in reading the *Philosopher*—because of his growing interest in science as such.

In composing this work Mather admitted his dependence on Ray, Derham, and other authors and only added that a number of "American Communications" were included.[51] The book summarizes the scientific learning of the early eighteenth century—with appropriate religious reflections thereon—under such headings as magnetism, minerals, vegetables and the like. Less attention is given to medicine than to the natural sciences, but there are some discussions of the chief features of human anatomy and physiology—of the skeleton, muscles, nerves, the sense organs, teeth, and so on.[52] There is little discussion of medical theory or practice, in which connection the "Curiosa" are more rewarding. Perhaps he was reserving such matters for systematic treatment in the forthcoming "Angel of Bethesda."

Certain medical doctrines were, to be sure, implicit in accounts of physiologic processes, as when humoralism is implied in the declaration that the animal spirits originate in the brain. And occasionally Mather's particular medical views stand forth, as in the statement that "the *caustick Salt* in the *Smoke*" of tobacco "may lay Foundations for Diseases in Millions of unadvised People." Much recent medical testimony would support him in this contention.

Quite apart from the light which *The Christian Philosopher* throws on Mather's knowledge of medicine and other sciences, the work is notable as indicating that science was influencing its author's theological perspectives. It was common enough, as Murdock points out, to view Nature as glorifying

---

[51] Such, again, as the observations on hybrid corn.

[52] See, *e.g.*, pp. 136, 165, 230, 234, 237 ff.

God. But Mather went further than this, in finding Nature so wondrous and beautiful as to suggest God's goodness and mercy rather than simply His dread power. This is all the more suprising because Mather was concerned with medicine as well as with astronomy, and much of his admonition on medical themes had exhibited a grim tone. Sickness is seen at close range and is rarely so inspiring as are the clean, vast reaches of the heavens. Yet Mather escaped or overcame the disillusionment which may be associated with the study of disease. Far from merely "ossifying" the early Puritan pessimism, this Boston clergyman actually looked forward to the coming optimism of the Enlightenment.[53]

Even in this respect, Mather was not strictly original, but he was sufficiently alert and open-minded to be the first American to transcend the traditional Calvinistic *Anschauung*. This merits emphasis here, since we will observe subsequently that the same mental qualities enabled him to introduce new concepts or procedures into American medicine as well as into American theology.

[53] Murdock, *Selections*, pp. 2 ff.

Chapter V

HISTORY OF "THE ANGEL OF BETHESDA"

By 1720, when Mather was approaching his sixtieth year, he had written at length on medical subjects, but this material was scattered widely in the works already noted, in various pamphlets, and in unpublished communications to the Royal Society. He finally decided, apparently, that his cumulative medical lore should be pulled together in some general compilation. This he desired to do not only for his own satisfaction but also in the belief that such a book would have definite utility. As a title for this he selected that of an earlier pamphlet, *The Angel of Bethesda*. The reference here to the healing pool was doubtless meaningful at the time, although present physicians would hardly look under this heading for the first American treatise in their field.[1]

The earliest surviving reference to "The Angel" was included in a letter of October 26, 1720, to John Winthrop, and during the next two years Mather forwarded several chapters for Winthrop's perusal.[2] The bulk of the writing was evidently completed in 1724, and it therefore represents the last of its author's major works. As is indicated in the preface, Mather was most anxious to have it published; just why he was unsuccessful in this is not clear. Perhaps the mere cost of publication, about which he was concerned at the start, was a serious obstacle. Perhaps, also, the fact that his general influence was waning had something to do with the matter. More specifically, considerable opposition

---

[1] The title was suggested by a reference in Boyle's writings, quoted by Mather in a letter to Dr. Woodward of November 22, 1712. Mather also refers to the Angel's healing powers in the *Magnalia*, I, 159.

[2] "The Mather Papers," Mass. Hist. Soc., *Collections*, series 4, VIII, 446 ff.

to Mather had been aroused among physicians during the inoculation controversy of 1721, and the aftereffects of professional tension may have made it difficult for him to publish in the medical field. This story will be considered shortly, but it is pertinent to recall here that his archopponent—Dr. Douglass—made clear the view that clerics should confine themselves to clerical matters.[3]

Whatever the explanation, Mather was never able to bring out his final compilation. A decade after his death, his son Samuel—the "little Sammy" of the diary—was still trying to secure its publication. The latter viewed "The Angel" as one of his father's chief claims to fame. In speaking of the ambiguous circumstances surrounding Cotton's election to the Royal Society, for example, he declared that "the Doctor" was nevertheless "very easy, as well he might be; for if he had not the due Title allowed him, he deserved it; as his *Christian Philosopher*, his *Curiosa Americana* . . . together with his *Angel of Bethesda* abundantly testify."[4] Samuel further remarked of the latter work that: "This is a considerable Volume, and cost the Doctor many Years study to fill and embellish it."[5] In 1739 he even issued a prospectus, announcing that "The Angel" was ready for the press and would "upon suitable Encouragement" shortly be published.[6] But no such encouragement was forthcoming.

Subsequently, as the years passed, the work became dated, and all prospects of issuing it faded away. The manuscript remained in the immediate family until 1816, when it was purchased by Isaiah Thomas from Cotton's grand-daughter,

---

[3] William Douglass, *The Abuses and Scandals of some late pamphlets In Favour of Inoculation of the Small Pox*, Boston, 1722, pp. 7 f.

[4] Samuel Mather, *op. cit.* p. 78.

[5] *Ibid.*, p. 72.

[6] In the *Boston Gazette*, December 24, 1739, quoted in T. J. Holmes, *op. cit.*, II, 739.

Mrs. Hannah Mather Crocker. Thereafter it came into the possession of the American Antiquarian Society, where it lay practically unnoticed until it came to the attention of Dr. Oliver Wendell Holmes in 1869.

There was every reason why Holmes should have reacted sharply against "The Angel." During the preceding century, the whole intellectual climate had changed; the occult had been ruled out of science, and the clergy had abandoned all thought of medical practice. Medical science had been reoriented; instead of involving a generalized humoral pathology, it was now related to localized pathology of a specific nature. And pharmacology, purged of most of the old remedies, had been reduced to a minimum by a generation that was "nihilistic" in its attitude toward therapy. In a word, Holmes found in Mather everything which the medicine of the 1860's had rejected or transcended.

The physician's impressions were doubtless colored also by the popular views of the mid-nineteenth century. It was during this same decade, as noted, that a revived discussion of the witchcraft trials had brought Cotton Mather into something approaching general disrepute. He thus became fair game, as it were, for a physician who had a clever pen and a complete confidence in the science of his own day. Holmes' ridicule of Mather has some value in bringing out the clergyman's more extreme weaknesses or absurdities. But it never seems to have occurred to the Boston doctor that Mather was to be judged by the standards of 1720 rather than by those of 1870.

Holmes first spoke at length on "The Angel" in a lecture before the Lowell Institute in 1869,[7] and returned to his criticisms in a later article of 1881. He found the treatise "full of pedantry, superstition, declamation, and mis-

[7] Published subsequently in his *Medical Essays*, Boston, 1883, pp. 312–69.

cellaneous folly."[8] He particularly objected to two features of the work, namely, its indication of clerical practice, and the absurdity or repulsiveness of its remedies.

On the first score, it is to be recalled that Holmes—writing in a day of much medical sectarianism—was hypersensitive to any encroachments on the realm of the regular profession. He was the arch-foe of homeopathy and the like, and was in no frame of mind to tolerate professional rivals even in the past. He therefore viewed "The Angel" as a horrible example of what happens when medicine is joined with religion:

The divine takes precedence over the physician in this extraordinary production. He begins by preaching a sermon at his unfortunate patient. Having thrown him into a cold sweat by his spiritual sudorific, he attacks him with his material remedies, which are often quite as unpalatable. . . . Everything he could find mentioned in the seventy or eighty authors he cites, all that the old women of both sexes had ever told him of, gets into his text, or squeezes itself into his margin. . . . He piles his prescriptions one upon another, without the least discrimination. He is run away with by all sorts of fancies and superstitions. . . . But when he comes to the odious class of remedies, he revels in them like a *scarabeus*. This allusion will bring us quite near enough to the inconceivable abominations with which he proposed to outrage the sinful stomachs of the unhappy confederates and accomplices of Adam.[9]

That there was some truth in this cannot be denied: the only point here is that it could have been said just as well of the official pharmacopeias of Mather's time.[10] There is more doubt about Holmes' assumption that the "regular" physicians of 1720 must have followed a more sane and cleanly practice. For this he offers no contemporary evidence. One cannot but recall again, in this connection, Mather's own reports of contemporary physicians' remedies—

[8] "History of Medicine in Boston, by Samuel A. Green, M.D. . . . with additional memoranda by Oliver Wendell Holmes, M.D.," in Justin Winsor (ed.), *Memorial History of Boston*, Boston, 1881, IV, 557 f.

[9] *Medical Essays*, p. 360.

[10] Holmes, in saying that Mather "revels" in repulsive materials, distorts the picture. The latter actually remarks that "Tis hardly good Manners to write so much about it." (Transcript, "The Angel," p. 420.)

such as the swallowing of leaden bullets for "the griping of the Guts"—which he himself rejected as absurd and dangerous.

Holmes was on surer ground when he condemned the ascribing of disease to original sin. This had become as foreign to most secular physicians of 1720 as it was to those of 1870. But he betrayed the limitations of his own medicine when he overlooked the possible values in Mather's efforts to influence the mental state of patients. In all this Holmes saw only theological intimidation. Although possessing unusual insight into medical psychology of a sort, he represented a type of medicine which had almost completely lost sight of psychosomatic relationships.[11] (At the very time he wrote, a woman in his native Boston was about to lead "Christian Science" into the breach so opened in the medical field.) In like manner, the doctor overlooked the significance of Mather's animalcular hypothesis, presumably because American physicians had lost interest in this theory after about 1850.[12]

Holmes had a few good things to say about Mather, as in approving such of his drugs as "quinquina" and "ipecacuanha" and in stating that the advocacy of inoculation "relates to the single medical suggestion which does honor to Cotton Mather's memory." Yet even here, he urges the reader to remember that this was the same man who had recommended the detection and punishment of witches![13]

Prior to the publication of Holmes' opinions, "The Angel" was also examined by Dr. Joseph Sargent of Worcester. The latter's views were similar to those of his Boston col-

---

[11] Cf. Eleanor M. Tilton, *Amiable Autocrat: A Biography of Dr. Oliver Wendell Holmes,* New York, 1947, p. 302 f.

[12] He mentions it casually at one point, *Medical Essays*, p. 361. Holmes wrote on Mather just before this theory was finally confirmed and reintroduced into this country via France and Germany. See Phyllis Allen (Richmond), "Americans and the Germ Theory of Disease," University Microfilms, Ann Arbor, Mich., 1949.

[13] *Medical Essays*, pp. 346 f, 362.

league, except that he was more direct in criticizing Mather for not having anticipated the medicine of the nineteenth century. He noted that the clergyman had treated common diseases "in no scientific manner. For there are no disquisitions on pathology and there is no account of morbid anatomy, nor of diagnosis, and no history of symptoms or of progress." Mather, he found, was concerned largely with "specifics and infallibles," and failed "to recognize the natural tendency in almost all diseases to recovery." As a result of this, the clergyman had urged treatments and then naïvely credited them with overcoming the illness.[14]

Dr. Sargent was the product of his own age, even as was Mather. Present-day medicine would approve the view that Mather overlooked the self-limited nature of many diseases,[15] but would reject Dr. Sargent's implication that there is little value in specific therapy. If the medicine of 1720 was at one extreme in this regard, that of 1880 had reacted to the other.

Except for some brief, descriptive comments made by Dr. William S. Thayer of the Johns Hopkins University in 1905,[16] no physicians thereafter seem to have taken any interest in "The Angel." That this was the result of Holmes' indictment, or that it simply indicated indifference, is impossible to say.

It remained for lay scholars to point out that the manuscript might at least be of interest in reflecting the medicine of its day. This had been noted as early as 1874 by S. F. Haven, Librarian of the American Antiquarian Society,[17] and the same comment was made by Wendell in 1891.[18] The Reverend Abijah P. Marvin, in his biography of 1892, went

---

[14] "Report of the Council," Amer. Antiq. Soc., *Proceedings*, No. 62 (April, 1874), 13 ff, 21.

[15] Even this was not always true; *e.g.*, Mather followed Sydenham in urging that smallpox be allowed to take its natural course without undue interference.

[16] "Cotton Mather's Rules of Health," *Bull. of the Johns Hopkins Hospital*, XVI (September, 1905), 296.

[17] "Report of the Librarian," Amer. Antiq. Soc., *Proceedings*, No. 62 (April, 1874), p. 35.

further in that he specifically repudiated the ridicule which had been heaped upon Mather's medicine. He recalled that the latter had prepared for a medical career and was no mere dabbler in this field. "His writings on the healing art," observed Marvin, "have furnished some merriment for the doctors of recent times, because of the curious and ridiculous remedies prescribed, but these were not invented by him. He was merely the exponent of medical science in his day."[19]

It is clear that Marvin was open-minded about the possible significance of Mather's medicine, but he provided little analysis thereof. Much the same can be said of several other scholars who subsequently commented on "The Angel." Thus Worthington Ford examined the manuscript in 1911 and prepared the transcript mentioned earlier. It was his opinion that this work, supplemented by Governor Winthrop's case histories, would provide a summary of the medical knowledge of more than a century.[20]

The analysis of "The Angel" in the ensuing chapter is based on premises similar to those implied in these earlier comments by Haven, Marvin, and Ford. It may be emphasized again, however, that one observes in "The Angel" not only a compilation of the medical knowledge of about 1720, but apparently the only such study ever prepared in the English-American Colonies. It is also unique among American works in its constant use—as in Mather's earlier medical writings—of a religious frame of reference. The study is less than a synthesis, since it is frequently discursive and disjointed, but it is certainly more than a mere hodgepodge or summary. It presents theory as well as

[18] *Cotton Mather, the Puritan Priest*, p. 276.

[19] *The Life and Times of Cotton Mather*, p. 13.

[20] Writing as editor of The Diary, I, 3 n. A volume of the Winthrop cases is preserved in the Massachusetts Historical Society. Both Kittredge and T. J. Holmes examined "The Angel," but their interest was primarily bibliographical rather than analytical in nature.

practice, interpretations as well as traditional lore. If
written a little later, Mather might have entitled it "a system of physic" or—still later—"a general text on medicine."

"The Angel" was also intended to serve as a "family medical manual," for in its long lists of remedies it amounts to a
popular pharmacopeia. In this respect it reveals Mather's
zeal for "doing good," whereas other sections reflect his scholarly and scientific interests. The work was thus addressed
simultaneously to physicians and to the public at large.
Perhaps this lack of differentiation provides a further clue as
to why the study was never published; it may have fallen
between the two stools of professional and popular appeal.

*　　*　　*　　*　　*

The chief sources for "The Angel" were the varied medical
works which were available to Mather in his own library and
in that of Harvard College. Many of these are indicated in
references scattered throughout the study, but a more co-
herent impression can be secured by recalling the nature of
the library collections themselves. Something has been said
of the Harvard materials;[21] it remains to note what was available to Mather on his own shelves.

The library of Increase Mather, which Cotton inherited,
had been unusual for its day in the Colonies. This was true
both of its extent and of the number of scientific works it
contained. Cotton early began to add to this family collection, as when he purchased volumes from the College—
presumably duplicates—in 1682.[22] Both the Mathers
viewed their books as among their most valued possessions,
and their combined holdings became one of the largest
private libraries in the English Colonies.[23]

[21] In Chapter II, above.

[22] The American Antiquarian Society possesses a list of these purchased works, which
Mather paid for between 1682 and 1684.

[23] It is sometimes termed the largest; e.g., Carl Bridenbaugh, Cities in the Wilderness
New York, 1938, p. 290.

The Mather library included many medical works, most of which were acquired by Cotton. It is possible to list, from the known fragments of the collection, the titles of some fifty authorities in this field. These included English, French, Swiss, Dutch, Danish, and German publications, chiefly in English or in Latin. Prominent among them were such classic works as those of Hippocrates, Pliny, Paracelsus, Boyle, Kircher, Thomas Browne, Fernel, Sydenham, Willis, Mead, and van Helmont.[24]

The internal evidence in Mather's writings indicates that he read in most if not all of these works, but it is not always clear when the reading was done. Much of it, undoubtedly, was the labor of his later years—after about 1710, and especially after 1720. Some evidence is supplied here by four of his commonplace books, which have survived from the large number originally composed.[25] Two of these, written during the late 1690's, contain only fragmentary medical references; the third—for about 1698 to 1709—refers to his reading of religio-medical works such as were cited in the "Biblia Americana." The fourth commonplace book, for 1720–1723, is rich in notes of medical reading which was done, presumably, in connection with the actual writing of "The Angel of Bethesda." Here are his original notes, for example, on the publications of Mead and Willis, as well as on pertinent materials in the Royal Society's *Transactions* between 1715 and 1720. There is also an implication that Mather picked up information wherever it could be found, as when he noted statements by van Helmont in Leigh's *Natural History of Lancashire.*[26]

[24] Various manuscript lists of the collection are possessed by the American Antiquarian Society, and are given in Tuttle, *op. cit.,* pp. 280 ff, 301 ff. Some of the books survive in the Society's library.

[25] See Samuel Mather's biography, p. 24. The four surviving are in the American Antiquarian Society collections.

[26] Charles Leigh, *The Natural History of Lancashire, Cheshire, and the Peak, in Derbyshire,* Oxford, 1700.

There is no evidence that Mather limited his purchases or reading to any one school of medical thought. He, as noted, favored the iatromechanical outlook, but his library was actually richer in the writings of the iatrochemists. Thus he possessed works by Paracelsus and van Helmont,the founders of the latter tradition. Van Helmont probably made an especial appeal because of his religious frame of reference. In some cases, the reason for Mather's dependence on particular authors is clear enough; for example, his interest in Kircher and Marten was aroused by their presentaion of the animalcular hypothesis. Again, it was presumably his concern about the public health which drew him to the writings of Mead.

When it came to composing "The Angel," Mather followed certain practices which seemed to exaggerate his actual productivity and range of reading. In the first place, various chapters simply reproduced earlier writings—with more or less change in the wording. Thus, chapter I is derived from a sermon of 1698;[27] chapters II, III, and IV also seem to come from earlier sermons; chapter VIII, *re* cures from the invisible world, incorporates a letter to Dr. Woodward of November 22, 1712; and chapter LIII is *Elizabeth in Her Holy Retirement* (1710) complete, plus a section on remedies. Occasionally, one can trace a Mather item through several writings. His theory of the *Nishmath* or vital principle, for example, was first expressed in "Tri-Paradisus," an unpublished paper of about 1720; with little change in form this reappeared in the pamphlet *Angel of Bethesda* (1722); and it was finally incorporated as a chapter in the large manuscript of the same name. At least a dozen chapters in "The Angel" simply reproduce earlier compositions.[28] Had the work been published, it would therefore

[27] *Mens Sana in Corpore Sano.*

[28] Other examples are chapters XXXII on the eye, and XXXIII on the ear, which abbreviate sections in *The Christian Philosopher*, pp. 235, and 244 ff.

have served—among other purposes—that of bringing together some of Mather's "collected papers."

The majority of the chapters, nevertheless, were newly composed, although their data or ideas often can be traced back into earlier materials. In a few cases, Mather derived an entire chapter from one or two authorities. In such instances, he cited the original works but then went on to use *their* references as if they were his own. The chapter on animalculae, for example, was taken largely from Benjamin Marten's *A New Theory of Consumptions*.[29] Mather gives credit to "Marten and Company" in general and then goes on to cite just the same authorities which were mentioned by Marten—Kircher, Martin Lister, Borellus, and others. He may be suspected here of appropriating the original references, a habit which was viewed more leniently in Mather's time than it is in our own.

Mather usually cited at least the direct sources of his information. In chapters apparently based on a number of authorities, each of them is noted. Chapter LXIII on tobacco, for example, refers to several Dutch and Danish authors as well as to George Cheyne's *Essay on Health and Long Life*.[30] Since all of these works were in Mather's library, there is no particular reason to doubt that he used them.

Here and there in "The Angel" the author injects what seem to be his own ideas or observations into the text. Chapter LXII on "Popery Ridiculed," for example, depended in part on a work by William Beckett which examined the claims made for healing by the saints.[31] The

---

[29] London, 1720. This was evidently one of the last additions to his manuscript.

[30] 4th ed., London, 1725.

[31] *A Free and Impartial Enquiry into the Antiquity and Efficacy of Touching for the King's Evil*, London, 1722.

latter discussed the question in a sober manner, but Mather added considerable ridicule of the whole idea. As a rule, his interpolations were of a moralistic nature.

"The Angel" seems in most respects a monument to Mather's eclecticism. It has been noted that in medicine—as in science at large—the clergyman usually displayed an open and encyclopedic mind rather than an original one, and this is most apparent in the chapters which he derived from only one or two sources. This does not mean, however, that he merely accumulated materials. The line between originality and "mere erudition" is not always easy to draw. In Mather's case, most of the data and basic ideas were derived from others in the first instance; nevertheless, there is no question that he thought out his own selections and interpretations.

This is well illustrated by some of his key concepts, such as that of the vital principle. That idea had had a long history,[32] and Mather's acceptance of it can be traced back in a general way to his early reading in Harvey, Grew, van Helmont, and others. But it is difficult to relate the formulation of the theory, as it finally appears in "The Angel," to any particular source. In other words, the concept had been thoroughly integrated by that time into the author's own thought.

Mather made no great claim to originality in "The Angel." One suspects that he would have been satisfied if this study had been recognized as a monument to his learning, and if, at the same time, it had broadened the outlook of physicians and been of some service to the public at large. They also serve in science, he doubtless believed, who only compile and interpret the work of others and make this knowledge as widely available as possible. Perhaps there was a peculiar

---

[32] See, e.g., Paul Diepgen, "Vitalismus u. Medizin im Wandel der Zeiten," *Klinische Wochenschrift*, Jahrg. 10 (August, 1931), 1433 ff.

need for this sort of service within a colonial culture.[33] In any case, a small, provincial population would hardly be expected to make many contributions to basic science.[34] Mather himself pointed this out in reference to mathematics. One need only substitute "scientists" for "mathematicians" in the following quotation, in order to sum up the whole matter.

Nor, can it be Expected, that while Colonies are yett so much in their Infancy as ours are, and have had so many Serpents also to crush while in their cradles as ours have had, they can be so circumstanced as to produce many acute mathematicians, or allow them the Leisure for extraordinary Inventions and Performances.[35]

What Mather here said of mathematics was true of the natural sciences in general, not only for the period in which he wrote but also for the entire eighteenth century. The colonial setting did not encourage many independent contributions, and the few Americans who made them were in most instances those who had enjoyed training or long residence abroad.[36] In medicine, not even this advantage produced any marked originality throughout the century.

There were, nevertheless, occasional exceptions to the rule, in the medical as well as in other fields. One of the earliest instances of this sort is to be noted in Mather's observations on genetics, and a further example is to be found in his theories of immunology as expounded in "The Angel." Such occasional evidences of originality are the more surprising, in Mather's case, because of the entirely provincial nature of his own background.

[33] In some connections, Mather was apparently seeking the same ends as are served today by "science writers," or others devoted to high-grade popularization.

[34] The widely scattered population of the so-called "American Colonies," c. 1715, was probably not over 400,000. Boston, the largest town, then numbered only ten to twelve thousand.

[35] Mather to Richard Waller, November 24, 1712, Royal Society.

[36] This was true of Logan, Colden, Franklin, Thompson, and Wells, all of whom were in varying degrees products of the European as well as of the American environment.

Chapter VI

THE NATURE OF "THE ANGEL"

One who knows something of Mather's earlier medical writings will encounter much that is familiar in "The Angel." To begin with, there is the same combination of religious and naturalistic elements in the later work as in the earlier. In writing to Winthrop about the manuscript in 1720, the clergyman explained that his book was to offer pious sentiments which the sick were "most Naturally and Rationally and Religiously to be led unto."[1] In a word, "The Angel" opens with a consideration of religious premises which the author felt were basic to all medical considerations.

Once again, Mather interprets sickness as divine punishment for original sin. Adam's descendants, inheriting his sinful tendency, continue in this way and thus ever renew the first cause of their tribulations. In introducing this theme in "The Angel," Mather presents disease as one aspect of the larger problem of evil. He rejects the ancient concept of good and evil principles in the universe—ignoring Satan in this connection—and declares that evil comes directly from God. *Isaiah* is quoted (XLV, 7), in which God declares: "I form the Light, and Create Darkness; I make Peace, and Create Evil." To which Mather adds "And now, Glorious God, We beleeve it: And yett the Thing remains unto us incomprehensible!" But he proceeds at once to point out that it is actually "our Sin" which is "the Root of Bitterness."[2]

The theologian might have stopped with this, but the medical thinker wished to explore the further question of

---

[1] "The Mather Papers," Mass. Hist. Soc., *Collections*, series 4, VIII, 446.

[2] p. 1 f. This and subsequent page citations from "The Angel" refer to the Ford transcript, certain chapters of which appear in the Appendix.

just how sin—current, individual transgression—brought on illness. Sin, he declared, results in "a Sickness of the Spirit," which in turn "will naturally cause a Sickness in the Body."[3] Here Mather found himself facing the old problem of mind-and-body. Why would the Spirit "naturally" influence the physical? In answer, the clergyman at first denied the implied duality altogether. "The Soul and the Body" he declares flatly, "constitute one Person."[4] But as is the case with some modern psychologists who take the same position in principle, he found it necessary to continue the analysis in dual terms.[5]

The interrelationships between mind and body were so obvious and yet so obscure that Mather, like many others before and after, felt it necessary to postulate some intermediary between them. This was the *Nishmath Chajim* or vital principle. In order to avoid semantic confusion, it were best to quote him here directly:

There is a Spirit in Man . . . which may be of a Middle Nature, between the Rational Soul ["mind" or "reason" in the ordinary sense?] and the Corporeal mass; but may be the medium of Communication, by which they work upon one another. It wonderfully receives also Impressions from both of them; and perhaps it is the Vital Ty between them.[6]

At this point it would have been logical for Mather to have pointed out how the *Nishmath* translated sin in the mind into physical illness, but the possibility that this principle could also explain other mysteries lured Mather instead into a discussion of biologic problems. Once again, the theologian in him seemed to be thrust aside by the scientist.

---

[3] p. 3.

[4] p. 4.

[5] The very word "psychosomatic," used over the last century to link body and mind, nevertheless implies a distinction between them.

[6] p. 40. Chapter V is in the Appendix. The philosophy here suggests Cartesian dualism, with the *Nishmath* playing much the same rôle as does the pineal gland in Descartes' writings.

The *Nishmath*, he explained, is located in various parts of the body and is composed of particles "which may be finer than those of the Light itself." It is not reason, but it is "the Life by which the several Parts have their Faculties maintained in Exercise." It provides sensation—sees, hears, and feels. It "leads to the Acts requisite in Generation" and guides the development of the embryo. It also directs instinctive behavior and such unconscious functions as those of digestion.[7]

Thus Mather first postulates a vital principle as an intermediary between mind (the "rational Soul") and the body, and then proceeds to employ it also as an explanation of biologic processes which are unconscious and yet seemingly purposeful in nature. This latter theme involves a classic problem: can teleologic behavior—the essential characteristic of "life"—be explained upon material grounds? Mather, despite his view of the body as a mechanism, felt that something more was involved. "There are many Things in the Humane Body, that cannot be solved by the Rules of Mechanism."[8] In an eloquent passage he declares:

In every other Machin, if anything be out of Order, it will remain so till some Hand from abroad should rectify it; it can do nothing for itself. But the Humane Body is a Machin, wherein, if anything be out of Order, presently the whole Engine, as under an Alarum, is awakened for the helping of what is amiss, and other Parts of the Engine strangely put themselves out of their Way that they may send in Help unto it. Whence can this proceed but from a *Nishmath-Chajim* in us, with such Faculties and such Tendencies from GOD imprinted on it?[9]

Here Mather aligns himself with an old tradition in biology. He clearly implies that a life-directing principle inheres in

---

[7] pp. 41–4. Mather's psychology, therefore, sharply distinguished between sensation and reasoning, assigning the first to the vital principle, the second to the "rational soul" or mind. He shows here no interest in epistemology, but the implication seems to be that the "rational soul" might possess innate ideas. Certainly, there is no indication—in his separation of sensation from reason—that he had been at all influenced by the current empiricism of Locke and others.

[8] p. 44.

[9] p. 47.

animals as well as men, since unconscious, purposeful behavior must be accounted for in all forms of life.[10]   As he
put it: "The *Nishmath-Chajim* is much like the Soul which
animates the Brutal World."[11]   Many able biologists and
physicians maintained such a "vitalistic" conception for
more than a century thereafter.

Having met the biological problem to his own satisfaction,
Mather returned to the original question of sin and illness.[12]
Sin, which presumably begins in the mind or "rational soul,"
is impressed upon the *Nishmath,* and the latter then exhibits
"a Sickness of the Spirit" which in turn is passed on to the
body in the form of physical illness.   In this sense, the *Nishmath* is "the Seat of our Diseases, or the Source of them."
All this is possible because that principle receives impressions from both mind and body and is "the vital Ty between them."   Hence it follows that to cure the body one
should first work upon the *Nishmath,* wherein the trouble
starts.   "Most certainly, the Physician that can find out
Remedies . . . that shall have a more immediate Efficacy to
brighten, and strengthen, and Comfort, the *Nishmath
Chajim,* will be the most successful Physician in the World.[13]

The most effective way of brightening the *Nishmath* is
through "Piety" in the "Rational Soul."   The latter, "in
its Reflections has powerful and wonderful Influences on the
Nishmath Chajim."[14]   If the "Rational Soul" can be brought

---

[10] It is possible, philosophically, to define "purpose" without reference to conscious-
ness—animal, human, or divine, but Mather assumed with most of his contemporaries
that teleologic behavior implied either human or divine guidance.

[11] p. 46.   Here Mather departs from the Cartesian view that animals are simply
machines.

[12] In the process, he suggests that the *Nishmath* will also explain witchcraft and other
occult phenomena.   In a word, he uses the principle as a philosophical catchall, to which
anything mysterious can be referred.

[13] p. 51.

[14] p. 56.

into "the Peace of God," it will brighten the *Nishmath*, and the latter in turn will then react upon the body in such a way as to promote a cure.

Although the religious appeal to the "Rational Soul" was Mather's main resource, he also advocated other measures to utilize mental factors in bodily health. He quotes Baglivi[15] as ascribing "a great part of our diseases" to mental cares and himself refers to: "what the Mind will do towards the Cure of the Body." The procedure advocated in this connection, in "The Angel," was more cheerful than that suggested by earlier sermons, and it implies some of the values which have been claimed for the confessional. "Let the Physician," declares Mather:

with all possible Ingenuity of Conversation, find out, what Matter of Anxiety there may have been upon the Mind of the Patient. . . . Having discovered the Burden, lett him use all the Ways he can devise, to take it off. Offer him such Thoughts as may be the best Anodynes for his distressed Mind; especially . . . the Ways to a Composure upon Religious Principles. Give him a Prospect, if you can, of sound Deliverance from his Distresses, or some Abatement of them.[16]

An awareness of psychosomatic relationships, as now understood, implies a two-way process: the body may influence the mind, as well as the reverse. Mather possessed the psychological apparatus for this in the view that the *Nishmath* was a "Ty" between them and was equally sensitive to each. Actually, he had relatively less to say about what physical (somatic) cures can do for the mind. Perhaps this was because cures which began with the body had no particular relevancy for his theology. But he did not overlook this theme entirely. Quite naturally, it received attention primarily in connection with mental states so extreme as to constitute insanity.

[15] Giorgio Baglivi, of Rome (1669–1707), an outstanding clinician.
[16] p. 52.

In discussions of mental illness, as might be expected, Mather leaned to some extent on theological or occult ideas. It was common enough for the medical thinkers of the seventeenth century, as well as for theologians, to ascribe such illness to Satan or his demons.[17] Felix Plater and Thomas Willis, for example, had held this view. Courageous protests had been made against it; indeed, the naturalistic concept of mental illness had been expressed from time to time for many centuries. But medical thinkers were turning to this outlook only gradually in Mather's time.[18]

The clergyman tried to combine occult and naturalistic approaches. In the *Magnalia*, for example, he had stated that the physical constitution of some individuals—the state of their humors—invites Satan or demons to take possession of them and so to cause insanity.[19] There were just two major forms of this condition as Mather recognized them—madness and melancholy. He assumed that these resulted, at least in part, from physical causes, but admitted uncertainty as to how these operate. In melancholy, for example, the animal spirits (generated in the brain) become "dull and soured;" but as to the occasion of this: "lett them, who know, declare; they who can only guess, will be modest and silent."[20]

The treatments recommended for mental illness were decidedly humane and were primarily of a psychologic nature. Melancholic patients should be endured, humored, and reasoned with.[21] Mather had intimate and bitter

---

[17] Mather, as noted before, also at times ascribed ordinary, somatic illness to Satan or his agents. He wrote, in Miltonic vein, about the Prince of Evil and his cohorts, who sometimes even work cures in an effort to steal the credit for this from God; transcript, pp. 492 ff.

[18] See Gregory Zilboorg, *A History of Medical Psychology*, New York, 1941, pp. 197 ff.

[19] I, 438 f.

[20] Transcript, pp. 220, 222, 225.

[21] pp. 220 ff.

experience with this process in the supposed mental illness of his third wife, as is revealed in detail in the diary.[22] Even in the cases of children whom he believed to be bewitched, his procedure had been primarily a psychologic and, apparently, a successful one.   But since he assumed that mental illness resulted in part from somatic conditions, he also recommended physical treatments.   These included the use of cold drinks, bathing, exercise, a soothing syrup, and moderate bleeding.[23]

The humane nature of Mather's psychotherapy is interesting, not only in itself, but in the fact that he makes no reference to the brutal treatments then in vogue. He seems almost to take a moderate, conciliatory attitude for granted. Nearly a century later, Benjamin Rush—often praised for the humanity of his psychiatry—would still urge far more severe measures.[24]

Occasionally Mather seemed to realize that, in ascribing mental illness to the humors and in following naturalistic therapy, he was forgetting his occult premises.   At one point, after discussing the animal spirits, he brings himself up short with the thought that—nevertheless—too much emphasis on these natural phenomena "ill becomes a Minister of the Gospel."[25]   Such awareness that his thought was moving from a theological to a scientific orientation was unusual.   Yet the trend itself can be observed in both negative and positive aspects of his medical writings.

It is notable, on the negative side, that Mather gave no credence to certain occult interpretations which had still

---

[22] Most critics have ascribed his increasing continence to the disturbed state of his wife's mind, but it is implied in the Boas' biography that the causal relationship here was the reverse, Ralph and Louise Boas, *Cotton Mather, Keeper of the Puritan Conscience*, New York, 1928.

[23] p. 226. Mather's general justification of somatic medicine will be discussed below.

[24] R. H. Shryock, "The Beginnings," in Gregory Zilboorg (ed.), *One Hundred Years of American Psychiatry*, New York, 1944, pp. 11 ff.

[25] p. 225.

been widely accepted during the preceding century. He largely ignored, for example, the astrologic tradition in medicine. Nor did he display interest in even the more or less naturalistic forms of divination; for example, in the common view that the secrets of mental, moral, or physical character can be discovered from examining a particular body part.[26]

More positively, Mather was beginning to be skeptical about cures by mystical means. Although convinced that wicked spirits were abroad and that people could invoke their favor by various charms, he was sure that it were better to depend on natural remedies. "Certainly," he wrote, "far from wise, are they that will go to Hell for Medicines.[27] He took special pains to repudiate the ancient notion that "a seventh son" possessed special healing powers and, in this connection, employed the logic of *reductio ad impossibile* in a manner which could have been used against mystical practices in general. There is no evidence, the clergyman noted, that God has given any such power to seventh sons, nor is there any reason to believe that this would inhere in the "natural Constitution" of such individuals. Perhaps, then, daemons are the source of this potency?:

But what an enchanted Field are we now brought into: and what a Door is opened unto ten thousand Sorceries! If Numbers are to be esteemed for the Healing of Diseases, why should not Figures be so too? And from Figures let us pass to Letters. . . . And why should not the seventh Son pronounce Words, and use his Lip as well as his Hand, for a Cure? . . . Would not a spell from him do as well as a Touch? I doubt it not! . . . I pray, lett us not foolishly leave the ordinary Ways of Cure, and run into impertinent, yea, very unwarrantable Superstitions.[28]

---

[26] See William A. Lessa, "Somatomancy—Precursor of the Science of Human Constitution," *Scientific Monthly*, LXXV (December, 1952), 357 ff.

[27] Transcript, p. 497.

[28] p. 500.

It would seem clear, from the foregoing discussion, that Mather was keenly aware of psychosomatic relationships and placed great emphasis upon the mental healing of somatic and mental illness. In the case of the latter, he also suggested material treatments. It remains to be shown, however, by what means he came to display such confidence in physical remedies for ordinary illness, that is, in medicine in the usual sense. Actually, it was the same religious outlook which justified, for him, the cultivation of somatic as well as of psychiatric medicine. In order to make this clear, one must recur momentarily to the theological background.

The theological interpretation of illness began, obviously, on a note which was grim and forbidding. The Old Testament doctrine of a God of Wrath finds frequent expression in "The Angel." Referring to infections, for example, Mather invoked a question which must have awed those who lived in constant fear of "visitations." "What unknown Armies," he inquired, "has the Holy One, wherewith to chastise, and even destroy, the rebellious children of Men?"[29] And he later suggests answers; as in stating that God, the commander of all disease, has vented His wrath upon the English nation with an all but universal plague of scurvy.[30]

Before such a God, men should prostrate themselves in an abject manner. Here Mather's masochistic tendencies, so apparent in early passages in his diary, are still in evidence. Those in pain should remember that they are suffering for their sins, just as Christ suffered on the cross for the sins of all mankind.[31] (In the chapter on childbirth, seventeen out of twenty-one pages are devoted to moralizing of this

[29] p. 71.
[30] p. 200.
[31] p. 85.

sort.[32]) And the proper thoughts for smallpox victims are those of self-abhorrence and self-abasement: such creatures are to be viewed as loathsome.[33]

It is difficult to say how far this attitude toward smallpox patients resulted from the nature of this particular disease and how far it was a product of Mather's theology. Abhorrence of the sick, or at least some degree of suspicion or disdain, was a logical corollary of the doctrine of theological pathogenesis. Recall only the Book of Job! Christianity is usually said to have replaced both this Old Testament view, and also the classical notion that the sick were inferior, by the thought that they were actually ennobled by illness and should be objects of respect and commiseration.[34] But the revived emphasis upon Old Testament teachings involved Mather—if not Calvinism at large—in something of a reversion to pre-Christian conceptions. For him, sickness was no sign of grace: it was sometimes viewed literally as a *dis*-grace.

It was not strange, therefore, that men—sinful as they were—often endured suffering from which there was no escape. In a discourse of 1714, Mather had declared:

We may have our Bodily infirmities, which may be grievous Diseases. But can they not be Cured? No: There comes that Message unto us from Heaven concerning them, "Thou shalt use many Medicines, and thou shalt not be Cured." We must lie under the Grief, as long as we are in the Body.[35]

Blunt as this statement may seem, it must still be echoed in the case of incurables, and Mather may have found it easier to reconcile this problem with a God of wrath than with a God of mercy.

[32] pp. 396 ff.

[33] p. 158.

[34] Henry E. Sigerist, *Man and Medicine*, New York, 1932, pp. 80 ff.

[35] *Insanabilia: An Essay upon Incurables*, Boston, 1714, p. 23.

In at least one aspect of sickness and death, nevertheless, the clergyman did find God's way inscrutable. There is a note of desperation when he comments, in "The Angel," on the appalling toll of infant mortality. Here the father, who had lost nearly all his own little ones, is moved to poetic language: "O how unsearchable the Judgements of God, and His Ways past finding out! The lamps but just litt up, and blown out again."[36]

This concern about infant mortality paralleled that of other divines over infant damnation, and it will be recalled that Wigglesworth—in his *Day of Doom*—did record that damned infants could be consigned to at least "the easiest room in hell." Mather envisaged no such concession, within *this* world, in the form of lessened mortality. But one cannot necessarily conclude from this that nothing ever would have been done for the health of children if they had been left only to the theologians. In the 1720's, neither they nor the physicians knew anything which *could* be done. Mather's exclamatory statement was probably as close to a protest as he dared come under the circumstances. And in so far as it was such, it looked forward to the infant welfare movement which was to ensue later in the century.[37]

This interpretation is the more plausible for the fact that Mather, despite his grim view of the origin and meaning of disease, was intensely anxious to do all that was possible to prevent, cure, or ameliorate this curse. And he was convinced that, within limitations already suggested, much could be done in these directions. The more optimistic outlook was based, even as was his pessimism, upon religious

[36] p. 456. Mather expressed his concern for children in various other ways; see Sister Monica Kiefer, O.P., *American Children Through Their Books, 1700–1835*, Philadelphia, 1948, *passim*.

[37] See Ernest Caulfield, *The Infant Welfare Movement in the Eighteenth Century*, New York, 1931.

principles. If Mather frequently spoke the language of the Old Testament, he by no means overlooked the implications of the New. Although God had sent disease into the world, He had also sent His Son that men might not perish. Christ redeemed men's souls, and so closely were these knit with men's bodies that in the very process there might be physical as well as spiritual healing.[38]

In a sermon of 1717, Mather had inquired: "But are not His People Distempered?" and had added:

Yes: But our SAVIOUR is a Shepherd who cures the distempers of his People. Sheep are liable to a Variety of Diseases. A Shepherd has his Medicines. He doth what we read in Ezek. XXIV. 4. "Heal that which is sick, and bind up that which is broken." 'Tis what our SAVIOUR does for His People, how Effectually, how Gloriously. . . . In Him we have, the Grand Physician of Souls. What is He but, the Lord our Healer?[39]

It was this hopeful doctrine which inspired Mather's faith in the efficacy of prayer as "the Universal Medicine."[40] Sinners who prayed for forgiveness might indeed be healed. No doubt Mather was convinced that he had seen this happen before his very eyes.

Once he had accepted the view that healing was part of the divine plan, moreover, Mather envisaged other means to this end which would supplement prayer. As already noted, he found evidence in the world about him that God helped those who helped themselves. (This was a seventeenth-century saying.) How else explain that in each part of the globe remedies had been made available for the illnesses peculiar to that region? It will be observed, in the statement just quoted, that "a Shepherd has his medicines" with which he cures his sheep and that this is "what our Saviour does

---

[38] The adjustment of the implications of the Old Testament to those of the New was a basic problem for New England as well as for other theologians. See, e.g., Joseph Haroutunian, *Piety Versus Moralism: The Passing of the New England Theology*, New York, 1932, pp. 157 ff.

[39] MS. sermon, Amer. Antiq. Soc.

[40] This is the subject of a "Mantissa" to Chapter IV in "The Angel," pp. 36–9.

for His People, how Effectually." In other words, God shows these natural remedies to those who will only search them out. And at this point, the whole realm of naturalistic medicine opens out before the seeker—the scientist—as a part of a larger whole. Such medicine is not only consistent with God's plan: it is an essential part of it.

With this religious justification ever in mind, Mather was able to give full play to the pleasure he derived from scientific observations and hypotheses. Present scientists may think that this theological approach to science followed a circuitous route, but it was the natural one to take in an age which sought to reconcile new revelations with the old. The process, as Mather participated in it, was not the "warfare" of which such later American critics as Draper and White would write at length. It was rather a joyous cooperation, from which science at least benefited much at the time.

It was in the course of giving play to scientific interests that Mather became more and more impressed with the wonders of Nature.[41] The resulting enthusiasms, which were most optimistic in tone, were no doubt inconsistent with pessimistic elements which persisted in his writings. This is quite evident in "The Angel," where the grim view of sinful man condemned to suffering appears side by side with almost ecstatic praise of the wonders of man's body and of all which may be done to preserve or restore its well-being. The eye, for example, is a marvelous organ devised for our use by a beneficent God—who, later, has also provided us with spectacles for making it even more serviceable.[42]

This, and many similar observations, are at one point summed up in a reference to "such a Divine Peece of

[41] This was carried so far that Isaac W. Riley, in his *American Philosophy, the Early Schools*, New York, 1907, pp. 197 ff, interpreted Mather as anticipating the transcendentalists' love of Nature for its own sake.

[42] Transcript, pp. 259, 261 f.

Mechanism as the Body of Man."[43]   This concept of the body as a mechanism implies a regularity in its functioning which is analogous to the regularity of astronomic phenomena—which also impressed Mather. And just as some recent authorities have seen in his astronomic views an indication of nascent deism, so similar conclusions could be drawn from his physiology. Mather was usually as unaware of such implications in the one case as in the other. Indeed, as mentioned earlier, he specifically denied that true science could be in any way inconsistent with true faith.[44]

In summing up Mather's integration of theology and medicine, as this is best presented in "The Angel," one may repeat that he was maintaining a tradition which had been expressed by physicians as well as clergymen during preceding centuries.[45] The parallel with the priest-physician van Helmont, whom Mather read, was particularly close. One finds in the former the same basic ideas about original sin and illness, and even much the same notions as to how spiritual healing may work through the vital principle within the body[46] to bring about physical cures.[47] The majority of physicians of Mather's day, however, had abandoned theological explanations of illness, so that his work may be interpreted as a persistence of already outmoded concepts. And it is easy to explain this survival in terms of his clerical outlook. At this point, one can understand that Holmes had more in mind, in objecting to clerical physicians, than their immediate attitudes toward patients.

[43] p. 58. The phrase itself was borrowed from Francis Fuller, *Medicina Gymnastica*, London, 1704, p. 12.

[44] *Manuductio ad Ministerium*, p. 51.

[45] See Chapter III, above.

[46] Through the *Archaeus* in van Helmont, and via the *Nishmath* in Mather.

[47] Walter Pagel, *The Religious and Philosophical Aspects of van Helmont's Science and Medicine*, Supplements to the *Bull. of the Hist. of Med.*, No. 2 (Baltimore, 1944), p. 12 f. An English translation of van Helmont was available in Mather's time; see *Oriatrike, or Physick Refined*, London, 1662, p. 553.

It is a nice question, nevertheless, whether Mather's religious medicine is to be viewed simply as a survival of outdated ideas, or whether it may be interpreted instead as a basic orientation which persisted or reappeared long after his time. One refers here not only to recent revivals of religious healing outside the medical profession, but also to later instances of a theological approach among physicians themselves. This was true, notably, of much of the medical writing in Germany under the spell of the *Naturphilosophie* a full century after Mather's death.[48]

*   *   *   *   *

So much for the religious, occult, and psychologic elements in "The Angel." Although these provide a general background and also permeate much of the work in the form of moralizing, the number of chapters devoted entirely to them is small.[49] Of the 66 original chapters, only three are centered on sin and spiritual healing, three on mental illness, and two on the occult. The greater part of the work, then, relates to somatic medicine.

"The Angel" includes no systematic account of anatomy or physiology, but—as in present, general texts on medicine—knowledge of these fields is implicit in the discussions. Thus, in commenting on the immediate cause of toothache, the author refers to the structure of teeth and to their supply of nerves. In another connection, he refers to the circulation of the blood as explaining how rapidly morbific materials may spread illness throughout the system. Since such references appear only sporadically, however, they do not in themselves indicate just what the range of Mather's anatomic and physiologic knowledge may have been.

[48] Thus, Heinroth and others then wrote on "Christian pathology," while Kerner viewed demons as the causes of disease; see Paul Diepgen, *Deutsche Medizin vor 100 Jahre: Ein Beitrag zur Geschichte der Romantik*, Leipzig, 1923, *passim;* and Georg Honigmann, *Geschichtliche Entwicklung der Medizin*, München, 1925, p. 66.

[49] No comment need be made on the incidental moralizing which occurs in many chapters throughout the MS.

The implication is that Mather's approach, like Sydenham's, was primarily that of a clinician. He focused on diseases—their description, history, causes, means of prevention, and possible cures. This perspective, within medicine, was analogous to his interest in natural history within the biologic realm. Conversely, there is no indication that a laboratory approach to medicine made much appeal to him. He appropriated the results of this when they seemed useful to the clinician's purpose, but showed no disposition to employ it in person.

The contrast here doubtless had its origins, to some extent, in two different types of mind, and the divergence between them has reacted on medical science down to our own day. But the contrast was also, in part, a reflection of the cultural environment; a pragmatic outlook naturally encouraged direct studies of disease rather than abstract biologic research. In aligning himself with the clinicians rather than with laboratory scientists, Mather was typical of nearly all American medical men throughout his own and the ensuing century.[50]

This did not mean that Mather was uncritical of the clinical literature. Like many others, both physicians and laymen, he had his say on the perennial theme of "The Uncertainties of the Physicians." In a chapter with this title,[51] he notes the many contradictions in which medical men are involved, ridiculing some of them almost as sharply as Holmes would later ridicule him. The literature on consumption is cited as a good example of the general confusion, since this disease ranked high in mortality and had therefore received wide attention.[52] And here, he remarks:

---

[50] R. H. Shryock, *American Medical Research: Past and Present*, New York, 1947, pp. 18 ff, 30 ff, 70 ff.

[51] Chapter XL. See Appendix; transcript, pp. 312 ff.

[52] Note that tuberculosis was viewed as a major menace well before the advent of what is conventionally called the industrial revolution.

we will not concern ourselves with the Differences among the Physicians, about the Cause of this Distemper; (whereupon, who can read the Collection made by Dolaeus,[53] and not cry out, the Diviners are mad!) but only see, how they differ about the Cure of it.

There follows a long list of remedies, each strongly supported by certain authorities and as violently opposed by others; for example:

Many hold, that no Good is to be done in a Consumption without Opiates. It is held by others, that they are pernicious Things, and no better than a Halter.... Lett Weikard[54] and Harvey engage one another upon the Juice of Turnips; the former with Panegyricks, the latter with Invectives. . . . Helmont . . . and Dolaeus, condemn the Letting of Blood in a Consumption.... Yett Galen and Mercatus[55] . . . approve it . . . Hippocrates would have us bleed in Distempers of the Lungs, as most as long as there is any Blood in the Body.[56]

And so on and on.

In the course of this analysis, the author cites the classical authors but makes it plain that he stands in no awe of them:

What an Oracle has Hippocrates been to our Physicians, who profanely enough use to putt the Title of Divine upon him! . . . And yett; what are the Aphorisms of Hippocrates; many of them trivial enough, and known to our Barbers; and those that are more important, many of them found false in very many Cases; many full of Uncertainty?[57]

What is the moral of all this? A physician, writing in this vein, was apt to claim that confusion had at last been resolved in his own particular therapy. But Mather, conscious of no guild loyalty, deliberately concludes that medical men—in and of themselves—are largely useless. Only if God guides them, can they be of service. This formula, so to speak, enables him to express his opinions of physicians and yet still advise patients to consult them.

---

[53] Joh. Dolaeus, 1651–1707, whose *Opera omnia* were published at Frankfurt a. M., 1703.

[54] Possibly Arnold Weickhard, 1578–1645.

[55] M. Murcatus, Italian physician, 1541–1593.

[56] p. 313 f.

[57] p. 317.

O thou afflicted . . . go to Physicians, in Obedience to God, who has commanded the Use of Means. But place thy Dependence on God alone to direct and prosper them. And know, that they are all Physicians of no Value, if He do not so.[58]

Perhaps one may be pardoned here for injecting a mildly cynical note. Observe that this same formula retained the clergyman, as the authority on matters divine, in a position to oversee physicians in some ultimate sense. Perhaps the former should decide, at least, who were the Godly doctors and who were not? Mather does not say this specifically, but a later clergyman—John Wesley—would urge his followers to consult only those doctors who met his standards of piety. Yet even cynics may recognize a valid element in this view; the physician should be a man of character as well as of learning.

All that Mather had noted concerning the uncertainties of therapy did not prevent him from recommending various drugs for various diseases. True, he occasionally qualifies this advice, but at other times is quite positive. In general, he was as much addicted to polypharmacy as were most practitioners of the age. These varied drugs were probably of little if any value, but it may be again noted that those which Mather suggested were not likely to do much harm. Here and there, as in any pharmacopeia, were items of real value. Thus, in discussing scurvy, Mather declares that a diet of salt meats is dangerous and urges the use of citrus juices.[59] Even his advocacy of opiates, as in smallpox cases,[60] may have had some ameliorative value.

The general plan of "The Angel" was to provide a chapter on each of the more important diseases as these were then recognized. As far as was possible, the author distinguished

[58] p. 316.

[59] p. 204. The value of citrus juice was certainly known long before its conventional dating in connection with the British Navy.

[60] p. 170.

between sharply different—that is, specific—disorders. But he still had to treat as distinct illnesses conditions which now would be viewed only as symptoms, for example, headache, dropsy, and jaundice. He also had to present as single diseases such conglomerates as "fevers" and "fluxes." Conversely, etiologic ignorance led to distinctions between diseases which are now integrated in terms of a common causal factor, for example, in the cases of scrofula and "consumption" (tuberculosis). Similar confusions persisted in medical thought until well into the nineteenth century.

Mather made little attempt to classify diseases. He occasionally followed the old method of assigning entities to body parts, as in the cases of toothache, headache, and sore throat. But he makes no use of anatomic systems, never referring, for example, to vascular or nervous disorders. Nor could he, for obvious reasons, classify by causal factors, as would be done now in reference to infectious or deficiency diseases. Hence his arrangement of subjects seems arbitrary, but it has at least the advantage of taking up one theme after another in much the form that these were known to the general public. There are none of the over-elaborate and meaningless classifications which came into vogue later in the century.

Most major illnesses, as then recognized, are considered in the course of the study. Using modern concepts, one may say that "The Angel" deals with a variety of infectious diseases, such as smallpox, measles, and venereal disorders.[61] Malnutrition is represented by ricketts and scurvy, and the chronic or degenerative diseases by cancer, kidney conditions, and rheumatism.[62] The author also uses age and sex,

[61] Other examples are "worms," "the itch," colds, sore throat, "fevers," and "fluxes."

[62] Other examples are gout, asthma, and apoplexy. Unfortunately, the chapters on fevers, agues, measles, scrofula, and cancer, as listed in what Mather called the "Bill of Fare," are now missing. Assuming that these were originally included, they may have been removed while the MS. was in possession of the Mather family.

as is still done, as special means for classifying, inserting chapters on the diseases of women, of infants, and of old age. There is, finally, a section on occupational disorders, taken largely from Ramazzini's famous work of 1700.[63]

The supposed entities which Mather includes in his survey, and also the emphasis which he accords to particular ones among them, provide some impression of the disease pattern of the age. As might be expected, there is emphasis upon acute infections, notably upon smallpox, measles, the "fevers," and the "fluxes." But scurvy also receives much attention as a widespread plague. This item, as well as the references to "worms" and to "the itch," has obvious implications for the living standards and hygiene of that era.

Notably absent are references to heart or vascular diseases as such. But it would be hasty to conclude from this that these conditions, now the greatest single cause of death in this country, were of little concern in 1725. For one thing, the concept of the hypertension complex had not yet emerged; although a decade after Mather wrote, Stephen Hales—another clerical scientist—would do pioneer work in this field. Vascular conditions doubtless lurked behind some of the other phenomena noted, such as dropsy, kidney disease, and apoplexy. Cancer was also of concern, though there is no way of telling how Mather treated it. One concludes that the degenerative conditions worried the elder portions of the population then even as now.[64]

In several instances, the medical text is almost lost in moral or religious considerations. In the case of consumption, this was because the author believed it to be usually

---

[63] Mather remarks that this work (De Morbis Artificium) deserves to be better known among "artificers." He advises here that sedentary workers should take exercise; transcript, p. 486 f.

[64] Mather himself, for example, most dreaded palsy, gout, the stone, cancer, and consumption, of which only the last is now viewed as an infectious disease. See Samuel Mather's biography, p. 62 f.

fatal; hence the victim should make his peace with God. Yet even here he adds a list of possible remedies.[65]

It was when he approached the venereal infections that the clergyman in Mather seemed to overwhelm his medical self. In offering some "clean Thoughts, on, the Foul Disease," he declined even to mention symptoms. He made it plain enough that guilty cases deserved their fate, but noted also the tragedy of the innocent victims. As was common at the time, he failed to distinguish clearly between syphilis and gonorrhea, although he implied on historical grounds that two diseases were involved.[66] This distinction would not be made finally until the nineteenth century.

The clergyman's disinclination to aid victims of these diseases is not surprising; indeed, general hospitals in the United States continued to take this attitude as late as 1850. At the conclusion of his chapter, however, he declares that there is mercy even for these sinners. And then, as though ashamed to offer advice but not stern enough to withhold it entirely, he says of the patient:

I'l do Nothing for you. . . . And I shall not care, if he take the Italian Cortegiana's Way for your Cure, (a Quarter of an Ounce of Coloquinesda infused in a Quart of proper Wine) which will keep you in Torment for three Days together. Gett ye gone to the Cheirurgeon. And when he has made a thorough Cure,—then, sin no more.[67]

In dealing with any particular disease, Mather usually identifies it by symptoms and then proceeds—if the information is at hand—to comment on its history.[68] Here one has the suggestion of specificity, that is, he is dealing with an entity which can be traced back in time. On rare oc-

---

[65] Transcript, pp. 306 ff. See Chapter XXXIX, "The Consumption," Appendix.

[66] pp. 193 ff. See Chapter XXI, Appendix.

[67] Transcript, p. 198. It is usually said that no distinctions were made between physicians and surgeons in the Colonies. Perhaps Mather was simply employing common English usage in this statement.

[68] As in ascribing syphilis to a Columbian origin.

casions, he implies that pathologic changes lurk behind the symptoms. Thus, in discussing consumption, he notes the wasting of the body, the lingering fever, and the tedious cough and then ascribes the latter to the fact that the lungs "are grievously corroded."[69] But, like most physicians of the period, he still failed to envisage any systematic correlation of pathologic anatomy with clinical phenomena.[70]

As has been noted, however, Mather was convinced that much illness originated in one peculiarly vital part of the body—an idea which would be exploited by later medical systems and sects. For Mather, this part was the stomach or "main wheel." In the language of the later eighteenth century, he viewed disturbances in the stomach as "the proximate cause" of many diseases. But not content with this, he also wished to know the ultimate cause (etiology) of these conditions. As he himself put it: "It may be one of the truest Maxims ever yett advanced by any of the Gentlemen, has been that. . . . A distempered Stomach is the Origin of all Diseases. . . . But, Syrs, whence is it, that the Stomach is distempered?"[71]

Casting about for an answer to this basic question, the clergyman encountered in the literature certain early expressions of the so-called "germ theory." His main source, as noted, was Benjamin Marten's *New Theory of Consumptions* (London, 1720), but he was also familiar with the similar writings of Kircher, "Lieuenhoek," and others.[72] Although he first presents this as a conjecture, it is clear from what follows that he became convinced of its validity.

[69] p. 301.

[70] This had been suggested by a number of great physicians during the preceding century, but would not be widely attempted until after 1800. See Esmond R. Long, *History of Pathology*, Baltimore, 1928, pp. 77 ff.

[71] p. 65.

[72] See Chapter VII in the Appendix, entitled "Conjecturalies or, Some Touches upon, A New Theory of many Diseases."

The theory fitted so nicely into known phenomena, and had such implications for prevention or cure, that he proceeded to discuss it with enthusiasm.

In introducing the hypothesis, the author notes that microscopes have revealed swarms of minute "animals" or "insects"[73] which inhabit all other animals and plants. These microscopic beings possess all the parts and functions of visible animals[74] and insinuate themselves into the latter through food and drink, through respiration, and even through the skin. Once in a host, the animalculae "multiply prodigiously" and injure the blood or "tender vessels." There is, moreover, a certain specificity about them, for "one Species of these Animals may offend in one Way, and another in another, and the various Parts may be variously offended: from whence may flow a Variety of Diseases."[75]

Many are the phenomena which can be explained by this hypothesis. Thus, hereditary disease results from the transmission of animalculae from mother to child. If vast numbers of them invade a community at once, they produce epidemics. And they also may be transmitted from one region to another in the bodies or goods of travelers (fomites). In one passage, Mather seems to imply that the insect swarms often observed during "plagues" are the actual causes of epidemics.[76] If so, he thought in this case of visible insects as causal factors. This concept is distinct from the later one concerning such insects as "vectors" of infection, but the former notion might still—if taken seriously—have been made the basis of preventive measures.

---

[73] In the vernacular, we still refer to "bugs" in this same sense.

[74] This was a common illusion. Even Leeuwenhoek thought that he actually saw heads, tails, etc. in his animalculae—a nice illustration of the subjective factor in scientific observations.

[75] Transcript, p. 66.

[76] p. 67. This idea was later used by American physicians who advanced the animalcular theory between about 1830 and 1850.

It is the migration of pathogenic animalculae which explains the history of epidemic diseases in man, domestic animals, and plants. This is the way in which measles, smallpox, and the plague reached Europe from Asia and Africa. These infections are therefore exotics in Europe and America. But routes may be reversed. Thus, the "Lues venerea" originated in America, but "Europe has paid its Debt unto America, by making unto it a Present of the Small Pox, in Lieu of the Great one" (syphilis).[77]

In two cases, "the Itch" and syphilis, Mather describes how the infecting animalculae may be transmitted from one person to another by contact or by using common towels,[78] a view which would subsequently be confirmed. The implications for preventive measures were clear enough.

It is true that pathogenic animals may invade a body without causing disease. Hence a theory is presented concerning what now would be termed "resistance" or "temporary immunity." If bodily secretions and evacuations are continued normally, the animalculae may be cast out as rapidly as they appear, so that no harm will be done. But "when the Emunctories thro' cold or any other Cause are obstructed, or any usual Evacuations are stopped; this prevents their passing off, and many Mischiefs ensue upon it."[79]

Once the animalculae have produced disease, the most effective way to cure is not merely to check but to eliminate them completely. Otherwise they will multiply again and become as troublesome as before.[80] This presented a serious problem, and Mather was awed by the panorama which the germ theory opened before his mind's eye. All about mankind were these invisible enemies, which

[77] p. 67. This quip has been ascribed to various medical men at one time or another.
[78] p. 68.
[79] p. 70.
[80] p. 68.

must somehow be met and overcome. Pondering this, he recalled his religious premises:

How much do we walk thro' unseen Armies of numberless Living ,Things ready to seize and prey upon us! A Walk, like the Running of the Deadly Garloup, which was of old called a Passing thro' the Brick-kiln! What unknown Armies has the Holy One, wherewith to . . . even destroy, the Rebellious Children of Men? Millions of Billions of Trillions of Invisible Velites! Of sinful Men they say, Our Father, shall we smite them? On His order, they do it immediately; they do it effectually.[81]

Yet this almost instinctive reference to the religious background did not deter Mather from proceeding at once to a strictly medical conclusion. Means must be found for destroying the villains of the piece, agents of the Holy One as these might be! In a passage of sonorous dignity, he faced at once the promise and the problems of chemotherapy:

But, O ye Sons of Erudition, and ye wise Men of Enquiry; lett this Enquiry come into a due Consideration with you: How far a potent Worm-killer, that may be safely administred, would go further than any Remedy yett found out, for the Cure of many Diseases! Mercury, we know thee: But we are afraid, thou wilt kill us too, if we employ thee to kill them that kill us.[82]

Mercury had indeed been widely used as a specific against syphilis, but had been found as dangerous as Mather implied.[83] Yet, despite this impasse in therapy, the clergyman clearly saw great possibilities in the future. In a word, he not only accepted the animalcular theory but explained clearly—following his European authorities—its application to disease phenomena, and its implications for prevention and cure.[84]

---

[81] p. 71.

[82] p. 72.

[83] Karl Sudhoff later cited this old use of mercury as supporting an historical view which Mather had rejected; *i.e.*, that syphilis was of pre-Columbian, European origin; see Sudhoff, *Der Ursprung der Syphilis*, Leipzig, 1913, pp. 6 ff. It is interesting that the first marked success in chemotherapy, which Mather envisaged, was achieved by Erlich after 1900—using other metallic compounds (arsenicals, "salvarsan") against this same disease.

[84] Of special interest, in connection with this hypothesis, is Chapter XX on "The Small-Pox encountered." This theme will be considered at length in the final chapter.

The clergyman's acceptance of the germ theory as a whole was an interesting performance. Although there was considerable European interest in the hypothesis during the late seventeenth and early eighteenth centuries, reference was rarely made to it in the literature of the English-American Colonies. There was, to be sure, a dearth of medical writings, and it is conceivable that some physicians knew of the theory but left no trace of this in the record. Mather himself remarked that "many" had come to accept it, but whether this term referred to Americans is not clear.

The only one of Mather's American contemporaries who is known to have referred in print to pathogenic organisms was his colleague Benjamin Colman of the rival Brattle Street Church.[85] Perhaps the latter had encountered the concept independently, or he may have derived it from Mather. In any case, the fact that *two* clergymen shared this view at the same time suggests that there may have been some discussions of it in Boston—at least in clerical circles. But Colman only mentioned the matter in passing. Its subsequent neglect by native physicians may be explained in part by a lapse of interest in Europe also during the latter part of the century.[86] Not until after 1800 was there a revival of much concern with the theory.[87]

Mather, then, was apparently the only American of the eighteenth century to give serious heed to the animalcular hypothesis. There is no evidence, however, that he exerted any influence on later American physicians in this connec-

---

[85] *Some Observations on the New Method of Receiving the Small-Pox*, Boston, 1721, p. 14 f.

[86] See Vilmos Manninger, *Der Entwickelungsgang der Antiseptik u. Aseptik . . . Aus dem ungarischen Originale übersetzt*, Breslau, 1904, pp. 26 ff.

[87] Even awareness of the theory remained very rare in this country, until after Dr. John Crawford of Baltimore wrote on it some eighty years after Mather's death. See his *Lecture . . . on the Cause, Seat, and Cure of Diseases*, Baltimore, 1811, as well as his periodical essays. There ensued a second period of interest in the U.S.A. to about 1850, then a second lapse, 1850–1875, then a final revival.

tion. "The Angel" was never published, and even if it had been, it is doubtful if the local medical men would have been in a mood to give it serious attention. Mather, then, failed in his effort to introduce the animalcular concept into American medicine. The significance of his theory lies rather in the indication of open-mindedness on his part—an attitude associated, also, with an ability to select out of contemporary science certain ideas which were to prove of lasting value.

This is, however, not quite the whole story. Mather did not merely accept theories which were then forgotten, only to be subsequently reaffirmed. He also, in the case of immunology, applied his ideas to experience. The approach to inoculation in 1721, which is usually assumed to have been purely empirical, was actually—on his part—a quite rational one in terms of animalculae. And in this context, his leadership helped to inaugurate a major preventive movement which continued into ensuing centuries. This aspect of Mather's medicine was not lost, and it merits a final chapter.

Chapter VII

The Advent of Preventive Medicine: Boston, 1721

Some four years before Mather completed "The Angel," there had occurred the Boston smallpox epidemic of 1721 in which he played a conspicuous role. It was during this experience that he made his major contribution to actual medical practice, and in order to understand this one must recall his background for dealing with such a public crisis. The circumstances of the epidemic itself need be noted only briefly, since these have been well described elsewhere.

Mather, as has been noted, was not only interested in medicine as such, but he saw in this field an immediate opportunity to apply science to the welfare of mankind. The desire to be of service to his fellow men seems to have grown on him over the years. This attitude evolved against the background of Christian benevolence in general, and of clerical leadership in particular, and was further encouraged by the example of contemporary German pietism.

Mather began his correspondence with the pietists of Halle in 1709. This exchange was but one instance of continuous intellectual contacts between colonial New England and Germany,[1] but it was an especially significant instance. Mather found in August H. Francke of Halle the very qualities to which he himself aspired: a combination of learning, piety, and devotion to the public welfare. Francke wrote in detail about his schools, orphanage, and hospital, and the Boston clergyman then published a glowing account of these for New England readers.[2] Mather felt that

[1] Harold S. Jantz, "German Thought and Literature in New England, 1620–1820," *Jour. of Eng. and Ger. Phil.*, XLI (1942), 5 ff.

[2] *Nuncia Bona e Terra Longinqua*, Boston, 1715; reprinted by Kuno Francke, "Further Documents Concerning Cotton Mather and August Hermann Francke," *Americana Germanica*, I (1897), 55–66.

Francke was serving God nobly in *this* World, and he was
especially impressed by the kindly piety of the latter's
works and by the numbers who were sent out from Halle
"to do good abroad." The Bostonian included in his comments the famous statement that: "The World begins to
feel a Warmth from the Fire of God, which thus flames in
the Heart of Germany, beginning to extend into many
regions; the whole World will ere long be sensible to it!"[3]

Here was a valid prediction of the influence which German pietism was shortly to exert in both England and its
American Colonies, and Mather seems to have been the
first New Englander to respond to this "Warmth" from
abroad. Although he was never a revivalist in the later
sense, his account of Francke breathes an enthusiasm
which was foreign to early Puritanism. In other words,
he became emotionally as well as rationally committed to
an expanded vision of good works. Jantz declares that this
same account provides the first sign that pietism was chang-
ing New England attitudes:

in the direction of easing and softening their harshness, their asperity,
their cold dogmatism, and their appeal to fear. Granitic Puritanism
was beginning to break up and allow the intrusion of that emotionalism
which first showed its power in the religious revivals a short time later
and continued to gather strength through the rest of the century.[4]

Mather can thus be pictured as the herald of the Great
Awakening, which had its social as well as its religious implications. Although some of his public activities may have
been petty or meddlesome, he clearly rose above this level
in his major interests and enthusiasms. Nor should these
enthusiasms be credited entirely to the German influence;
room must be left for his own genius in these matters. Note
that his chief publication in this field, *Bonifacius* (*Essays*

[3] *Ibid.*, p. 62.

[4] *Ibid.*, p. 22.

To Do Good), appeared in 1710, when he had just begun to establish contact with Halle. T. J. Holmes terms this work "warm, friendly, helpful" and notes that Mather—despite his reputation for vanity and pedantry—published it anonymously. It apparently exerted wide influence, since it went through at least eighteen editions. Indeed, Moses Coit Tyler remarked that it held "the germs and hints of nearly all those vast organizations of benevolence that have been the glory of the years since it was written."[5] Mather's concern for social welfare was undoubtedly genuine and fruitful.

There is no better illustration of this fruitfulness than is afforded by Mather's efforts to improve the health of his community. Here his concern was reinforced, as it were, by his particular interest in medical problems. He devoted himself to those various aspects of local health which are, today, distinguished under such headings as "medical care," the "refresher" training of physicians, and "public health" in the ordinary sense. His desire to provide medicines for the poor (medical care) has been mentioned. So, too, has his inclination to impart the latest medical knowledge to apprentice-trained "doctors" ("refresher" training). When it came to public health activities, he always consulted physicians before urging any particular course; and it was only during the crises of two epidemics, and in the face of the indifference or opposition of that profession, that he undertook independent action.

This latter attitude was first displayed in the publication of Mather's pamphlet on measles in 1713.[6] He was con-

---

[5] Quoted by Holmes, *Cotton Mather: A Bibliography*, I, 92. Benjamin Franklin's testimony of how this work influenced his own conduct "through life," in his letter of 1784 to Samuel Mather, is viewed by Schneider (*History of American Philosophy*, 1946, p. 39 f) as a "joke," but we are unable to find evidence to justify this interpretation.

[6] *A Letter, About a Good Management under the Distemper of the Measles, at this time Spreading in the Country. Here Published for the Benefit of the Poor, and such as may want the help of Able Physicians*, Boston, 1713. This work shows a reasonable knowledge of the distinct symptoms of the disease, and recommends moderate treatments and good nursign. The chapter on measles in the later "Angel" has been lost.

vinced that there were many who did not secure the services of physicians, and felt that—with a serious epidemic at hand —something must be done about this. But, like some later reformers, he was somewhat apprehensive about the attitude which the medical profession would take in the matter. After having himself lost his wife, three children, and a maidservant from the disease, he finally suggested to physicians that they distribute directions on its treatment. The doctors declined to do this, but Mather—upon issuing the pamphlet— then declared that he did so with professional approval.[7]

Aware that he might be criticized for such action, he took pains to explain that he was not merely meddling in professional affairs. "I know not," he declared, "(. . . and I care not) what Censures this Action may meet withal." And he added:

I am sure, nothing but a pure Act of Charity to the Poor, where Physicians are wanting, is now intended; nor anything offered, but what a Number of our most Eminent physicians have approved of . . . and the helping, tho' of but one or two Miserables, weighs down, against all that may be said, against the Freedom which this Letter has taken. I am satisfied, The Angel of Bethesda would Esteem it so.[8]

The clergyman was not so fortunate in his relations with the medical profession eight years later, when the next health crisis was precipitated by a more sinister disease. Smallpox had become more widespread and virulent during the preceding century, and was by 1700 an object of intense fear throughout Europe and America. Associated with it were circumstances which met all the criteria for arousing popular alarm. The disease was loathsome, it was highly fatal, it spread in epidemic form, and the scars it left on those who recovered served as a perpetual reminder of its menacing nature. Like certain other historic plagues, it was therefore more calculated to arouse demands for public

[7] *Diary*, II, 256 ff; 272.

[8] *A Letter*, p. 4.

action than were endemic ills which—no matter how serious—were apt to be taken for granted.

Smallpox, like the similar but already differentiated measles and chicken pox, seemed obviously contagious. Hence it was common to combat it by the isolation procedures inherited from earlier struggles against so-called leprosy and the bubonic plague. Such procedures, while helpful at times, failed to check major epidemics. It is against this background that one can understand the growing interest displayed in Europe after 1700 in reports about the oriental folk practice of inoculation. This was said to result in mild cases and to convey immunity thereafter. Reports were also made of similar folk practices in remote parts of Europe. But apart from the doubtful nature of these latter stories, it was certainly the information from the East which aroused serious attention.[9]

As early as 1700, Dr. Martin Lister, F.R.S., received from a kinsman a report on inoculation as it was practiced in China. During the same year, Dr. Clopton Havers brought the matter to the attention of the Royal Society. Subsequently, in 1713, there was some discussion of the matter before that body, and in 1714 Dr. John Woodward communicated to it the famous letter of Dr. Emanuel Timoni recommending the procedure as practiced in Turkey.[10] There followed more discussion and requests for further information. As a result of all this the Society published in 1716[11] an independent Latin account of Turkish practice by one Pylarini, which had already appeared in a Latin version at

[9] There is a considerable literature on the early history of inoculation. See, *e.g.*, "The History of Inoculation and Vaccination," *Lecture Memoranda, XVIIth International Congress of Medicine*, London, 1913, Chapters 1–3; Arnold C. Klebs, "Historic Evolution of Variolation," *Johns Hopkins Hospital Bull.*, XXIV (March, 1913), 70; and his similar *Die Variolation im achtzehnten Jahrhundert*, Giessen, 1914, pp. 5 ff.

[10] Much of this was published in the Society's *Trans. No. 339*, XXIX (1714), 72ff.

[11] *Philosophical Trans.*, No. 347.

Venice in 1715. Pylarini's account tended to confirm that of Timoni.[12]

In this manner, reports of an old folk practice gained access—under the pressure of increasing fear—to the literature of Western science. Yet no English physicians seem to have attempted inoculations between 1714 and 1721; indeed, Dr. William Douglass of Boston later wrote that "the communications of Timonius and Pylarinus in England were regarded as Virtuoso-Amusements until April, 1721."[13]

Far otherwise was the attitude adopted by the Reverend Cotton Mather, F.R.S., in provincial Boston, who, upon seeing Timoni's communication in the *Transactions*, wrote Dr. John Woodward in 1716 that he could confirm the latter's favorable impressions of this statement.[14] The truth is that Mather, in contrast with most English physicians, was already familiar with the idea of inoculation. At this point, curiously enough, there entered into the situation what might be termed an African background to American culture. As Mather himself explained:

many months before I mett with any Intimations of treating the Small-Pox, with the Method of Inoculation, any where in Europe; I had from a Servant of my own, an Account of its being practiced in Africa. Inquiring of my Negro-man Onesimus, who is a pretty Intelligent Fellow, Whether he ever had the Small-Pox; he answered, both, Yes, and No; and then told me, that he had undergone an Operation, which had given him something of the Small-Pox, & would forever praeserve him from it; adding, That it was often used among the Guramantese . . . and his Description of it, made it the same, that afterwards I found related unto you by your Timonius.[15]

---

[12] Raymond P. Stearns, "Remarks Upon the Introduction of Inoculation for Smallpox in England," *Bull. of the Hist. of Med.*, XXIV (March, 1950), 106 ff.

[13] Quoted, *ibid.*, p. 113.

[14] Mather was then in regular correspondence with Woodward, *re* the "Curiosa Americana."

[15] Letter of July 12, 1716, to Dr. Woodward, British Museum, quoted in George Lyman Kittredge, "Some Lost Works of Cotton Mather," Mass. Hist. Soc., *Proceedings*, XLV, 422.

Mather, incidentally, was not the only Bostonian who became familiar with African practice, for the Reverend Benjamin Colman also spoke later of a "poor Negro" who gave him information about this.[16]   More than one slave probably communicated these ideas to his master.   Indeed, it is stated that further questioning of Negroes and slave traders confirmed the original story told to Mather.[17]

In any case, Mather found his previous interest in inoculation further encouraged by the materials in the *Transactions*. And this emboldened him to raise some questions of Dr. Woodward.   "How does it come to pass," he inquired,

that no more is done to bring this operation, into experiment and into Fashion—in England?   When there are so many Thousands of People, that would give many Thousands of Pounds, to have the Danger and Horror of this frightful Disease well over with them.   I beseech you, syr, to prove it, and save more Lives than Dr. Sydenham.   For my own part, if I should live to see the Small-Pox again enter into our City, I would immediately procure a Consult of our Physicians, to Introduce a Practice, which may be of so very happy a Tendency.[18]

The idea of seeking "a Consult" of physicians, should smallpox again appear, was the same as that which Mather had followed in the epidemic of measles in 1713.   But in 1716 he planned to suggest to them not simply a statement on treatments,[19] but rather a basic new procedure in medicine— that of active immunization.   Without analyzing it in these terms, Mather sensed—as did many others—that he was here advancing into an unknown and perhaps dangerous area of practice.   Could not some guidance be obtained?   He therefore concluded his letter to Woodward with the excla-

[16] *Some Observations on the New Method Of Receiving the Small-Pox by Ingrafting or Inoculating*, Boston, 1721, p. 15.

[17] John B. Blake, "The Inoculation Controversy in Boston: 1721–1722," *New England Quart.*, XXV (December, 1952), 2.

[18] Letter of July 12, 1716, quoted in Kittredge, "Some Lost Works," p. 422.   As Kittredge implies, this letter was one of the "Curiosa."

[19] Such a statement, in the case of smallpox, had already been made in Thacher's *Brief Rule*, Boston, 1677.

mation: "But could we hear that you have done it [inocula-
tion] before us, how much would That embolden us!"

It was common enough for provincials to look to London
for guidance; but as noted, there was no response to this
appeal before 1721. Such hesitancy in the home country is
understandable. It was obviously a risky business to inject
the actual virus of smallpox. And even if mild illness *did*
then ensue, there was uncertainty whether this was true
smallpox and whether, therefore, any immunity to the latter
was provided.[20]

It has also been suggested, in explanation of delays in
London, that the disease was so common in that city as to be
almost endemic in character. Hence there was lacking
there, between 1716 and 1721, such an urge to experiment as
might be provided by an epidemic.[21] As a matter of fact,
it rarely occurred to anyone at this early stage to attempt
inoculations *in advance* of clear and pressing danger.

The next definite outbreak of smallpox in London came in
1721. It was then that, at the instigation of Lady Montagu,
inoculations were performed in some twenty scattered cases.
But there was much opposition; and when two deaths ensued, the practice seemed discredited.[22]

Far otherwise was the outcome in Boston, where an
epidemic appeared almost simultaneously with that in
London. Whether Mather heard of and was encouraged
by the few English inoculations at the last moment, is a
matter of interpretation.[23] But this is of small moment,

---

[20] See Peter Kennedy, *An Essay on External Remedies*, London, 1715, p. 155, cited in
John Thomson, *Historical Sketch of . . . Small Pox*, London, 1822, p. 32 f.

[21] This is Miss Genevieve Miller's suggestion.

[22] Stearns, *op. cit.*, pp. 113 ff.

[23] Kittredge says nothing about such news having reached Mather; and Reginald H. Fitz,
in his "Zabdiel Boylston, Inoculator," *Johns Hopkins Hosp't. Bull.*, XXII (September 1911),
likewise makes no statement to that effect. But Klebs surmises ["The Historic Evolution
of Variolation," *ibid.*, XXIV (1913)] that Mather did hear of the London experiments.

since Mather—unlike the London physicians—had committed himself in advance to experiment whenever the next visitation occurred. Kittredge sums this up effectively in declaring that:

when Cotton Mather urged inoculation . . . in 1721, he was not acting upon a sudden and whimsical impulse, he was not plunging headlong into an unconsidered experiment on the strength of something he had just come across in a scientific journal. On the contrary, he was proceeding in accordance with a matured plan—he was carrying out a resolution which he had formed and announced *five years before*. The significance of this fact requires no emphasis.[24]

*　　*　　*　　*　　*

When a ship from the West Indies brought smallpox cases into Boston in April, 1721, the town authorities responded in the usual manner. Playing safe, they assumed that the disease might be spread either by contagion or by unsanitary conditions (noxious miasms)—the traditional explanations—and they therefore ordered both the isolation of cases and the cleaning of streets. But since smallpox was usually viewed as contagious, it was isolation which received major attention.[25]

During May and early June of that year, the Selectmen ordered the offending ship down the harbor and placed guards over houses in which cases appeared. But by mid-June so many were suffering from the "distemper" that the guards were removed, and thereafter—so far as the authorities were concerned—the disease was free to take its natural course.[26] One has here a nice illustration of the ineffectiveness of isolation procedures as then practiced, once a serious infection had spread beyond a few original foci.

[24] "Lost Works of Cotton Mather," p. 427.

[25] The theory of contagion well explained the spread of smallpox, so that no debate arose over this subject in 1721. Quite different was the more complex behavior of certain other epidemic diseases, notably yellow fever, which would later arouse serious controversies about the means of transmission. See C.-E. A. Winslow, *The Conquest of Epidemic Disease*, Princeton, 1943, pp. 181 ff.

[26] Blake, "The Inoculation Controversy," p. 3.

Mather, meantime, was observing the ominous spread of
the epidemic. He noted in his diary, May 26, 1721, that
since inoculation had "never been used in America, nor
indeed in our Nation," he would now suggest this procedure
to the physicians.[27] The letter which he then addressed to
that group was of a cautious nature, and was apparently
intended to appease professional sensibilities. The experiment should be made "warily," and only under the management of skilful practitioners. And it was to be hoped that
"whoever first begins this practise, (*if you approve that it
should be begun at all*) may have the concurrence of his
worthy Brethren to fortify him in it."[28]

Among those to whom copies of this address were forwarded was Dr. William Douglass, the only Boston practitioner who held the M.D. Mather had hitherto had pleasant
relations with Douglass and had borrowed from him a
scarce copy of the *Philosophical Transactions* containing
material on inoculation. But Douglass, according to Fitz,
felt aggrieved that the clergyman "should borrow his books
and select therefrom communications upon a medical subject and recommend them to . . . the physicians of Boston
without consulting with the owner of the books in question."
Douglass also intimated, later, that Mather had persuaded
Dr. Zabdiel Boylston to begin inoculations before the
physicians had had time to consult on the matter.[29] It seems
probable that Douglass immediately opposed Mather's
recommendations and used his influence to prevent any

[27] II, 620 f.

[28] Quoted in Fitz, *op. cit.*, p. 8 f. On the various published portions of this "Address,"
see Kittredge, *op. cit.*, pp. 428 ff. The latter also identifies portions of it, including the early
specimen of Negro English in the account of African practice, in a pamphlet published by
Boylston, Boston, 1721. *Cf.* Holmes, III, 994 ff. This particular section reppeared later
in "The Angel," Chapter XX.

[29] Fitz, *op. cit.*, p. 9, citing Douglass, *The Abuses and Scandals of some late Pamphlets in
Favour of Inoculation*, London, 1722.

action being taken thereon.[30]   Hence, despite his apparent caution, Mather probably did arouse professional ire at the start of this episode.   No conference was held, and the clergyman was thus left with only the alternatives of abandoning his project or of taking independent action.

Mather never forsook his original intentions, though he was beset with doubts and fears.   What of the safety of his own children?   On June 22, he declared he was preparing a treatise on inoculation, and on June 23 he apparently made a second appeal to the physicians.   On the next day, he wrote to Dr. Boylston as an individual, submitting the evidence in favor of the practice and urging him—if "you should think it advisable"—to undertake it.[31].   In a word, he now decided to support the experiment if even one practitioner could be persuaded to attempt it.

This letter seems to have convinced Boylston, for on June 26 he inoculated his son and two Negro slaves.   These cases proving successful, he performed the operation on several others—reaching a total of ten by July 17.   The popular opposition which was immediately aroused is understandable: what could be more dangerous than to deliberately infect healthy persons with a serious disease?   Was not this an offense against God and man?   It is no wonder that both Boylston and Mather promptly became objects of popular denunciation.

Mather noted in his diary, July 16, that he derived "an unspeakable Consolation" in having at last persuaded one physician to try "the New Method," but he was disturbed by the popular outcry.   "The Destroyer," he decided, was alarmed lest lives be saved, and had therefore taken pos-

[30] *Ibid.* Douglass, as later appeared, had scientific as well as professional reasons for his opposition.

[31] Fitz, p. 10, citing Mather's diary, and Peter Thatcher's memorial of Boylston in the *Mass. Mag.*, I, (1789), 778

session of the people. "They rave, rail, they blaspheme. . . . And not only the Physician who began the Experiment but I also am an Object of their Fury."[32]

Boylston, for his part, took notice of the clamor by announcing in the *Boston Gazette*, July 17, that all his experiments had succeeded and that he would announce further results shortly.[33] Unfortunately for him, all his colleagues were now in opposition. They were led by Dr. Douglass, who likewise appealed to the public through the press. On July 24, he entered a statement in the *News-Letter* which summed up the essential indictments of inoculation, as these would be employed thereafter throughout the controversy. First, the process was dangerous. Second, it was irreligious to interfere with God's "Providence" in such matters. And, third, it was doubtless criminal from the viewpoint of public law.[34]

The medical indictment had some merit: the indiscriminate practice of inoculation might under some circumstances spread infection. Would it not be safer, if inoculation must be tried, to operate only upon patients who could be isolated? Presumably, such considerations helped to line up Douglass' colleagues almost solidly behind him.

If the physician expected to secure clerical support in addition, however, he was much mistaken. Had the leading clergy been as stuffily orthodox and conservative as they have been pictured, they might well have endorsed the religious indictment. That they did not do so is so much further evidence of the distortions inherent in the popular tradition. What actually occurred was that six of the most prominent ministers replied to Douglass on July 31 in the *Gazette*, defending Dr. Boylston and the righteousness of his

[32] *Diary*, II, 632.
[33] Cited by Blake, *op. cit.*, p. 4.
[34] *Ibid.*, p. 5.

experiments. The statement was prepared largely by Colman and was signed by Increase as well as by Cotton Mather.[35]

This reply was both a moving and a logical statement. The clergymen recalled Dr. Boylston's excellent reputation and resented Douglass' reference to him as "a certain cutter for the stone" who lacked a degree. "We that have stood by," they declared, "and seen his tenderness, courage and skill in that hazardous operation cannot enough value the Man and give praise to God." As for the slur on Boylston for lacking the M.D., this was also a slight on all the other practitioners who were Douglass' supporters:

tho' he [Boylston] has not had the honour and advantage of an Academical Education, and consequently not the Letters of some Physicians in the Town, yet he ought by no means to be called Illiterate, ignorant, etc. Would the Town bear that Dr. Cutler or Dr. Davis should be so treated?[36]

This exchange had its implications for the status of the medical profession at the time. But the most interesting and telling portion of the clerical reply dealt with the religious indictment. Claiming that able and pious persons were by now convinced of the value of inoculation, they inquired:

Cannot they give into the method or practice without having their devotion and subjection to the Al-wise Providence of God Almighty call'd in question? . . . Do we not in the use of all means depend on GOD's blessing? . . . For, what hand or art of Man is there in this Operation more than in bleeding, blistering and a Score more things in Medical use? which are all consistent with a humble trust in our Great preserver, and a due Subjection to His All-wise Providence.[37]

Thus was the religious argument refuted in medical terms, but this had small influence on the physicians. Only one of

---

[35] Fitz, *op. cit.*, p. 15. It is rather striking to find Increase, despite his advanced years, here standing with his son on the unpopular side. The father even entered into the pamphlet warfare which ensued, in his *Several Reasons Proving that Inoculating . . . the Small Pox, is a Lawful Practice*, Boston, 1721. In this, Increase notes that certain clergymen "and many other younger Divines, not only in *Boston*, but in the Country," share his views, p. 1.

[36] Fitz, p. 13.

[37] *Ibid.*, p. 14.

them would accept Boylston's invitation to observe the results of his operations. Here was a strange spectacle indeed. On the one side, it was the physicians who opposed the advent of preventive medicine without even deigning to observe the results, and opposed this on religious as well as on scientific grounds. On the other, it was the clergy who not only aided Boylston, but who also defended a liberal theology against the doctors and the populace at large.

The physicians had more success in appealing to the town authorities than they had with the clergy. Indeed, the Selectmen consulted with the doctors as to proper action—an unusual procedure at the time.[38] Having heard tales of the terrible results of inoculation in Europe from one of the doctors, the Selectmen and Justices reprimanded Boylston and forbade any further use of the procedure.[39]

Boylston, nevertheless, continued his work—as Douglass put it, "in Contempt of the Magistrates and in Contradiction to the Practitioners."[40] During August, Boylston inoculated seventeen persons, in September thirty-one, in October eighteen, and in November over one hundred.[41] On the whole, it was the better educated who sought inoculation and the masses who feared and continued to oppose it.

By this time, a newspaper and pamphlet warfare was under way, led by the ministers on the one hand and the physicians on the other. The latter found just the organ they needed in the appearance of the anti-clerical *New England Courant* in August —published by James Franklin, with the youthful Benjamin

[38] Blakes notes ("Medical Profession and Public Health in Colonial Boston," *Bull. of the Hist. of Med.*, XXVI [1952], 225), that this indicated the growing prestige of the profession.

[39] *An Account of the Method and Success of Inoculating the Small-pox in New England*, London, 1722, p. 11. Holmes states (*op. cit.*, I, 13) that the text of this work, or at least the matter, was by Cotton Mather. Much of this also later appeared in "The Angel," Chapter XX.

[40] *The Abuses and Scandals*, p. 9.

[41] Blake, "The Inoculation Controversy," p. 6.

hovering in the background. The Franklins apparently welcomed the issue as a means of attacking the clergy, and the latter responded by condemning the *Courant* as a "wicked paper."[42] Cotton Mather alone contributed some seven published statements to the total debate,[43] but it is unnecessary here to follow all the ramifications of the controversy.

When the epidemic became more severe, the Selectmen attempted to remove all infected persons who came into the town to the pesthouse. And the General Court entered the picture by voting funds for the relief of the sick poor[44]—a procedure to be followed in many later American epidemics. The provincial legislature, however, does not seem to have taken sides in the inoculation furor. When, in November, popular feeling reached such a point that a bomb was thrown into Cotton Mather's home, the General Court offered a reward of £50 for finding the perpetrator of this "Villany."[45]

The number of deaths from smallpox had been low during the Summer months, the greatest being twenty-six in August, but in September these rose to one hundred and one and reached their high point in October with four hundred and eleven. There were two hundred and forty-nine deaths in November, and thereafter the epidemic rapidly declined. All told, 5,889 persons are reported to have "taken" the smallpox out of a total Boston population of about 12,000—an incidence of almost fifty per cent. Of those infected, there were 844 deaths, that is, a case mortality of nearly fifteen per cent.[46]

What then, of the number inoculated, and of the case mortality in *this* group? The value of that process, assuming that it resulted in true smallpox, would turn in large measure

[42] Fitz, *op. cit.*, p. 17.

[43] See Holmes, *Bibliography*, I, Chronological List.

[44] Council Records, VII, 319.

[45] *Ibid.*, p. 316 f. For Mather's account of the episode, see Fitz, *op. cit.*, p. 20 f.

[46] Bridenbaugh, *Cities in the Wilderness*, p. 143; Blake, *op. cit.*, p. 8.

on the comparative mortality in natural and artificial infection. Both Cotton Mather and Boylston realized the significance of this statistical approach, which involved one of the first historical instances of the quantitative analysis of a medical problem. They assumed that inoculation would stand or fall on the basis of the "calculus of probabilities" of death under the two types of infection.[47]

Boylston subsequently reported that he had inoculated 242 persons, of whom six died.[48] There was much debate over whether these deaths resulted from infection previous to inoculation, or perchance from some other disease altogether. But assuming the worst, this gave a mortality ratio of only about 2.5 per cent after inoculation, in comparison with about 15 per cent in the "natural" cases. In other words, the danger of death was at most only one-sixth as great in artificial as in natural infection.

Cotton Mather also reported on the risks of inoculation, in a letter of March 10, 1721/2, to Dr. Jurin of the Royal Society. The clergyman gave the same number of deaths as did Boylston, but using a higher estimate of the number of inoculations (300), he calculated a lower mortality ratio of about 2 per cent.[49] Jurin, meanwhile, had already figured the risks involved in some later English inoculations, which he found to involve a mortality of only about 1 per cent. He concluded that the Boston operations had been done less carefully than those in England.[50]

In most infectious diseases even a mortality of 2 per cent after inoculation would, regardless of what protection was

[47] This matter of smallpox mortality, indeed, thereafter provided data for the development of the calculus of probabilities by mathematicians; see R. H. Shryock, *Development of Modern Medicine*, New York, 1947, p. 137 f.

[48] *An Historical Account of the Small-Pox Inoculated in New England*, 2d ed., London, 1726, reprinted Boston, 1730, p. 50.

[49] Kittredge, "Lost Works," pp. 475 ff.; Klebs,' 'Historic Evolution of Variolation," p. 11.

[50] *Ibid.*

provided, be considered a serious risk. But the risk appeared relatively slight, for the individual, in the case of the almost certain exposure and infection involved in a major smallpox epidemic. This is probably the most infectious of all diseases, and natural immunity is very rare at best. It will be noted that, although most of the older portion of the Boston population had probably already had the disease and were therefore immune, almost fifty per cent of the townspeople acquired the disease naturally in 1721. The implication is that nearly all residents who had not already had the disease acquired it in the natural way in 1721.

Another argument in favor of inoculation, in addition to that of the low mortality, was the mild nature of the attacks so induced. As Colman graphically described it, these patients: "found ease and sweetness and lay praising God in their Beds or rather sat up in their Chairs doing so. Their friends stood smiling about them. Their tongues were filled with laughter and ours with Thanksgiving on their account when we went to see 'em."[51]

Implicit in such an account, however, was the danger to which Douglass had already called attention. These inoculated patients entertained their friends quite freely. Hence the operation, it was claimed, became a source of further infection, and it is still held that Mather and Boylston deserve censure for their failure to protect the community by isolating the inoculated cases.[52]

There is no question that inoculation could have, under some circumstances, started or further spread an epidemic. Nor is there any doubt that, in principle, the inoculated cases should have been isolated. But it is a nice question whether, under the circumstances which actually obtained at

---

[5] *Some Observations on the New Method of Receiving the Small-Pox*, Boston, 1721, p. 3.

[52] Blake, *op. cit.* pp. 16, 18.

Boston in 1721, there was much danger in the practice. It
will be recalled that the epidemic had been steadily increasing, by natural means, for more than a month before the
first inoculations were performed in June and that as late
as the month of August, Boylston operated upon only
seventeen persons.[53] Compared to the number who already
had the natural disease by that time and who also were not
isolated, these inoculated cases provided a relatively small
pool of infection.

This, at any rate, was the view of the clergy, who were
indignant when accused of spreading the disease. Colman
declared it outrageous "to bear us down as some would:
'That the Inoculation has caus'd the dreadful Malignity and Infection
which has been in the Town.'" To say this to Us who have been call'd
from day to day to the many noxious Chambers, each of which has had
poison eno' in 'em to have spread the Town over, and which have been
continually by day and night filling the Air with Infection . . . requires
an Assurance indeed. . . . Besides, In fact, the Malignity and Mortality
has not been now so great, in proportion to our present numbers, as it
was three and forty Year agoe, when in about fourteen Months, we are
told Eight hundred People died of it; which I suppose was a greater
mortality than if Eighteen hundred had died of it now. . . . And we at
last find too by sad experience, that They understood as well the managing the Distemper as we do now: For . . . we find that we know very
little or nothing what to do.[54]

The argument here is clear enough; nearly everyone had
been or would be exposed to infection anyway, by the time
the inoculations were undertaken. And in a previous epidemic, when no inoculations were attempted, the incidence
and mortality had been even higher than they were *with* inoculations in 1721. *Ergo*, these operations could not be viewed
as a major factor in the spread of this later outbreak.

The public, nevertheless, was disturbed by the possible
danger of spreading contagion through inoculations. Hence

----

[53] Incidentally, this delay in inoculating may have, for technical reasons, weighted the
statistics unduly on the side of inoculation. But there was in any case a large margin in its
favor.

[54] Colman, *op. cit.*, p. 11 f.

their fears were aroused when Boylston resumed inoculations in May, 1722—in the absence, now, of any epidemic. The Selectmen thereupon ordered the inoculated persons isolated and secured Boylston's promise to proceed no further without official approval. This seemed to be a final victory for Douglass, who observed with evident relish that:

Last January Inoculation made a Sort of Exit, like the Infatuation Thirty Years ago, after several had fallen Victims to the mistaken Notions of Dr. M—r and other learned Clerks concerning Witchcraft. But finding Inoculation in this Town . . . beginning to crawl abroad again last Week, it was in time, and effectually crushed in the Bud. . . .[55]

Douglass, however, spoke too soon; indeed, he came in time to approve inoculation himself. For Mather, Boylston, and their allies had inaugurated a program that was not to be stopped by a temporary setback in Boston. Although there was much to be said for the 1722 action of the Boston authorities in placing inoculations under public control, this was far different from attempting to suppress the entire program.

In view of the long-run outcomes, the Boston experience of 1721 proved to be a major triumph for Mather and Boylston. The former's part in the story has been praised even by those scholars who have held a generally unfavorable opinion of him. The chief criticism still made of Cotton and his father, in this connection, is that they were motivated by a desire to maintain a clerical right "to interfere with and control the life of the community." Douglass, on the other hand, is said to have been "defending the integrity of the medical profession against the interference of those whom he considered to be credulous laymen."[56]

---

[55] Quoted in Blake, *op. cit.*, p. 9. The attempt to provide public control of inoculation seems to have broken down again when another smallpox epidemic occurred in Boston in 1752. A local resident, Abigail Greenleaf, wrote on July 24 that "Contrary to Law, when it was at but five or Six houses they began to inoculate. . . ." She reported that "about 25 hundred have been inoculated & thirty two died." (1.3%); Mass. Hist. Soc., courtesy of Stephen T. Riley, Librarian. On subsequent experience in Boston, see Blake, "Smallpox Inoculation in Colonial Boston," *Jour. Hist. of Med.*, *VIII* (1953), 284 ff.

[56] Blake, "The Inoculation Controversy," p. 15.

There is no doubt that the Mathers were conscious of the dignity of their position and resented anti-clerical criticisms. Both were inclined to see the work of the Evil One in the opposition. But to view their activities as primarily an expression of a right to "interfere" overlooks or interprets as rationalizations their constant appeals to the *medical* evidence—to the African reports, to the European literature, and most of all to the actual results of inoculation. It also overlooks the whole background of Cotton Mather's concern for the public welfare. This concern, far from merely reflecting the pretensions of a theocrat, was inspired by a nascent and far-reaching humanitarianism.

Dr. Douglass probably did resent Mather's "encroachments" on the medical field. Fresh from Europe and with a European degree, the former was doubtless more sensitive about professional status than were the other local practitioners. And Douglass may have felt that it was time to put an end to the clerical concern with medicine. In this sense, he can be viewed as the herald of a more self-conscious profession. Unfortunately, he attacked as obsolete a clergyman who was probably more widely read in medicine—as well as more open-minded—than he himself.

Douglass' scorn of Mather as a layman dabbling in medicine was obvious enough. Writing to a British colleague during the epidemic, he referred to "a certain credulous Preacher of this place called Mather" who "preached up Inoculation."[57] Now just how "credulous" was Mather in this whole matter?

It is generally known that the clergyman was familiar with the African and Oriental reports, as well as with the Boston experiments. It is not so well realized that he also thought out a rational explanation for the phenomena of

[57] Douglass to Dr. Alexander Stuart, September 24, 1721; Royal Society

infection, both natural and artificial. Parts of this analysis are available in certain of his writings published in 1722, but since these materials were assembled two or three years later in "The Angel," it is also in the latter that his theories are to be noted. Mather's views regarding the processes involved in infection and in immunization deserve some attention.

* * * * *

In the chapter on smallpox in "The Angel," Mather discusses the disease in the manner usual in that volume. He echoes Sydenham in recommending moderate treatments, in the expectation that Nature—so abetted—may effect a cure.[58] But what was the external cause of this dread malady? As early as the epidemic of 1721, Mather had begun to suspect that this would be found in pathogenic animalculae.[59] Two or three years later, when he had completed "The Angel," he had become more positive about this. Although he referred there to the "contagion" or the "miasm" of the disease, he also stated plainly:

It begins now to be vehemently suspected that the Small-Pox may be more of an animalculated Business than we have been generally aware of. The Millions of — which the Microscopes discover in the Pustules, have confirmed the Suspicion. . . . And so, we are insensibly drawn into new Sentiments, about the Way of its Conveyance, and the Cause why tis convey'd but once.[60]

The author had a ready explanation for the first problem posed here. The animalculae—or "the contagion"—entered the body through the respiratory passages, and so gained direct access to the blood and through it to vital organs.[61]

[58] *Cf.* Colman's candid phrase: "We know very little or nothing what to do."

[59] In a pamphlet of 1722, he refers to smallpox as an invading enemy. He then adds that—since many now think this "an animalcuated Business"—there is "less of Metaphor in our Account, than may be at first imagin'd." *An Account of the Method and Success of Inoculating the Small-Pox in Boston in New England*, London, 1722, p. 7 f. See Holmes, *Bibliography*, I, 11.

[60] Chapter XX; Transcript, 154. See Appendix.

[61] This is still viewed as the common route of infection.

The second query, however, required a general theory of immunity for its answer. Mather approached the problem in the light of his own observations in 1721, when he had been convinced that those who were inoculated experienced only slight attacks of the disease and were thereafter immune. Why was this the case? Since Mather was a pioneer in this field, the problem was a novel one and provided an opportunity for original solutions.

In modern immunization procedures, vaccines are deliberately attenuated or killed in order to render them safe. In the first inoculations, mild reactions were secured without any knowledge of how this was brought about. Mather, unlike most physicians, could not rest content with the mere fact; his mind demanded some rational explanation. He was not unique in this respect, since Timoni had raised the problem—at least implicitly—in his letter to the Royal Society of 1714. Subsequently, when this procedure became a practical issue in 1721 and 1722, several European writers suggested answers to the problem of mild reactions. Mather seems to have been the only American who participated, so to speak, in these discussions.

Obviously, if inoculated cases of smallpox were mild, the virus used must have been weakened in some way, either (1) before it was injected, (2) by the method used in injecting it, or (3) by what occurred within the body thereafter.

On the first score it was suggested, for example, that in natural infection the effluvia were made more virulent by exposure to air and sunlight, whereas during inoculation, no such exposure occurred and the virulency therefore remained low.[62] Another suggestion was that inoculators used less virulent portions of the virus taken from patients,

---

[62] Jacob à Castro Sarmento, *A Dissertation on the Method of Inoculating the Smallpox*, London, 1721, pp. 47 f. We are indebted to Miss Genevieve Miller for references to this and to several other of the contemporary European writings on inoculation. The word "virus" is used above, and throughout, in its present sense.

that is, they selected "the more vicid Pus" which was less poisonous than were the more subtle fluids in the pustules.[63] Rarely if ever expressed, however, was the thought that the virus might have been attenuated by drying, or by derivation from late-stage cases in which it had already been weakened by exposure to the natural resistance of a host.

With regard to the circumstances under which an inoculated virus entered the body, it was pointed out, first, that only a relatively small amount of it was injected, whereas there was more massive exposure in natural infection through the respiratory passages. The latter process also involved large surfaces, with direct access to the blood and thus to vital organs, whereas inoculation was made at only one or two points on the limbs.[64]

As for what occurred within the body *after* inoculation, there was, first, the notion that "the system" tended to resist injected poisons and could do this more effectively if it were in good condition when exposed. Hence it was viewed as an advantage of artificial infection that this could be timed by the physician—the patient meantime undergoing whatever preparation was deemed appropriate. More specifically, it was claimed that the small quantity of virus injected was diluted and tempered by the watery part of the blood, so that it produced only a mild case of the disease.[65] This thought suggests the modern view of the rôle of antibodies in the blood serum.

Although one can cite several of these instances in which physicians pondered this problem at the time, there was no

---

[63] W. Wagstaffe, *A Letter to Dr. Freind, Showing the Danger and Uncertainty of Inoculating the Small Pox*, London, 1722, p. 21. (Dr. Wagstaffe, F.R.S., was on the staff of St. Bartholomew's Hospital.)

[64] A. Vater, *Das Blatter-Beltzen oder die Art u. Weise die Blattern durch künstliche Einpfropffung zu erwecken*, Wittenberg, 1721, p. 32 f. Vater was commenting on the original communications of Timoni and Pylarini to the Royal Society.

[65] *Ibid.*

general awareness of its significance. When Dr. Thomas Fuller of London later surveyed the "Eruptive Fevers" as a whole, he posed the question: "Why Inoculation giveth a more kindly Small-Pox than common Infection"; and then calmly asserted that "This is a Problem, the Solution of which none hath hitherto attempted."[66]   If a physician, particularly concerned with smallpox, had never heard by 1730 of any of the views just noted, it becomes clear that the authors of these theories were a select group indeed.

Mather presented his own ideas about the mildness of inoculated cases in his London pamphlet of 1722. He may have taken hints from Timoni's letter of 1714, but it seems unlikely that he had seen such contemporary publications as those of Sarmento and of Vater cited above. At any rate, he overlooked or ignored all circumstances connected with the handling of the virus and concentrated rather on the place of injection and on what subsequently occurred within the body. The virus, he held, ordinarily reached the blood via the lungs and thus was carried directly to the vital organs. So attacked in its very "citadel," the body had great difficulty in resisting the invader. Under inoculation, on the other hand, the virus entered only the periphery of the body and could not reach the vital parts. Hence it was relatively easy to overcome it and a mild case ensued. Such a mild case, at the same time, enabled the body to resist successfully any later infection—just as did a natural attack of the disease.

In describing this process, Mather declared that:
the Miasms of the Small-Pox, being admitted in the Way of Inoculation, their Approaches were made only by the Out-Works of the Citadel,

---

[66] *Exanthematologia*, London, 1730, pp. 418 ff. Fuller also referred to the less virulent nature of the "vacid Part" of the pus, to the small amount employed, etc. He added a theory that during the incubation period in the body, the virus remained cool and relatively harmless at the point of incision; whereas in natural infection it was heated and so activated for some five days within the body as a whole.

and at a considerable Distance from it. The Enemy, 'tis true, gets in so far as to make some Spoil; even so much as to satisfy him, and leave no prey in the Body of the Patient, for him ever afterwards to seize upon; but the vital Powers are kept so clear from his Assaults, that they can manage the Combat bravely; and . . . oblige him [the Invader] to march out the same Way he came in, and are sure of never being troubled with him anymore.[67]

In the light of later knowledge of infection and immunity, this theory of Mather's is at least intriguing. It might be suggested, today, that the skin is more resistant to the infection than are the respiratory passages and that resistance at the point of inoculation may arouse the body's whole defense mechanism before the disease has been generalized through the blood—thus assuring a milder case when the vital parts are finally attacked. In this sense, there was plausibility in Mather's view that the virus gets in so far as to make "some spoil," but that the vital parts are "kept so clear" as to "manage the Combat bravely."

There seems no doubt, then, that the clergyman recognized the essential problems presented by the novel phenomena of artificial immunization. And he provided what was at least a plausible explanation of these data. There is no evidence that any of the Boston physicians, or even any other Americans of the time, envisaged the questions which were involved. Moreover—and this merits emphasis—Mather was unusual, if not unique, in holding that the virus was probably composed of living organisms.[68] For Douglass to scorn the clergyman, under these circumstances, as a "credulous" layman, seems so naïve as to require no further comment. Mather was not technically a physician, but he was certainly the outstanding medical thinker as well as the moral leader throughout the epidemic of 1721.

---

[67] *An Account of the Method and Success of Inoculating*, p. 7 f.

[68] This cannot be stated with finality, since various materials in the European literature, 1715–1722, have doubtless escaped us.

It is quite true, as Stearns points out, that credit for introducing inoculation into western practice cannot be ascribed
"to any single person or organization."[69]   As in all such cases,
many individuals and groups were involved.   No small rôle,
for example, was played by Lady Montagu and by the officers
of the Royal Society.   The same can be said of the subsequent activities of various European medical men.

Yet it so happened that Mather and Boylston provided the
first test of inoculation which was carried out on a significant
scale.   Whatever statisticians might now say of the ade-
quacy of their "sample" of cases, or of any undue "weight-
ings" which may have been involved, the data they reported
were extensive in comparison with any others then available.
Their findings therefore made a marked impression at the
time and thus became one essential link in the sequence that
led eventually to a considerable adoption of the practice in
both Europe and America.

No attempt will be made here to trace the subsequent
history of inoculation during the eighteenth century.   But
certain essential facts may be recalled briefly, in order to
suggest the place of the Boston experience in the larger
story.   It has already been noted that both Mather and
Boylston reported their statistics, as well as their general
observations, to London observers.   These reports made a
favorable impression in many circles.[70]   Thus Dummer, in ad-
dressing Mather's anonymous pamphlet of 1722 to Sir Hans
Sloane and the London College of Physicians, declared that:
as all new Discoveries . . . are received at first with Opposition, none has
met with greater than this [inoculation] in New-England.   A vast Number of honest People quarrel'd with it upon religious Scruples; and they

---

[69] "Introduction of Inoculation for Smallpox in England," *Bull. Hist. of Med.*, XXIV
(1950), 121.

[70] John Thomas, in his *Historical Sketch of the Opinions Entertained by Medical Men . . .
of SmallPox* London, 1822, implied (p. 37) that it was the reputation of the Boston
leaders (Mather, etc.) for learning and integrity, which made their reports so influential.

were strongly supported by the Physicians of the Place, for reasons of a very different Kind, which it is not at all necessary to mention. But as Truth is mighty . . . the great and suprizing Success of this Practice, has convinc'd every reasonable Adversary, and silenced the most obstinate.[71]

It is to be remembered that inoculating had been practically abandoned in England after several deaths, and Stearns observes that—without the New England evidence—"the case for inoculation could hardly have been sustained or the practice extended" in the mother country.[72] After the receipt of the Boston reports, inoculations were resumed in various parts of the British Isles. And Dr. Jurin, of the Royal Society, began a systematic collection of the results in statistical form. His annual *Accounts*, continued until 1728, eventually related to nearly a thousand cases. He concluded, statistically, that natural infection involved an average mortality of about one in six (16.6 per cent), whereas that for inoculated cases was about one in fifty (2 per cent).[73] These British results were fairly close to those reported earlier by Mather and Boylston.

Inoculation subsequently had many ups and downs in Britain. Interest in it apparently lessened there during the 1730's and then was revived again by further American experience.[74] This second Colonial episode related to a smallpox epidemic in Charleston, South Carolina, in 1738, when a Dr. J. Kilpatrick[75] reported many inoculations with a mortality as low as one per cent. The latter, in presenting

[71] Preface, *An Account of the Methods and Success of Inoculating.* Boylston exerted an even more direct influence in London, through lectures there before the Royal Society and the London College of Physicians. Viets terms his report on inoculation on these occasions as a "masterly clinical presentation," "Some Features," *Isis,* XXIII (1935), 389 ff.

[72] *Op. cit.,* p. 117.

[73] See, *e.g.,* James Jurin, *An Account of the Success of Inoculating the Small-Pox in Great Britain, for the Year 1725,* London, 1726, pp. 55 ff.; Stearns, *op. cit.,* pp. 118 ff.

[74] Klebs, "Historic Evolution of Variolation," *Johns Hopkins Hosp't. Bull.,* XXIV (1913), 14.

[75] Later "Kirkpatrick." See his *Analysis of Inoculation,* London, 1754, p. 107 (printed originally in Charleston, first London printing, 1744, according to Klebs).

his evidence, referred back for substantiation to the earlier reports by Cotton Mather.

By the 1740's, in addition to a cumulative literature for and against inoculation, much material had been printed in Britain on the methods of preparing patients, on the procedures employed, and so on. Economic factors entered the situation, when some found it profitable to serve as inoculators at high fees, and in consequence the poor could not afford the operation. Since smallpox was almost endemic, the custom developed of resorting to inoculations in the absence of any epidemic. And in order to guard somewhat against the danger of precipitating outbreaks, more or less isolated "inoculating hospitals" were established. Kirkpatrick, in the work mentioned, refers to as many as 309 inoculations in one of these places in less than a year.[76]

Meantime, the practice was employed sporadically in the American Colonies, chiefly during epidemics, and it is refreshing to note that Benjamin Franklin—as well as Dr. Douglass and various other earlier opponents—came to support it. By the time of the Revolution, moreover, it was beginning to be employed on general preventive grounds even as in England. Washington's orders, in having his troops inoculated, served as a convenient reminder.[77] While there is no evidence that any large proportion of the population was ever inoculated in either Britain or the Colonies, the practice was widely accepted by the latter part of the century.[78] Indeed, as Klebs points out, inoculation became

[76] *Ibid.*, Preface. See also Michael Kraus, *The Atlantic Civilization*, Ithaca, N. Y., 1949, pp. 208 ff.

[77] On Colonial experience after 1721, see John Duffy, *Epidemics in Colonial America*, Baton Rouge, La., 1953, pp. 34 ff. An illustration of mid-century support of inoculation in the English Colonies will be found in Laughlin Macleane, *An Essay on the Expediency of Inoculation*, Philadelphia, 1756, which—like Kilpatrick—cites Mather's original data, p. 17.

[78] On the actual values of inoculation for the public health, which seem to have been greater in America than in Britain, see Duffy, *op. cit.*, pp. 27, 41.

so popular that when Jenner's safer "vaccination" was discovered (1798), it "had first to subdue variolation before it could make any appreciable headway." Not until 44 years later did Parliament forbid the earlier practice.[79]

Inoculation on the Continent of Europe derived largely from England. One of the first protagonists was Voltaire, who learned of it in London during the early excitement of the 1720's. There were the same debates, for and against, as had occurred in the British Empire. There was, in Paris, even a curious repetition of the Boston experience, in that at first the clerical authorities favored experiments, while the medical opposed them.[80] There was some lag in introducing inoculation on the Continent, but by the 1750's and 60's it was being slowly adopted in most of the western European countries.[81] Credit was usually given, on the Continent, to the immediate English example, but the debt of the latter to American experience was also noted.[82]

It should be pointed out, in conclusion, that the later practice of vaccination against smallpox grew out of the earlier inoculation procedure. It was inoculation which drew Jenner's attention to his subject, and in the light of which he worked out his investigation. Indeed, since he viewed cowpox as essentially the same disease as smallpox in a milder form, vaccination could be viewed as "inoculation" which employed a safer virus attenuated by passage through cattle.[83] Seen from this perspective, vaccination

---

[79] *Op. cit.*, p. 21.

[80] *Lettres De M. De La Condamine A M. Le Dr. Maty. Sur L'État Présent De L'Inoculation En France*, Paris, 1764, pp. 78 ff.; John Thomson, *Historical Sketch of the Opinions Entertained by Medical Men . . . of Smallpox*, London, 1822, p. 50.

[81] Klebs, *op cit*, pp. 12 ff.

[82] Thus Condamine, writing in 1764 on inoculation, declared that "*l'insertion REVINT triomphante de l'Amerique en Angleterre, & commença dès-lors à s'éntendre en Europe.*" He referred here (p. 6) to the Charleston results, 1738, but also noted the pioneer Boston experiments, p. 36 f.

[83] Edward Jenner, *An Inquiry into the Causes and Effects of the Variolae Vaccinae*, London, 1798, pp. 2 ff.

appears as simply a much improved form of inoculation.

The common impression is, however, that empirical immunizations had their advent only with Jenner's discovery of 1798, and the significance of inoculation as the original chapter in this story is thus commonly overlooked. No doubt this distortion results, in part, from the fact that vaccination was so much safer—particularly in that it involved no danger of infecting others—that it seemed in practical terms a new dispensation. In so far as cowpox and smallpox have at times been viewed as distinct entities, moreover, this also may have led to the view that Jenner's work represented an essentially new departure.[84]

One may add here a curious note of at least historical interest. Jenner's program was an empirical one, and this remained true of the subsequent practice of vaccination and of analogous experiments with other diseases—now forgotten—over the first three quarters of the nineteenth century.[85] Yet Mather had suggested a rational explanation of artificial immunization, in terms of pathogenic organisms, as early as 1722. Here, as in so many cases in medical history, scientific circumstances were such that effective use of this early theory was long delayed. Not until the 1870's, in the days of Pasteur and Koch, did this bacteriologic approach to immunology finally come into its own.

---

[84] There was subsequently a long debate over whether the virus of cowpox was a distinct organism from that of smallpox, or only a variation thereof. At least some medical authorities have accepted the latter view—which implies, by the etiologic criterion, that the two diseases are really one. See, *e.g.*, H. G. Garland and W. Phillips (eds.) *Medicine*, I (London, 1953), 913.

[85] See Shryock, *Development of Modern Medicine*, 1947, p. 76.

Chapter VIII

Conclusions: Mather's Place in Medicine

It seems well, in conclusion, to pull together the various aspects of Mather's medicine in order to see the pattern as a whole. This pattern was woven of many strands, taken not only from medicine as such but also from theology, ethics, and science at large. As with all leaders, the design reflected Mather's distinctive thought and personality as well as the culture of the times.

Any analysis of Mather's medicine must begin with its background in Christian thought and morality. It was Christianity which encouraged, if it did not originate, his interest in science, and it was Christianity—especially Calvinism as leavened by pietism—which inspired his concern for social welfare. These two, science and humanitarianism, were the mainsprings of his more distinctive work, and they reinforced one another with particular effectiveness in the medical realm. Had Mather been simply a scientist, he would never have done as much as he did for the public health. This required moral enthusiasm as well as scientific understanding. Had he, on the other hand, been only a benevolent preacher, he would have lacked the technical knowledge necessary for these same accomplishments.

There was nothing unique, of course, in deriving inspiration simultaneously from science and from humanitarianism. Franklin, Jefferson, and others shared this dual orientation, in a century characterized by close interrelations between natural philosophy and social reform. But observe that Mather anticipated these later leaders; he was the herald of the Enlightenment as well as of the Great Awakening. It will be recalled that Franklin, although usually viewed as the antithesis of Mather, testified to the direct influence

which the latter's idealism exerted upon him.   Even the
deists had a Christian background.

*   *   *   *   *

When one examines Mather's natural philosophy and
medicine in strictly scientific terms, he is at once confronted
with those theological and occult elements which seem so
incongruous to the modern reader.   Perhaps these actually
were more out of place in the Mather of 1725, than they
had been in the van Helmont of 1640.   Yet there is no doubt
that the Boston clergyman was moving with, and at some
points ahead of, his times.   Hence we have in his medicine
a nice illustration of how a man's mind *begins* to make its
way from one pole of thought to another.   This stage of
things involves juxtapositions of elements old and new, which
later seem unaccountable once we have arrived at the other
pole.   Such transitional thinking is more difficult, but in
some ways more interesting, than is that to be observed
after the new *weltanschauung* is finally established.   It may
be added that Mather, in the process of feeling his way
toward a new orientation, provides us with the only American example of a complete medico-theological synthesis.

*   *   *   *   *

There is no question about the quantity of Mather's
scientific writings, just as there is no doubt of the scale of
his other outpourings.   On medicine, in particular, he wrote
at length, and was unique in this respect in his time and
place.   There has been considerable skepticism, on the other
hand, with regard to the quality of his scientific work.   He
usually seemed more learned than original, more a theorist
than observer.   Yet there were some remarkable exceptions
to these generalizations, as in his observations on hybrid
corn, or, again, in his apparently original view that the
phenomena of immunization could be best explained in
terms of pathogenic organisms.

It would, in any case, be wide of the mark to think that Mather possessed a merely eclectic mind. He did much more than to soak up, in miscellaneous fashion, all the learning which was available. He read omnivorously, to be sure, and—like many *virtuosi*—reported all sorts of odds and ends picked up in this manner. But he also read, at times, with much discrimination. Probably the most striking aspect of Mather's scientific thought was his ability to select, from the maze of "natural philosophy," those discoveries and problems which were eventually to prove of major importance.

Cohen calls attention to this discernment in regard to science at large and illustrates it by a comparison between Mather's *Christian Philosopher: a Collection of the best Discoveries in Nature, with Religious Improvements* (1721) and an earlier science text by Charles Morton. The latter work, although long standard in England as well as at Harvard, misinterpreted some discoveries and subordinated all of them to a preconceived system. Mather, in comparison:

actually gathered together a collection of "the best discoveries in nature," as his title indicates. . . . The result is that Mather's book is a very interesting one and still makes exciting reading. It is imbued with a modernity of feeling, despite the "quaintness" of the "religious improvements," and is characterized throughout by the natural freshness that derives specifically from the fact that Mather intended to present the "best discoveries" and actually did so.[1]

This same discernment is evident in the clergyman's medical writings. It has been overlooked, apparently, because of the presence therein of many trivial or extraneous materials which caught the eyes of later readers. Oliver Wendell Holmes was typical in this respect; he saw only the surviving anachronisms. Yet interspersed with Mather's ramblings and moralizings were many prescient observa-

[1] I. Bernard Cohen, "The *Compendium Physicae* of Charles Morton (1627-1698)," *Isis*, XXXIII (June, 1942), 659 f.

tions. He not only sensed the importance of the animalcular hypothesis, for example, but promptly recognized its basic implications for immunology and for chemotherapy. Within these areas lay some of the most significant problems of the future. Whether or not these ideas were original with Mather, what other American of his era—or for some time, thereafter—displayed such insight?

* * * * *

Although Mather's medical theories exerted little if any influence on the subsequent course of scientific thought,[2] certain aspects of his applied medicine were calculated to have lasting value. This might well have been true of his psychiatry, for example, which anticipated the kindly treatments which finally came into professional vogue during the nineteenth century. But since "The Angel" was never published, there is no way of telling what impact it might have had on American attitudes toward mental illness.

The one instance in which Mather's applied medicine did exert lasting influence, however, was a most significant one. Inoculation was the first positive achievement in preventive medicine, and the principle involved remains valid at the present time. The history of immunology, with all its ultimate values in overcoming infectious diseases, began—above the folk level and on a meaningful scale—in the Boston of 1721. Seen in this perspective, as well as in relation to his theoretical insights, Cotton Mather emerges as the first significant figure in American medicine. He deserves, moreover, a place in the history of western medicine as a whole.

---

[2] How completely unknown or ignored was his animalcular theory of smallpox, later in the century, is illustrated in Laughlin Macleane's *Essay on the Expediency of Inoculation,* Philadelphia, 1756. It is simply stated therein (p. 35) that the cause of smallpox is "utterly unknown."

Proposals

for printing a BOOK entituled:—
THE ANGEL OF BETHESDA.

An Essay upon the Common Maladies of Mankind: offering, first, The Sentiments of Piety, whereto the Invalids are to be awakened in and from their bodily Maladies. And then, a rich Collection of plain but potent and approv'd Remedies for the Maladies.

Accompanied with many very practicable Directions, for the Preservation of Health, to such as enjoy a good Measure of so great a Blessing.

And many other curious, and grateful and useful Entertainments, occasionally intermixed.

The whole being, a Family-physician, which every Family of any Capacity may find their Account in being supplied withal.

Tho' the Title of the Book thus exhibited, may somewhat explain the Design and the Value of it, yett for a further and fuller Explanation, here shall be given the Contents, and some Account of what is contained in the sixty six Capsula's into which it is divided. Capsula I. *Salvianus,* or some Remarks of Piety on the grand Cause of Sickness. II. *Valerianus,* or, Points of Health to be always attended to: and famous Methods for the Prolongation of Life proposed. III. *Therapeutica Sacra,* or, The Symptoms of an Healed Soul, with the Methods of coming at it. IV. The *Tree of Life.* Whereto there is annexed, *Panacaea;* or, A Proposal of an Universal Medicine, to them that would consult their Health under and against All Diseases. V. *Nishmath Chajim,* The probable Seat of all Diseases, and a general Cure of them, further discovered: more particularly for Splenetic and Hysteric Maladies, which make so great a Part of our Distempers. VI. The *Gymnastick,* or, An Exercitation upon Exercise. VII. *Conjecturalia,* or, some Touches upon a New Theory of many Diseases. VIII. *Raphael,* or, Notable Cures from the Invisible World. IX. *Stimulator,* or, Considerations upon Pains, Dolours, Aches, in general. X. *Cephalica,* or, Cures for The Head-ache. And, The Ague in the Head. XI. *Dentifrangibulus,* or, The Anguish and Releef of the Tooth-ache. XII. The *Prisoners of the Earth,* under the Gout; with some Notable and Instructive Entertainments for them.

[127]

XIII. The *Gouts* younger Brother, or, A Rheumatism, and Sciatica, quieted. XIV. *Flagellum.* The Stone; And other Diseases of the Kidneys and Bladder. XV. *Magor-Missabib*, or, The Cancer. XVI. *Scrophularia.* or, The Kings-Evil touch'd upon. XVII. *Pyretologia.* or, Fevers extinguished. XVIII. *Febrifuga.* or, Agues conquered. XIX. The *Inevitable.* or, The Measles managed. XX. *Variolae triumphatae.* or, The Small-Pox encountred. And, a Poem upon it, by one coming out of the Jaws of the Destroyer. XXI. *Kibroth Haltaavah.* or, some Clean Thoughts on the Foul Disease. XXII. *Malum ab Aquilone.* or, The Scurvy discoursed on. XXIII. *Moses.* or, one drawn out of the Dropsy. XXIV. *Bethlem* visited. or, The Cure of Madness. XXV. *De Tristibus.* or, The Cure of Melancholy. XXVI. *Paralyticus resuscitatus.* or, The Palsey-struck, taking up his Bed, and walking. XXVII. *Attonitus;* or, The Apoplexy considered. XXVIII. *Caducus*, or, The Falling-Sickness considered; with a New Discovery of a most unfailing Remedy for all Convulsive Diseases in old or young. XXIX. *Vertiginosus.* or, How to steer under Dizziness. XXX. *Dormitantius.* or, The Lethargy; and other sleepy Diseases. XXXI. *Ephialtes.* or, The Night-mare beaten off. XXXII. The *Oculist;* considering Diseases of the Eye; especially, Blindness. With a Poem upon it. XXXIII. *Colaphizatus.* or, Diseases of the Ear; especially Deafness. With an Appendix, of, Advice to the Lame. XXXIV. *Stiptica.* or, Bleeding at the Nose. XXXV. *Suffocatus.* or, A Sore Throat; and Quinzy. XXXVI. *Adjutoria Catarrhi.* A Catarrh; And what we call, A Cold, how to stop it. XXXVII. The *Breast-beater;* or, A Cough quieted. XXXVIII. *Breath struggled for.* or, The Asthma, and Short-windedness, releeved. XXXIX. *Desector*, The Consumption, the Grand Mower, felt by the Grass of the Field. XL. *Medicina Medicanda.* A Pause made upon the Uncertainties of the Physicians. XLI. *Icterus* look'd upon; or, The Jaundice cured. XLII. The *Main Wheel* scour'd and oil'd. or, Help for the Stomach depraved; And Vomiting. XLIII. *Edulcorator.* Help for the Heart-burn. And, Stomach-ache. XLIV. The *Vermine-killer;* upon Worms. XLV. *Intestina Omnia Recta.* or, The Disorders of a Flux rectified. XLVI. *Jehoram* visited. or, The Bloody-flux remedied. XLVII. *Miserere mei.* or, Compassions for the Cholic; and the Dry-Belly-ache. XLVIII. *Ashdodes.* or, The Piles. XLIX. *Scabiosus.* or, The Itch safely and quickly chas'd away. L. *Singultus finitus.* or, A Stop to the Hiccough. LI. *Ephphatha.* or, some Advice to Stammerers; How to gett Good by, and how to gett rid of, their grievous Infirmity.

The ANGEL of BETHESDA.

An ESSAY
Upon the Common Maladies
of mankind

Offering

First, The SENTIMENTS OF PIETY
which the Invalids are to be awakened,
in and from their MALADIES.

And then, a Rich collection of Plain, Potent
and Approv'd REMEDIES
for the MALADIES.

Accompanied with many very practicable
DIRECTIONS for the PRESERVATION
of HEALTH, to such as enjoy a
good measure of so Great a Blessing.

And many other curious, and Grateful & useful
ENTERTAINMENTS, occasionally
intermixed.

Or a Family-Physician, which Every FAMILY
of any Capacity may find their account
in being supplied with.

By a FELLOW of the ROYAL SOCIETY.

Gal. VI.10.
As we have opportunity, Let us do good
unto all men.

LII. *Muliebria.* or, Foeminine Diseases.   LIII. Retired *Elizabeth.*   A
Long, tho' no very Hard, Chapter for a Woman whose Travail ap-
proaches; with Remedies to abate the Sorrows of Childbearing.   LIV.
Great Things done by *Small Means;* with some Remarks on a Spring of
Medicinal Waters, which every Body is at Home an Owner of.   LV.
Mirabilia et Parabilia. or, more Great Friends to Health, very easy to
come at.   LVI.   The Eyes of poor Hagar opened. or, A Discovery of
unknown Stores, for Cures, which every body is Master of.   LVII. A
Physick-Garden. or, A Consideration of the admirable Vertues in certain
Plants which every common Garden may be furnish'd with.   LVIII.
Thaumatographia Insectorum. or, Some Despicable Insects of admirable
Vertues.   LIX. *Infantilia.* or, Infantile Diseases.   LX. *Paralipomena.*
or, Cures and Helps for a Cluster of Lesser Inconveniences.   LXI.
Medicamenta sine quibus. or, Certain Remedies, that People of any Con-
dition, may always have ready at hand for themselves and their Neigh-
bours.   LXII. *Fuga Daemonum.* or, Cures by Charms considered; And a
Seventh Son examined.   LXIII. *Miso-capnus.*   Taking the Use of
TOBACCO under Consideration with a Pinch upon the Snuff-box.
LXIV. *Restitutus.* or, A perfect Recovery, in the wise and good Conduct
of one Recovered from a Malady.   LXV. *Liberatus.* or, The Thanksgiving of one advanced in years and praeserved from grievous and painful Diseases.   LXVI. *Euthanasia.* or, A Death Happy and Easy.

You see the Bill of Fare.   It would be too great a Reproach upon
Humane Understanding to imagine, that a Treatise of such Intentions,
and composed with such a Variety of Good Things both for Soul and
Body, and of such universal Benefit for all Sorts of People, Sick or Well,
High or Low, Old or Young, would not find a General Acceptance.   What
Gentleman would not be willing to have such a Companion with him?
Or what Family would not be willing to save Life, and Health, and
Money too, and serve a greater Interest than all of These, by having
such a Counsellour alwayes at hand?   The Book paies all due Regards to
our Skilful and Faithful Physicians; our Necessary Friends.   The
Divulgation of Medicines, is no more than what has been made by
charitable Physicians times without Number.   The Medicines in this
Book are very many of them such as the Best Physicians have already
published.   And as They will not be, so tis incredible that any others
can be Enemies to this Publication.

The *Angel of Bethesda* is now lying at the Pool; and waiting to be
called forth.

It can't well be carried on, but in the ordinary Way of Subscription.

It shall be delivered unto Subscribers, at the Price of Twelve Shillings the Book; which is as cheap again as a Book of the like Bulk from Europe is usually sold for. And very probably it will at some time or other save the Expense of more than as many Pounds unto the Purchaser.

He who sends in Subscriptions for Six Books, may expect a Seventh gratis. The Subscribers also (except any of them forbid it) may expect their Names to be published with the Work, as tis now become customary.

The Subscriptions are taken in, by
To—

Sir; You have here putt into your Hands, Proposals of a Work, which you cannot but be a Well-wisher to. By procuring such a Work to have its Operation in your Neighbourhood, you will very much do them an unknown Service, both in Spiritual and their Temporal Interests; and many will both in Soul and Body fare the better for you. Your known Good Will towards Men, and Zeal to do Good, unto Men, has encouraged the Undertakers, to lodge these Proposals, more particularly in your Hands, that by your Means a Number of Subscriptions may be obtained, for the enabling of them to go thro' the Undertaking; which is thought necessary by,

Your Servants,
The Booksellers.

Capsula I.

Some Remarks
on the Grand CAUSE of Sickness.

Felix qui potuit rerum cognoscere causas.

Mankind has been sadly puzzled about the Origin of Evil. The quaestion, Πόθεν τὸ κακόν, *whence Evil comes,* has been as vexing a Problem as ever was in the World. The Opinion of the old Magians (before the Reformation of Zoroaster, in his Revived *Magianism,*) which was afterwards followed by the Manichees, as numerous a Sect of Hereticks, as almost any that ever was upon the Face of the Earth, was of old strongly imbibed among the Persians. But our Glorious God, speaking about the Affairs of Persia, will have two Gods no longer beleeved among them. No, He sais, Isa. xlv. 7. *I form the Light, and I create Darkness; I make Peace, and create Evil; I the Lord do all these things.* And now, Glorious God, We beleeve it: And yett the Thing remains unto us incomprehensible!

If we enquire after the Origin of Diseases, we shall not enquire wisely after this Matter, if we do not find our Sin against the Holy and Blessed One, to be the Root of Bitterness, from whence they have all arisen.

I will chuse to express my Sentiments of this matter, in the Terms, which in a Treatise entituled, *Mens Sana in Corpore Sano,* I gave unto the public above twenty Years ago.

Lett us look upon Sin as the Cause of Sickness. There are it may be Two Thousand Sicknesses: and indeed, any one of them able to crush us! But what is the Cause of all? Bear in Mind, That Sin was that which first brought Sickness upon a Sinful World, and which yett continues to sicken the World, with a World of Diseases. Our Sickness is in short, *Flagellum Dei pro Peccatis Mundi.*

First, Remember, That the sin of our First Parents, was the First Parent of all our Sickness. All our Sicknesses are but the Execution of that primitive Threatening in Gen. II.17. *In the Day that thou sinnest thou shalt surely Dy.* If Crudities, and Obstructions, and Malignities, are the Parents of our Sicknesses, tis very sure that Sin is the Grand Parent of them; and the sin of our First Parents is the First Parent of them all. We read in Eccl. IX.18. of *One Sinner destroying much Good.* I find, some Jewish Rabbis take our Father Adam, to be meant by that One Sinner. Our Health is no small Part of the Good which has been de-stroy'd by him. Had our First Parents eaten of the Tree of Life, doubt-less a confirm'd state of perfect Health, both in themselves and their off-spring, had been the Fruit of it. But our First Parents criminally applied themselves to the forbidden Tree of Knowledge. This proved a Tree of Death, both to themselves and their Offspring; and Sicknesses are among the Punishments of that nefandous Crime. *Alas, our Father did eat soure Grapes, and our Teeth are sett on Edge.* When that Expression is used about our Lord Jesus Christ; (Heb. II.9.) *He TASTED Death for us;* I make no doubt, that it is an elegant Allusion unto the Way whereby Death at first came into the World; This was by tasting the forbidden Fruit. As Death, so Sickness, the Inchoation of Death, is but the bitter Taste of that unhappy Action! Yea, the Breath of the Old Serpent, whereto Mankind in our first Parents hearkened, has poisoned us all. The Poison, which that Serpent who is The Angel of Death, has insin-uated into us, has disturbed our Health, as well as depraved our Heart. Sin, Sin, was that which opened the Floodgates for a Flood of Wretched-ness to rush in upon the World; And Sickness is one Instance of that Wretchedness. Cursed Sin; I Indict thee this day, for murdering of the World!

Secondly, Remember, that the Sin of every individual Man, does but Repeat and Renew the Cause of Sickness unto him. We are informed, in Psal. CVII.17. *Fools, because of their Transgression, and because of their Iniquities, are afflicted,* with Sickness. Indeed Sin sometimes is Naturally the Cause of Sickness. A Sickness in the Spirit will naturally cause a Sickness in the Body. Inordinate Passions burn the Thread of Life. Immoderate Courses drown the Lamp of Life. The Wise Man sais about Unchastity, *It consumes the Body.* It has been said, *plures occidit Crapula quam Gladius,* The Cup kills more than the Canon. And, *multos Morbos Fercula multa faciunt.* Many Dishes will breed many Diseases. Alas, when will Men Beleeve it? The Board slayes more than the Sword. And one may say *By Suppers and Surfeits more have been killed than all the Physicians in the World have cured.* The Apostle sais about the worldly Grefs and Cares; *They work Death.* We may add, *Ignavum corrumpunt otia corpus.* The Humours of the Body stagnate and corrupt in Idleness. But Sin is yett oftener a Moral Cause of Sickness. What are Sicknesses, but the Rods wherewith GOD corrects His own offending Children? Pious Asa takes a wrong Step; and he is diseased in his Foot for it; God sends the Gout upon him. And, what are they, but the vindictive strokes of Wrath, wherewith God Revenges Himself upon the Children of Wrath? Jehoram did a Bloody Thing; and, so, his Bowels fell out by Reason of his Sickness: God smites him with a Bloody Flux for it. Hence, our Sicknesses are in the New Testament called by a Name that hath Scourges in the Signification of it. (Ponder also at Liesure, Exod. xv. 26. and Deut. xxviii. 21. 22. 27. 35. 60. 61. And say not, as he to whom the Book of Happiness was presented, *I am not at Liesure.*) Ah, Sin; How mischievous art thou! A Man may say of every Sin, when he meets with it, *Have I found thee, O mine Enemy?* The Soul and the Body constitute one Person; and the Body is unto the Soul, the Instrument of Iniquity. Hence for the Sins of the one, there come Sufferings on the other. Syrs, Be afraid of Sin. I tell you tis a very unwholesome Thing. When you are gorne to drink the stolen Waters of Sin, there's Death in the Pott.

Thirdly. Hence, under Sickness, we should make a solemn Enquiry after Sin. As upon other Disasters, there was that Call given: Hag. i. 5. 7. *Consider your Ways:* Tis to be heard most sensibly in our Sicknesses. There is a Self-examination incumbent upon All Men: upon sick Men it is peculiarly incumbent. I pray, Lett our Sickness itself, be such an Emetic as to make us Vomit up our Sin, with a poenitent Confession of it. A Time there was when Sacramental Profanations were chastised with Sicknesses among the Corinthians: They had not come in an orderly Manner to the Body of the Lord, and God rebuked it with Disorders upon theirs. (Compare 2 Chron. xxx. 20.) Now, sais the Apostle, *Judge yourselves.* Indeed, Sickness does not always come to manage a Controversy of GOD with us for some Iniquity. A Job, that perfect and upright Man, may have his *Ulcera Syrraca* (so tragically described by Aretaeus and admirably answering the Diagnosticks which the Sacred Writ has given us of Job's Distemper:) to try his patience. Tis said of that man of God Elisha, He *fell sick of the Sickness whereof he died:* It seems he had been sick some Times before. Our Lord may have a Lazarus, of whom it shall be said, *One whom thou lovest is sick.* Strange! Diseases may be Love-tokens! A Timothy, that rare Minister, whom one of the Ancients calls *an Admirable young Man,* may be troubled with often Infirmities. Our Lord Jesus Christ is to be visited in the Sickness of His dearest Brethren. (Lord, That ever thou shouldest call them so!) But yett, it becomes us to be very inquisitive and sollicitous, lest there be Wrath in our Sickness; and Thoughtful what is the Controversy?

Wherefore, both under our Sickness and after it, we should be more concerned for being saved from Sin than from Sickness. Our Sins, indeed what are they, but the terrible Sicknesses under which our Souls are fearfully languishing and perishing. A sinful Soul is a sickly Soul. Original Sin is a Leprosy. Every Lust is a Distemper of the Soul. An unsteady Soul has a Palsey. A wanton Soul has a Fever. A worldy Soul has a Dropsy. Anger in the Soul is an Erisypelas. Envy is a Cancer in the Soul, Sloth, a Scurvy. Whenever we have sinned, we have cause to say, *Lord, Heal my soul, for I have sinned.* Now, Sickness is to awaken our Concern, first, for the Pardon of the Maladies in our Souls; and so, for a Power against them all.

First: Under Sickness, what should be our chief Concern? It should be that: Psal. xxv. 18 *Lord, look upon my Affliction and my Pain, and forgive all my Sin.* If it be then putt unto us, *what lies Heaviest now upon you?* Say not, *my Sickness,* but say *my Sinfulness: That I have done so little Service for my Lord Jesus Christ; That I have mispent so much of my precious Time; That I have made no more Provision for Eternity; And, that I am still so sottish, and slothful, and sensual, and carnal, and alienated from the Life of God.* And for to quicken this our Concern under our Sickness, we are to think, *What will become of me, if I dy unpardoned; what will become of me throughout eternal Ages?*

Next, After Sickness; what should be our chief Concern? It should be that: Psal. CIII. 3. *Bless the Lord, O my Soul, who forgiveth all thine Iniquities; who releeveth all thine Infirmities.* The Iniquities are to be taken away first; and then the Infirmities. Lett us not count our Sickness well gone, except our Sin be gone too. But lett us now putt this unto ourselves; *Am I now more Assured of my being pardoned, than I was before? Am I in better Terms with Heaven? Can I see and say, Tis in Love to my Soul that GOD has brought me back from the Pitt of Corruption?* It should now be more of our Care, That our Sickness be removed in Mercy, than ever it was that it should be removed at all.

In fine; The Sickness that enfeebles us, must make us fly more vigorously than ever unto the expiatory Sacrifice of our Lord Jesus Christ, for the Forgiveness of our Sins. Our Sickness is utterly lost upon us,

if it render not a Christ more precious unto us than ever He was, and
instruct us not how to make more Use of Him. As the Sick in the Gos-
pels much cried out for a Christ, so Sickness is to teach us, the Worth of
a Christ, and cause us more to see, that without a Christ we are undone
forever. There is a Ransome which a sick Man is to be minded of; that
Ransome, Job. xxxiii. 34. *He is chastened with Pain upon his Bed, his
Flesh is consumed away, his Soul draweth nigh to the Grave. Then God is
gracious to Him, and saith, Deliver Him from going down to the Pitt. I
have found a Ransome.* Syrs, when we are sick, lett us behold our Lord
Jesus Christ as going down to the Pitt for us, and plead that Ransome
that we may not ourselves go down. In the Directories for Visiting the
Sick, used many Ages ago, the Sick were directed to say, *Lord, I place
the Death of my Saviour Jesus Christ between Thee and my Sins.* Tis
impossible to say a better Thing than that!

Upon Sickness, our Address must be made unto our Lord Jesus Christ;
of whom it is said, Matth. viii. 17. *Himself bare our Sicknesses.* Indeed,
we cannot say, that there were any proper Sicknesses among the Sufferings of our Saviour. We do not find that he was ever properly sick. His
Body being formed by a special Efficacy of the Holy Spirit, seems to
have been of so exact a Temper, as to be less liable to Diseases than other
men. But our Saviour bore our Sicknesses, because, as tis elswhere said
for it, He bare our sins, which are the Cause of our Sicknesses. Wherefore, in every Sickness lett us repair to the Death [of] our Lord Jesus
Christ, and struggle with our Unbeleef more than our Sickness, until we
are able to say, *Lord, my whole Dependence is on my Saviour, who has
made Atonement for the Sins, for which thou hast made me sick in smiting
me.*

I will recite you a Contemplation of the blessed Austin, which under
Sickness may be the sweetest Anodyne of our uneasy Minds. "There
lay extended over the whole World a great Instance of Sickness; That
is to say, All Mankind, subject unto many Diseases both of Soul and
Body. And therefore there is come into the world that great Physician,
by whose Wounds we are Healed. Indeed, we see that the Soul of man
labours under the numberless Diseases which are its Vices. And the
Body of Man suffers more Diseases than any other Creature. But O
Admirable and Amiable Matter! and a Thing full of compassionate Goodness! (*Fusus est sanguis Medici, et factum est medicamentum phrenetici.*)
The Blood of the Physician being shed, becomes the Cure of the Distempered.

In fine, There were malignant Ulcers which Galen sais, the Greeks called Chironian, because none but Chiron could cure them. The malignant Mischiefs which our Sin has brought upon us, we are sure, are such that None but Christ can cure them!

It was a mistake in some of the Ancients to make Jesus a Greek Name, carrying of Healing with it. But it will be no Mistake in us to look on our Jesus as The Lord our Healer.

The Design of all this Essay is to lead the Reader unto Him. And therewithal to prosecute that grand Maxim, The Cure of a Sin-sick Soul is what all Invalids ought to reckon their grand Concern. I will express it in the Words of Rhegius translated from the High-Dutch by Lorrichini, in a Treatise entituled, *Psychopharmacon. Adversa Valetudo, membrorumque intentus ac Mors, Terribilis quodem judicatur: sed omnium quae accidere poterunt homini rerum est horrendissima aegritudo et exitium Animarum. Quod si membris languentibus et infirmo corpori salubria Medicamenta Studio diligentiore quaerimus, cur non cura majore, quae sanant atque vivificant Animas adlaboramus indagate?* And we will up-braid many Christian People with the Words of an heathen Poet,

> *Ut corpus redimas, ferrum patiens, et ignes;*
> *Arida nec sitiens ora Lavabis Aqua.*
> *Ut valeas Animo, quicquam tolerare negabis!*
> *At praemium pars haec corpore majus habet.*

Thus Englished.

> To save your Bodies, Cutts and Burns you'l chuse;
> And you're parched, to quench your Thirst refuse:
> Your Soul to keep in Health bear any Thing!
> For This a greater Happiness will bring.[1]

It is a Thing strongly pressed by the noble Morney, that Julian himself beleeved Aesculapius the Son of Jupiter to have descended from Heaven, to be Incarnate, and have appeared among Men as a Man, in order to the Restitution both of their Spirits and of their Bodies, to their pristine Perfection. O Invalids, I am leading you to your true Aesculapius!

---

[1] The above five lines are not in Mather's writing.

Cap. V. *Nishmath-Chajim.*

The probable Seat of all Diseases,
and a general Cure for them,
further discovered.
More particularly for Splenetic
and Hysteric Maladies, which make so great a part
of our Distempers.

I. There is a Spirit in Man; a wonderful Spirit, which from very good Authority may be called *NISHMATH-CHAJIM;* (or, The Breath of Life:) and which may be of a Middle Nature, between the Rational Soul, and the Corporeal Mass; but may be the Medium of Communication, by which they work upon one another. It wonderfully receives also Impressions from both of them; and perhaps it is the vital Ty between them. The scriptural Anatomy of Man, into Spirit, and Soul, and Body, seems to favour and invite the Apprehensions, which we are now proceeding to.

When our Saviour so excused His drowsy Disciples, *The Spirit is willing, but the Flesh is weak;* doubtless, by the Spirit, he means, what His Apostle afterwards called the Mind, and the Spirit of the Mind, and, the Inner-Man. But there being also in Man, that which is called, the Soul, or, the Heart, or that Principle and Passion, which is concerned most immediately for the Praeservation of the Life, and of the Comforts that may sweeten it. This Principle is called The Flesh. The Flesh of the Disciples here, which now so rebelled against the Spirit, was not the Lust of Pleasures and Riches and the like; but it was that most Natural Affection of the Soul which lay in a Desire to shun Death and Grief. And this Flesh here is called weak, not because it wanted Strength, for it was in Truth, too strong: But because it wanted Health; it was out of order. For the Health of the Soul, it lies in its obeying and not opposing the Empire of the Mind.

II. The Great GOD who formed all things, and who after a singular manner forms the Spirit of Man within him, has endued this *Nishmath-Chajim*, with marvellous Faculties; which yett are all of them short of those Powers, which enable the Rational Soul, to penetrate into the Causes of Things; to do curious and exquisite Things in the mathematical Sciences; and above all, to act upon a principle of Love to GOD, and with the Views of Another World.

III. Some Rays of Light concerning this *Nishmath-Chajim*, have been darted into the Minds of many learned Men, who have yett after all remained very much in the Dark about it.

Famous have been the Sentiments of Helmont (and some other Masters of Obscurities) about it; who would exhibit it under the name of the Archaeus; and with much of Reason press, that in the Cure of Diseases, there may be more of Regard paid unto it.

According to Grembs (writing *De Ortu Rerum*) it is *Medium quid inter Vitam et Corpus, et veluti Aura nitens splendensque.* A sort of Luminous Air which is of a Middle Nature, betwixt spirituous and corporeous.

It has the Denomination of the aerial Spirit, with some Philosophers, who trouble the Stars, more than there is any Need for.

Even the Galenists themselves, have not been without some Suspicions, yea, some Acknowledgments, of our *Nishmath-Chajim*, and have given very broad Hints concerning it. And no doubt, they may thank the old Platonists for instructing of them. The great Fernelius, one of the most illustrious Men that ever shone among them, (writing, *De Abditis rerum Causis*) gives a very lively Description of it. Yea, he finds it in the τὸ ἐνορμῶν or, *Inciter*, of Hippocrates; and having a great Power of Incursion, like the Wind, he allows it some Affinity with the Nature of Body; but inasmuch as it is invisible, it must also have some Affinity with what is incorporeal: So, he will have it of a Middle Nature between Both. But he supposes it the Vehicle, and proper Seat of the Soul, and all its Faculties; and if we call it, their Body, we shall have his Permission for it.

And indeed, the old Platonists had a Notion, of a certain excellent Body, pellucid and ethereal, subservient unto the Faculties of the Soul, and uniting it unto the more terrestrial Body.

Heurnius, whom some reckon and value next unto Fernelius, (in his *Institutions*) describes it as, *A Kind of Ethereal Spirit, elaborated out of the purest Part of the Blood, and changed into the Substance of a very subtil Air; and the prime Instrument of the Soul for the Performance of its Functions.*

IV. Our *Nishmath-Chajim* seems to be commensurate unto our Bodies; and our Bodies are conformable to the Shape which God our Maker gives to that plastic Spirit, (if we may call it so). But by what Principle the Particles of it, which may be finer than those of the Light itself, are kept in their Cohaesion to one another, is a Thing yett unknown unto us.

V. And how it fares in the case of Amputations on our Bodies; Whether like a Flame violently struck off, what is so, may not nimbly, as by Sort of a Magnetism, reunite with what it belongs unto: but then, how far it becomes for the present folded up into it: or, whether it be not entirely lost, but what remains, may have the power to produce a Recruit, when there shall be a Lodging again provided for it; this also is yett unknown unto us.

VI. The *Nishmath-Chajim* is the Spirit of the several Parts, where it has a Residence; and it is the Life by which the several Parts have their Faculties maintained in Exercise. This, tis, that sees, that hears, that feels; and performs the several Digestions in the Body. And the Animal World, having *Animam pro Sale*, if it were not for this, would quickly putrify.

VII. We have sometimes been led by our Microscopes, into some Apprehensions, that our Bodies are originally folded up, in inconceivably minute *Corpusculicumcules;* and that Generation is nothing but the Evolution of the Stamina so involved: which Operation is carried on, by filling them up with a Matter agreeable to them, till they have an Augmentation to the utmost extent of the Dimensions, that they can reach unto: and that the Resurrection of the Dead, which is in the Sacred Scriptures called, a Filling of the Dead Bodies, will find out the old Stamina of the Forsaken Body, again shrunk up into its first Parvity, and replenish it with a more Ethereal Matter, fitt for the coelestial Employments and Enjoyments intended for it. But this Hypothesis is encumbred with Difficulties which drive us into a *Nish-math-Chajim*, either to support and perfect the Hypothesis, or to yeeld us a Better upon the failing of it.

VIII. The *Nishmath-Chajim* is indeed, *Generationis Faber ac Rector;* and as it leads to the Acts requisite in Generation, without any further Instructor, so it is the Spirit, whose Way we know not, for shaping the Bones and other Parts, in the Womb of her that is with Child.

IX. There are indeed many Things in the Humane Body, that cannot be solved by the Rules of Mechanism. Our *Nishmath-Chajim* will go very far to help us, in the Solution of them. Indeed we can scarce well subsist without it.

X. There is an astonishing Operation, and indeed some Illustration and Explanation, of the *Nishmath-Chajim*, in praegnant Women; whose Imagination frequently makes Impressions on the unborn Infants, that would exceed all Beleef, if we had them not continually in View before our Eyes. The Instances are so numerous and so various, that one might compile a large Volume of them; and almost ask a Palaephatus to afford a Title for it. But in what other Way to be accounted for?

XI. For the *Nishmath-Chajim* we may safely be Traducians. It is a Flame enkindled in, and so derived from, the Parent. And this Traduction (which is *luminis e lumine*) may help us considerably, in our enquiries, *How the Dispositions of our original Sin are convey'd and infus'd into us.*

XII. It was of old, yea, it is at this day, a prevailing Opinion, among the Strangers to the glorious Gospel of the Blessed God, that the Manes, which remain after Death, have still an humane Shape, and all the Parts both external and internal, which there were in the Body that is now deserted: yea, that there is a Food which this departed Spirit craves for and lives on. Homer inflicts punishments on the wicked after Death, which there must be a Sort of Bodies to be the subjects of. And Plato speaks of those that are punished in Hell, as having such Members and Faces as they had once upon the Earth. Indeed Justin Martyr argues from it that these old Gentlemen must needs have some

Knowledge and Beleef of our Doctrine of, the Resurrection of the Dead. But what shall we say, when our Glorious Lord-Redeemer, in His Parable of the Rich Man, supposes his Body in the Grave, and yett, being in Hell, he cries out of a Body, and particularly, of a Tongue, that is tormented there? Many of the Ancients thought there was much of a real History in the Parable: and their Opinion was, that there is, Διαφορὰ κατὰ τὰς Μορφάς a Distinction (and so a Resemblance,) of Men as to their Shapes after Death. We find this was the Opinion of Irenaeus; who proves, from what our Saviour speaks of the dead Man, that the Souls which have putt off their Bodies, do yett *Characterem Corporum custodire*, preserve the Shapes of the Bodies, to which they were united. And from the same Speech of our Saviour, Tertullian does infer: *effigiem Animae et corporales lineas*, the Shape and corporeal Lineaments of the Soul. I will say nothing of what Thespesius returning to Life reported about the τὰ τῶν ψυχῶν χρώματα the Colours of Souls and the Ulcers by their Passions left upon them.

On this Occasion the Words of M. Dacier, in her Notes upon Homer's Odysses, are not unworthy to be considered: which give us the Observation, that a fine subtil Sort of Body, accompanied the Intellect after the Separation of the Soul by Death from the grosser Body.

XIII. The *Nishmath-Chajim* is much like the Soul which animates the Brutal World: even that Spirit of the Beast, which goeth downward unto the Earth; but is by the Hand of the Glorious Creator impraegnated with a Capacity and Inclination for those Actions, which are necessary for the Praeservation of themselves, and the Propagation of their Species. The Nidification of Birds, the Mellification of Bees, and a thousand such Things, how surprising Works done in the Brutal World, without any rational Projection for them! And hence, there are also many Actions done by us, that have a Tendency to our Safety and Welfare, which are not the Effects of any rational Projection; but such as we do by what we call, a meer Instinct of Nature, fall into. The sucking Infant, yea, and the nursing Mother, too,

do very needful and proper Things, without consulting of Reason
for the doing of them.

It is a Thing, which who can observe without Astonishment?
In every other Machin, if anything be out of Order, it will
remain so till some Hand from abroad shall rectify it; it can do
nothing for itself. But the Humane Body is a Machin, wherein,
if anything be out of Order, presently the whole Engine, as under
an Alarum, is awakened for the helping of what is amiss, and other
Parts of the Engine strangely putt themselves out of their Way
that they may send in Help unto it. Whence can this proceed
but from a *Nishmath-Chajim* in us, with such Faculties and such
Tendencies from God imprinted on it?

XIV. Having at some Time or other felt a considerable Smart,
or been considerably sick, from something that we have mett
withal, we have an Abiding Horror for that thing perhaps all our
Days. Tho' we certainly know that the Thing will now do us no
Hurt, but rather do us much Good, yett no conviction of Reason
will overcome our abiding Horror. We cannot swallow the Pill,
or take the Meat or the Drink, and do an hundred Things,
which we have heretofore been horribly frighted at. Our *Nishmath Chajim* has an incurable Aversion for them.

XV. Tis the *Nishmath-Chajim*, that is the Strength of every
Part in our Body, and that gives Motion to it. Here perhaps the
Origin of muscular Motion may be a little accounted for. And
this is the Spirit, and the Balsams, and one might almost say, the
Keeper, of each Part, which is occupied and befriended with it.
Yea, what Construction shall we make of it, when People have
lived without any Brains in their Heads, and after the Destruction of almost all the Bowels in their Bodies? We are supplied
and surprised with many most credible Relations of such Things.
And I quaestion, whether anything will do so well, or go so far,
as our *Nishmath-Chajim*, to account for them.

XVI. The principal Wheel in the animal Oeconomy, is the
Stomach. And we shall now find that which above all things
the Digestion there, is to be ascribed unto. Dispute, O Philosophers, and Physicians, how Digestion is performed in the

Stomach. Tis the *Nishmath-Chajim* after all, that is above all, the main Digester. Else, how could a Stomach that is actually cold, and has in it no very tastable or notable Humour for this Purpose, Digest the very Stones that are taken down into it?

The taking of some Repast is in our Sacred Scripture sometimes called, the Establishing of the Heart. The Heart, is not seldome, a term for our *Nishmath-Chajim*.

XVII. It is the *Nishmath-Chajim*, that is more eminently the Seat of our Diseases, or the Source of them. To pass by what they quote of Herophilus, we find Plato eloquently demonstrating that all Diseases have their Origin in the Soul. Yea, as long ago as the Days of Hippocrates, the Essentials of Diseases began to be discovered; and the Pacifying and rectifying of the Enforcing Spirit was proposed as the most ready Way to cure them.

Quaere: How far the Decays of old Age are to be found in the Circumstances of the *Nishmath-Chajim* falling under Impairments? And whence it came to pass that when Moses was very old, yett his Eye was not dim, nor his natural Force abated?

Is not this the true Humidum Radicale they use to talk of? and Is not this the Microcosmic Air whereto Tachenius ascribes the Cure of the Gout by a strong Perturbation of the Mind; upon which he concludes it animated?

XVIII. It is probable, that when we dy, the *Nishmath-Chajim* goes away, as a Vehicle to the Rational Soul; and continues unto it an Instrument of many Operations. Here we have some Solution for the Difficulties about Place and the Change of it, for such an immaterial Spirit as the rational Soul: And some account for Apparitions of the Dead; the Spectres, which are called both Spirits and Phantasms, in our Gospel. Yea, we are certain of it that Persons before they have died, upon strong Desires to visit and behold some Objects at a Distance from the Place to which they were now confined, have been thrown into a Trance, wherein they have lain some considerable while without Sense or Breath; and then returning, have reported what they have seen. But incontestible Witnesses have deposed that in this Time, they were actually seen at the Place, which they affirmed they had gone unto.

And here also we do a little understand how our Apostle in the Raptures (which the Scoffing Lucian derides him for) wherein he supposes he might be out of the Body, yett he heard Words: he was yett sensible of occurrences.

In reading of Homer, (as has been already in Part observed) we find his Notion to be the same with what was in the Egyptian Philosophy; which supposed that Man was compounded of three Parts: an intelligent Mind, called φρήν or ψυχή; a Vehicle, called εἴδωλον the Image, or the Soul; and a gross Body, called σωμα the Soul, in which they look'd on the Mind as lodged they supposed exactly to resemble the Body in Shape, and Bulk, and Features; being in the Body as the Statue in the Mould; and so after its Departure keeping the Image of the Body. Plutarch very distinctly delivers this Doctrine, and sais, when the Soul is compounded with the Understanding, it makes Reason; and when compounded with the Body, it makes Passion. The one Composition is the Principle of Pleasure and Pain; the other of Vertue and Vice. He adds, Man dies two Deaths: the first Death makes him two of three; the second makes him one of two.

XIX. In the indisputable and indubitable Occurrences of Witchcrafts (and Possessions) there are many Things, which, because they are hard to be understood, the Epicurean Sadducees content themselves, in their swinish Manner, only to laugh at. But the *Nishmath-Chajim* well understood, would give us a marvellous Key to lett us into the Philosophy of them.

XX. And now, for some important Consequences.

Most certainly, the Physician that can find out Remedies (particularly in the Mineral or Vegetable Kingdome) that shall have a more immediate Efficacy to brighten, and strengthen, and comfort, the *Nishmath-Chajim*, will be the most successful Physician in the World. Especially, if he can irradiate the Spirit in the Stomach, he will do wonderfully.

The things also, which fortify the Blood, and restore a volatil Ferment, in the vapid and languid Blood, will do wonders for us. It is impossible to kill a Man, (the *Nishmath-Chajim* will never leave him), till the Circulation of his Blood be ruined.

He who will best keep in Heart the *Nishmath-Chajim*, will be, ἸΗΤΡὸΣ ᾿ΑΝῊΡ ΠΟΛΛῶΝ ᾿ΑΝΤΆΞΙΟΣ ῎ΑΛΛΩΝ.

XXI. We read, *Heaviness in the Heart of Man makes it stoup, but a good Word makes it glad.* We read, *A cheerful Heart does Good like a Medicine, but a broken Spirit dries the Bones.* The Invigoration, or the Debilitation of the *Nishmath-Chajim*, is that wherein those ancient Observations are accomplished. Dr. Aurbachius, after forty Years Practice, made this Declaration, *Reipsa comperi plures homines moestitia ac Dolore Animi mori, quam violenta Morte.* It is a Remark of Baglivi, but it may have been made by ten Thousand more, "That a great part of our Diseases, either do rise from, or are fed by a Weight of Cares, lying on the Minds of Men. Diseases that seem incureable, are easily cured by agreeable Conversation. Disorders of the Mind first bring Diseases on the Stomach; and so the whole Mass of Blood gradually becomes infected. And as long as the Passions of the Mind continue, the Diseases may indeed change their Forms; but they rarely quitt the Patients." A Bonifacius heretofore address'd the Physicians on this Occasion, in such Terms as these. "Tranquillity of Mind, will do strange Things towards the Releef of Bodily Maladies. Tis not without Reason, that Hofman in his Dissertation Des Moyens de Vivre Longtems, does insist on Tranquillity of Mind as the Chief among the Ways to Live Long. And that this is the Cause why we read, the Fear of the Lord tendeth to Life. They that have practised, the Art of Curing by Expectation, have made an Experiment of what the Mind will do towards the Cure of the Body. By practising, the Art of Curing by Consolation, you may carry on the Experiment. I propound then: Lett the Physician with all possible Ingenuity of Conversation, find out, what Matter of Anxiety there may have been upon the Mind of the Patient; what there is that has made his Life uneasy to him. Having discovered the Burden, lett him use all the Ways he can devise, to take it off. Offer him such Thoughts as may be the best Anodynes for his distressed Mind; especially the right Thoughts of the Righteous, and the Ways to a Composure upon religious Principles. Give him a Prospect, if

you can, of sound Deliverance from his Distresses, or some
Abatement of them. Raise in him as bright Thoughts as may be;
and scatter the Clouds, remove the Loads, which his Mind is per-
plexed withal; especially, by representing and magnifying the
Mercy of God in Christ unto him."

XXII. It is well known, that if one third of our Diseases,
be those which we call, Chronical, more than one half of this
third, will be those, which in Men go under the Name of Splenetic,
and in Women go under the Name of Hysteric; the Spleen and the
Womb are often enough unjustly accused in these Denominations.
It is marvellous to see, in how many Forms we undergo Splenetic
and Hysteric Maladies; the very Toothache itself often belongs
unto them: and marvellous will be the Success, marvellous the
Esteem, of the Physician that can discover them and encounter
them.

The sagacious Dr. Sydenham, seems to have the Scent of our
Nishmath-Chajim, when he tells us, that as the Outward Man
is framed with parts, obvious to Sense, thus the Inward Man
does consist of a due Series, and as it were a Fabric of Spirits, to
be view'd only by the Eye of Reason: And as this is united with
the Constitution of the Body, so the Frame of it is more or less
easily disordered, by how much the Constitution of the Spirits
is more or less firm within us. And that the Origin of the Splenetic and Hysteric Ataxy in the Body is a feeble Constitution of the
Spirits, and the breaking of their System, so that they are easily
dissipated, or have an unaequal Distribution.

These Maladies have many Symptoms, which may serve as
Diagnosticks for them; especially these two: That the Urine is
clear, limpid, and copious. And, That the Patient is chiefly
affected with his Indispositions, when he has just had his Mind
under some Disturbance and Affliction.

It is plain, that these Diseases are not mainly in the Humours;
inasmuch as Evacuations do not releeve, but fearfully produce
and increase the Diseases. Only indeed, when the Ataxy of the
Spirits, has by its Continuance at last considerably vitiated the
Humours,—then a little Purging and Bleeding may be allowed of.

The Cure is: first, quiet the Spirits with proper Anodynes. Then bring them to Rights, and revive them and refresh them, and bring a new Strength into them. In short, confirm the System. Chalybeates do Wonders this Way; and usually the Steel in Substance, more than many of the common Preparations. Corroborating Plants, infused in generous Wine, or a Tea of them, have also done wondrously, yea, Venice-Treacle alone (our Sydenham sais) as contemptible as it may seem, yett if often used, and a long while, it is a great Remedy in this, as well as very many other Diseases, and perhaps the most effectual that has hitherto been known in the World.

The Force of the Peruvian Bark regularly administered, for giving a Vigour to the Blood, and so to the Spirits, has also been very surprising, and for the recovering of people to an healthy Constitution out of splenetic and hysteric Diseases.

But there is nothing like the Exercise of Riding on Horse-back every Day, when the Weather will allow it; and increasing the Journey by Degrees, till one comes in a Score of Miles in a Day.

XXIII. Upon the Whole:

Of all the Remedies under Heaven, for the conquering of Distempers, and for the Praeservation of Health, and Prolongation of Life, there will now be found none like serious Piety. Many Remedies have done virtuously, (and had their Virtues) but thou excellest them all. The Rational Soul in its Reflections has powerful and wonderful Influences on the *Nishmath-Chajim*. Now, in the Methods of Piety, gett a Soul into the Peace of God, with Assurance of a Reconciliation to Him; and walk in the Fear of God, and the Comfort of the Holy Spirit; keeping always in, and filled always with, His Love; and indulge none of those Lusts, which render the Wicked like the troubled Sea. Keep a Conscience, which in a continual Aim at what is Right shall make a continual Feast. Be not Anxious about Futurities, nor Disturbed upon Provocations; but lett the Strong Faith of a faithful Saviour performing the Thing that is appointed for us in all that happens, produce a perpetual Tranquillity and Serenity in the Soul. Go on singing in the Ways of the Lord, and casting all

Burdens on Him, and, rejoicing in the Hope of the Glory of God. Thus, I show you a most excellent Way.

XXIV. Lett this be Remembred: moderate Abstinence, and convenient Exercise; and some Guard against injurious Changes of the Weather, with an Holy and Easy Mind, will go as far, in carrying us with undecay'd Garments thro' the Wilderness, to the promis'd and pleasant Land, which we are bound unto, as all the Praescriptions with which all the Physicians under Heaven, have ever yett obliged us.

Cap. VII. *Conjecturalies,*

or, some Touches upon,
A New Theory of many Diseases.

Faelix qui potuit Rerum cognoscere causas! Of a Distemper we
commonly say, *to know the Cause, is Half the Cure.* But, alas, how
little Progress is there yett made in that Knowledge: Physicians
talk about the Causes of Diseases. But their Talk is very con-
jectural, very uncertain, very ambiguous, and oftentimes a meer
Jargon: and in it, they are full of Contradiction to one another.
It may be one of the truest Maxims ever yett advanced by any
of the Gentlemen, has been that: *Ventriculus malis affectus est
Origo omnium Morborum.* A distempered Stomach is the Origin
of all Diseases. I am sure tis as useful a Caution as ever they
gave, and it is the very Sum of all prophylactic Physick. But,
Syrs, whence is it, that the Stomach is distempered?

Since we are upon Conjectures, I pray lett us allow some Room,
to those of Dr. Marten and Company.

Every Part of Matter is peopled. Every green Leaf swarms
with Inhabitants. The Surfaces of Animals are covered with other
Animals. Yea, the most solid Bodies, even Marble itself, have
innumerable Cells, which are crouded with imperceptible Inmates.
As there are infinite Numbers of these, which the Microscopes
bring to our View, so there may be inconceivable Myriads yett
smaller than these, which no Glasses have yett reach'd unto.
The Animals that are much more than thousands of times less
than the finest Grain of Sand, have their Motions; and so, their
Muscles, their Tendons, their Fibres, their Blood, and the Eggs
wherein their Propagation is carried on. The Eggs of these
Insects (and why not the living Insects too!) may insinuate themselves by the Air, and with our Aliments, yea, thro' the Pores of
our Skin; and soon gett into the Juices of our Bodies. They may
be convey'd into our Fluids, with the Nourishment which we
received, even before we were born; and may ly dormant until the

[149]

Vessels are grown more capable of bringing them into their Figure
and Vigour for Operations. Thus may Diseases be convey'd
from the Parents unto their Children, before they are born into
the World. As the Eggs whereof Cheese-mites are produced,
were either in the Milk before it came from the Cow, or at least
the Runnet with which the Cheese was coagulated. If they meet
with a proper Nest in any of our numberless Vessels, they soon
multiply prodigiously; and may have a greater Share in producing
many of our Diseases than is commonly imagined. Being brought
into Life, then either by their spontaneous Run, or by their dis-
agreeable Shape, they may destroy the Texture of the Blood, and
other Juices: or they may gnaw and wound the tender Vessels. It
may be so, that one Species of these Animals may offend in one
Way, and another in another, and the various Parts may be
variously offended: from whence may flow a Variety of Diseases.
And vast Numbers of these Animals keeping together, may at
once make such Invasions, as to render Diseases epidemical; which
those particularly are, that are called, pestilential. Epidemical
and almost universal Coughs, may by this Theory be also accounted for.

Strange Murrains on Cattel seem to have been sometimes of
this Original. Dr. Slate observes, of the famous one that passed
from Switzerland thro' Germany to Poland, that in its Progress,
it spred still two German Miles in twenty-four Hours, and he sais
'It were worth considering, whether this Infection is not carried
on by some volatil Insect, that is able to make only such short
Flights as may amount to such Computations.'

As for the Distempers in humane Bodies, Kircher and Haupt-
man assert, that Malignant Fevers never proceed from any other
Cause than little Animals. Blancard affirms, that the Microscope
discovers the Blood in Fevers to be full of Animals.

Ettmuller sais, unwonted Swarms of Insects resorting to a
Countrey, foretell a Plague impending.

And thus we may conceive, how Diseases are convey'd from
distant Countreys or Climates, by the Animalcula, or their Eggs,
deposited in the Bodies or Cloathes or Goods of Travellers.

Tis generally supposed, that Europe is endebted unto America for the Lues venerea. If so, Europe has paid its Debt unto America, by making unto it a Present of the Small Pox, in Lieu of the Great one.

Dr. Lister having observed, that the Plague is properly a Disease of Asia, and still comes from thence; he adds, that the Small Pox is an exotic Disease of the Oriental People, and was not known to Europe, or even to the Lesser Asia, or to Africa, till a spice Trade was opened by the latter Princes of Egypt, unto the remoter Parts of the East Indies; from whence it originally came, and where at this Day it rages more cruelly than with us. Dr. Oliver likewise gives it as his Opinion, that we received the Small Pox and Measles from Arabia; and that Europe was wholly unacquainted with them, until by the frequent Incursions of the Arabians into Africa, and afterwards into Spain, the Venom came to be spred as now it is.

The essential Cause of the Itch, appears to be a vast Number of minute Animals, that make Furrows under the Scarf-skin, and stimulate the nervous Fibres; as may be demonstrated by a Microscope, examining the Humour in the little Bladders rising between the Fingers. The Insects contained in a very small Part of that Humour, fixed upon the Skin of a sound Person, either by shaking Hands with the Mangy, or using a Towel or a Glove after him; these do soon insinuate into the Pores, and then quickly multiply enough to occupy almost all the Surface of the Body. Hence, if the Cure be not so closely followed, as not only to check, but also to kill, all the Animals, they soon increase and become as troublesome as they were before. In the like Manner is a yett more filthy Disease communicated. Thus tis that God judges you, O ye Whore-mongers and Adulterers!

M. Hartsoeker does not scruple to say, *I beleive that Insects occasion most of the Diseases which Mankind is attack'd withal.*

Dr. Marten suspects, that there is possibly no Ulcer, or ulcerated Matter, but what may be stocked with Animals, which being of different Species, the Ulcerations may be more or less violent according to them.

The learned Borellus assures us, that several times he hath seen Animals upon Plaisters taken from fistulous Ulcers; and he adds, *Thus we are held of many Diseases which come from invisible Animals or such as can only be perceived by Microscopes.*

The famous Mayern also observed a cancerous Breast, full of these Animals.

Dr. Andry found, that the Pustles of the Small-Pox are full of them; and so is the Blood and Urine of them that have it: that in the venereal Distemper, there is hardly any Part of the Body that is not gnaw'd by them; that in the *Fistula Lacrymalis* the Water that comes from the Eyes is full of them; that our Cancers are horribly replenished with them, which gnaw upon all the Sieves of the Glands with prodigious Consequences. And, that as these Animals grow old, they assume New Forms, which would be very terrible unto People, if they could but see the terrible Spectacles.

Dr. Marten is not without Suspicion, That a Consumption may often be of this Original; and that these Animals or their Seed, may sometimes be by Parents haereditarily conveyed unto their Offspring; or communicated by sick Persons to sound ones, that are too conversant with them. He also supposes, that tho' great Quantities of these Animals, or of their Eggs, may be lodged in our Blood and Juices, yea, and in our Vessels find a Nest which may bring them into Life; yett while our Secretions are duely performed, or usual Evacuations continued, the Animals may be cast out of our Bodies as fast as they are bred there; and their own very Motion may contribute unto it. But when the Emunctories thro' cold or any other Cause are obstructed, or any usual Evacuations are stopped; this prevents their passing off, and many Mischiefs ensue upon it.

While I was thus entertaining myself with the Speculations of Dr. Marten, and his Auxiliaries, upon this new Theory of Diseases, I litt on Mr. Bradly's new *Improvements of Planting and Gardening;* who maintains, that the Blights upon the Vegetable World are owing to Insects: whereof he discovered some (a thousand times less than the least Grain of Sand) which found the Cold so agreeable an Element unto them, that at a Yard's Distance from a slow Fire the Heat would burn them to Death. But those Insects he thought overgrown Monsters, to those which have been discovered by M. Lieuenhoek (and other Ey-witnesses) whereof above eight Million may be found in one drop of Water: And Mr. Hook proceeded so far as to demonstrate Millions of Millions contained in such a mighty Ocean. A very gentle Air may carry these from one Place to another, and so our Plants become infested with them.

On this Occasion I find his Friend Mr. Ball, modestly but very learnedly offering his Apprehensions, that our pestilential Diseases may be of the like Original. In Europe, the Plagues are brought by long, dry, easterly Winds, which Mr. Ball thinks, may bring infinite Swarms of these Destroyers; and that most probably they come from Tartary: For he has never heard of properly pestilential Distempers any where in the World, but where the Tartarian Winds have reached them. When the Plague raged in London, those Places which had Scents that probably kill'd or chas'd away these Animals, were kept from the Infection.

This Conjecture about the Origin of Diseases, may be as good as many that have been more confidently obtruded and more generally received.

But what Remarks are to be made upon it; what Sentiments of Piety to be produced?

"How much does our Life ly at the Mercy of our God! How much do we walk thro' unseen Armies of numberless Living Things, ready to sieze and prey upon us! A Walk, like the Running of the Deadly Garloup, which was of old called a Passing thro' the Brick-kiln! What unknown Armies has the Holy One, wherewith to chastise, and even destroy, the rebellious Children of Men? Millions of Billions of Trillions of Invisible Velites! Of sinful Men they say, *Our Father, shall we smite them?* On *His* order, they do it immediately; they do it effectually.

What a poor Thing is Man; That a Worm inconceivably less than the light Dust of the Balance, is too hard for him!

How much is it our Interest and our Prudence, to keep Resolves in the Love of God!"

But, O ye Sons of Erudition, and ye wise Men of Enquiry; lett this Enquiry come into a due Consideration with you: How far a potent Worm-killer, that may be safely administred, would go further than any Remedy yett found out, for the Cure of many Diseases!

Mercury, we know thee: But we are afraid, thou wilt kill us too, if we employ thee to kill them that kill us.

And yett, for the Cleansing of the small Blood-Vessels, and making Way for the free Circulation of the Blood and Lymph, and so to serve the greatest Purposes of Medicine, there is Nothing like mercurial Deobstruents; of which, the Cinnabar of Antimony, Aethiops Mineral, and the Antihectic of Poterius, may be reckoned the principal.

But after all, tis time to have done with the metaphysical Jargon, which for a long Time has passed for the Rationale of Medicine. How much would the Art of Medicine be improved, if our Physicians more generally had the mathematical skill of a Dr Mead or a Dr Morgan, and would go his Way to work, mathematically, and by the Laws of Matter and Motion, to find out the Cause and Cure of Diseases.

The Words of one of them are worth recieving: "Since the Animal Body is a Machine, and Diseases are nothing else but its particular Irregularities, Defects, and Disorders, a Blind Man might as well pretend to regulate a Piece of Clock-work, or a deaf Man to tune an Organ, as a Person ignorant of Mathematicks and Mechanism, to cure Diseases, without understanding the natural Organization, Structure, and Operations of the Machine, which he undertakes to regulate."

Cap. XI. *Dentifrangibulus,*

or, the Anguish, and Releef, of
The Tooth-ache.

The Tooth-Ache, how frequent a Malady! Two Twigs of the external Carotid Artery running under the Ear and entring into the Inferior Maxilla, are disseminated thro' all its Length into the Roots of every Tooth, to carry Blood for their Nourishment. In those Vessels, acrid Humours (together with the Blood) pass to the Teeth and gnaw and vellicate the exquisitely sensible Membrane that coats their interiour Medulla, and hence the intolerable Twinges of the Tooth-ache.

Tis a very surprising Thing, which the learned Raw has observed and affirmed: that the Seeds of all the Teeth ly hid in the Socketts of the Gums, or Jaws of a Foetus; and that as many Seeds as lay latent there, so many Teeth a Man should have in his Life. He was able to demonstrate unto the Eye, the Seeds that were hid in the Gums of a new born Infant. Every Foetus contains the Seeds of the compleat Number of Teeth, which are ever to appear upon Room occasionally made for them, as long as he lives; and they are precisely fifty-two. Besides the thirty-two Teeth, which are found in a perfect Man, there are the Trace of twenty more, which are to be found in every Infant.

So then, there are Fifty-two Tormentors in thy Gums alone, O Man, to which thy Sin has made thee liable, as in the Course of thy Life, they may arise and appear and corrupt; and the Nerve at the Bottom of each becomes uneasy.

If I go to read unto one under the Tooth-ache, a Lecture on our Philosophy of his Distemper, he will give but a poor Attention to it; He will cry out, *Rather tell me what shall be done to give some Ease unto me.*

But I will first advise him how to gett Good by his Pain, before I direct him how to gett out of it.

Under the Torments of this Malady, there are some Truths to be chew'd upon: some Thoughts that if being intensely pursued,

they won't at all divert or abate the Pain, yett they may cause
what is thus painful, to become as useful unto the Sufferer.

Think: "The Teeth, wherein I suffer so much Torture, how
much have I sinned with them! The Sin of my first Parents was
perpetrated by the Teeth. An horrid Sin; a Sin that is mine; and
forever to be bewayled.

"I have employ'd my Teeth in Eating irregularly, inordinately;
and without a due Regard unto the Service and Glory of God, in
my Eating.

"How often have I dug my Grave with my Teeth. And how justly
am I punished with Pains in the Teeth, which have been so abused!

"My Teeth are used in my Speech. Some of the Letters pro-
nounced in Speaking are the Dentals. In Speaking amiss, how
many Sins have I been guilty of!"

Think: "Among the Sufferings wherein my dear Saviour made
Expiation for my Sins, the Pains which the Fist of Wickedness
gave to His Cheek-bone, were particularly sensible.

"O my Saviour, may the Sins of my Teeth, as well as all my
other Sins, thus expiated, be all forever pardoned. And may I
have the Grace for the Time to come, always to eat and speak
in the Fear of God!"

Think: "If the Pains of the Teeth, are so intolerable; if the
Continuance of these Pains for one Year together upon me,
would make me so very miserable; how can I undergo the Pains
of them who dy in their Sins! the Pains in the strange Punishment reserved for the Workers of Iniquity! the Pains which will
cause *Weeping and Wailing and Gnashing of Teeth*, unto those
that are thrown into them! Pains which are, no Mortal can say
how great, and of how long a Continuance. Oh! Tis a *fearful
thing, to fall into the Hands of the living GOD!* If His Immediate
Hand inflict Pains upon us, how can my Heart endure them! O
my Saviour, deliver me from those direful Pains! Enable me to
repent of the Sins that will expose me to the Pains! How in-
finitely am I endebted unto the Saviour, who has delivered me!"

Finally: The Pains of the Teeth, hasten the Destruction of
them. And, O Man, when thou dost perceive thy Teeth agoing,

wilt thou not infer, that thou art thyself agoing after them? Thy perishing Teeth give this Admonition to thee; *O Man, since the hardest and strongest Things thou hast about thee, are so fast consuming, do not imagine that the Rest of thy Body will remain long unconsumed, or that any Bones of thy Body shall not soon moulder into Dust.*

It is a Passage that Austin has in his Confessions, L. 9. c. 4. "Lord, thou doest afflict me with Pain of the Teeth; and when it was so great that I could not speak, it came into my Mind, to admonish my Friends present, that they should pray for me, unto the God of all Health. Writing this on Wax I gave it 'em to read, and as soon as we kneel'd down, the Pain went away. I was amazed, I confess, my Lord, my God; for I had never found any thing like it, in all my Life."

Tis a marvellous Indiscretion in People to be no more careful of praeserving a good Sett of Teeth; in the Contrivance whereof the wise Design of the Glorious Creator has been so conspicuous! And in the Continuance whereof, the Speech is much concerned; the Breath kept sweet; the Beauty sett off; and insupportable Pains prevented.

If People would betimes use to wash their Teeth with fair Water every Day; and wash behind their Ears, and about their Temples, yea, their whole Heads, with cold Water, (and avoid some scurvy Courses and Follies!); they might enjoy a good Sett of Teeth all their Days.

Yea, tho' they have suffered much in their Teeth, by the Neglect of this Praeservance, lett them now take it up, now make Use of it. They may find the Benefit of it the Rest of their Days.

Tot Remedia ad sedandos Dentium dolores prostant, quot Homines.

Bartholin.

The Number of Remedies for the Tooth-ache is almost as large as that of St. Apollonia's Teeth, which being brought in from the several Churches in the Kingdom, at the Order of an English King who was troubled with the Tooth-ache, were found enough to fill several Hogsheads.

To prevent the Tooth-ake and keep the Teeth sound, frequently rub the Teeth with the Ashes which remain in Tobacco-pipes, after the Rest of the Body has been consumed in Smoke; and then wash the Mouth with fair Water, but lett it not be too cold.

It looks like some Disgrace to the Physicians, that so many People, even of their own dearest or nearest Relatives, do so commonly ly whole Days, perhaps Weeks together, under the Torments of the Tooth-ache unreleeved. It seems to say, *Syrs, you are Physicians of how little Value! You can't so much as cure the Tooth-ache!*

Thrust the Eye of a Needle into the Bowels of a Sow-bug; and the Matter which it fetches out, putt in the hollow Tooth, if it be such an one that akes. This I have heard cried up as an Infallible for the Tooth-ache, and I have seen some Success of it.

A Thigh-bone of a Toad, applied unto an aking Tooth, rarely fails of easing the Pain.

Borellus tells of a poor Countryman, whose intollerable Tooth-ache threw him into Convulsions; that he was cured with Betony thrust up his Nose.

Willius writing *De Morbis Castrensibus*, promises rare Effects from a Decoction of the Shavings of fir Wood in Beer, held hott in the Mouth.

Two or three Drops of the freshly expressed Juice of Rue dropt a little warm, into the Ear and the Ear stop lightly with Wool upon it. This does Feats in the Tooth-ache.

Take Allum and melt it; while tis melting mix a little powdered Ginger with it; make it into little Pills, and hold it between the Teeth, so as to bear on the Aking Tooth. It seldom fails of giving ease.

If the aking Tooth be in any Degree an hollow one, melt a little Beeswax and mix with it a little Tobacco Ashes, and stop the Tooth with it. It eases marvellously.

If the Tooth-ache be from a Defluxion manifestly cold, boil the inner Bark of Elder, with a strong Vinegar, till all the Liquor be boil'd away. Of this Bark, while it is yett hott, putt in the Tooth which is afflicted. Monsr. D'ube sais, It will infallibly ease the Pain.

If it be from a Defluxion evidently hott, the same Gentleman directs a Gargarism, with fair Water and strong Vinegar mixed; or, the use of Whey; or Blood-letting.

For this Purpose, Fuller has an aluminous Epithem. Take burnt Allum powdered, half an Ounce; Nutmeg one Dram; Honey of Roses enough to make it an Ointment. Spread it on Paper, and with a convenient Cloth bind it unto the Side of the Face which is in Pain. It repels powerfully, when it is not a rotten Tooth, but a sharp Rheum affecting the whole Jaw, and one Side of the Face.

To check the Defluxion which causes the Tooth-ache, Shavings of Comfrey-root made a Paste and applied unto the Temples, may do well. Diverse little Plasters, especially one of Mastick, have been advised for this Purpose.

Or, Shepherds-pouch, bruised, and putt into the Ear.

A little Bag of Featherfew, bedewed with Rhum, and made hott between two Plates over a Chafing-dish. Apply this.

Or apply a Plaster of Burgundy-pitch mixed with powdered Nutmeg, to the Artery in the Temple.

Blisters drawn behind the Ears, and repeted, have done Wonders in the Tooth-ache.

What shall one think of Hipps gathered in the Wane of the Moon, in August, and worn on the Arm of the same Side with the aking Tooth?

They praescribe a thousand Things, to be held in the Mouth, especially to chew Pellitory of Spain.

And Things to be putt into the hollow Tooth, espccially, a Bit of Lint which is tinged with Oyl of Cloves, or of Origanum.

Among the Scots, they use a green Turf, heated among Embers as hott as can be endured, and applied unto the Side of the Head affected.

If there's nothing else to be done, *draw the Tooth!*

The Cerecloth you'l find in the Chapter of the Sciatica, laid under the Ear, does wonders in the Toothache.

Cap. XX. *Variolae triumphatae,*

The
Small-Pox encountred.

It is an hard Chapter that we have now before us. There is a great Plague which we call the Small Pox, wherein the Misery of Man is great upon him: a Distemper so well known, and so much felt, that there needs no Description to be given of it.

So few among the miserable Children of Men do now escape it, that the Enquirers after Causes have suspected the Original of this Malady to be some Venom connate with every Man (derived, they'l tell you, from the Maternal Blood unto him) which lies dormient and buried, until it be fired by Contagion, and then furiously breaking out from its unknown Lurking-Place, it mixes with the whole Mass of Blood, and makes the terrible Disturbance, and even Destruction, the Fear whereof holds Mankind in a very uneasy Bondage.

But this old Notion loses much of its Authority, by our considering that it is a new Distemper. Tho' the learned Bartholinus to that Quaestion *an deformis hic Morbus antiquis fuerit notus?* answers, *Non ausim dubitare,* yett, all that is quoted from Hippocrates and from Aetius and Galen will not remove the Doubt of other learned Men upon it. Nor will they see that Celus (the Tully of the Physicians) has described so livelily our Small-Pox that one may say, *Ovum ovo similius non sit.* Tis evident unto us that the Ancients were unacquainted with it. It is one of those new Scourges whereof there are several, which the Holy and Righteous God has inflicted on a sinful World. It is not many Ages ago, that it was brought into Europe thro' Africa; on the Wings of those Arabian Locusts which in the Saracen Conquests did spread over the Face of the Earth. It seems as if the Constitution of the Earth, and of the Air, and of humane Bodies, has altered in successive Ages; from whence new Maladies have arisen, which the praeceding Ages were Strangers to; (and the Symptoms

[160]

and Effects of old ones have mightily altered;) and probably more will yett arise. Hence (as the Leprosy grows less common, so) new Fevers appear. But the proper Plague has never yett visited the vast Regions of America: howbeit pestilential Fevers little better than that, have there made most fearful Ravages.

It begins now to be vehemently suspected that the Small-Pox may be more of an animalculated Business than we have been generally aware of. The *Millions* of —— which the *Microscopes* discover in the Pustules, have confirmed the Suspicion. (What would a *Nieuentyt* now say, reading Job. VII. 5. upon it?) And so, we are insensibly drawn into new Sentiments, about the Way of its Conveyance, and the Cause why tis convey'd but once; all which,—*Non sunt hujus Loci.*

The Sentiments of Piety to be raised in and from this grievous Disease, are what I am first and most of all to be now concerned for.

And now, O Mankind in general, wilt thou not from the View and Sense of this new Evil devised against thee, humble thyself under the mighty Hand of God?

Glorious GOD, such a sharp, and indeed such a new Rebuke of thine upon us, correcting us for our Iniquity, and consuming our Beauty as Moth, (yea, as a Lion,) why, why must it come upon us? Righteous art thou, O Lord; yett lett us reason with thee of thy Judgments! The Answer which Heaven thunders down upon us, is: *Ah, sinful Generation, a People laden with Iniquity, a Seed of Evildoers, Children that are Corrupters; they have forsaken the Lord: And why are ye stricken more, even with Strokes that were unknown to the more early Ages? Tis because ye revolt more and more!*

The distressed Children of Terror having such a fearful Expectation of this fiery Indignation to devour them, and seeing that, *Sceptra Ligonibus aequat,*—even Stars, yea, Crowns, are struck down by it; they are certainly stupid out of Measure, and more foolish than the wild Asses Colts, if they do not immediately turn and live unto God, and gett into such a State of Safety for Eternity, that they may be ready for whatever Event this Distemper may have upon them, and not be *afraid with any Amazement.*

The Advice is: And, oh! *behold an Angel with a flaming Sword* over thee giving of it; *praepare to meet thy God*, O thou Traveller thro' an *Hatzar-Maveth*, a Land where *fiery flying Serpents* are hovering every where about thee!

Be restless until the Things that accompany Salvation, and the evident Tokens of it, be plainly to be found upon thee: until thou art able to say, *My Mind by a new and a strong Biass given from Heaven unto it, is come to make the Serving and Pleasing of the Glorious God, the chief End of my Life; and I now go to God, for that which I have heretofore gone to Creatures for. The Blessed God is now more to me than this World. The Enjoyment of Him is a Blessedness praeferrible with me to all the Pleasures and Riches and Honours of this World.* Able to say, *Every Thing of a Glorious Christ is precious to my Soul. I prize Him in all his Offices; I prize Him with all His Benefits. I would fain have Him to fulfil in me all the Good Pleasure of His Goodness.* Able to say, *There is no known Course of Sin, condemned by the continual Reproaches of my Conscience, wherein I indulge myself; if I am surprised into any gross Act of Sin, I feel my Bones broken, till a repenting Faith has restored me to the Peace of God. The Lusts of indwelling Sin, I seek, I sigh, I long for a Deliverance from them.* Able to say, *I love my Neighbour; I am glad when it goes well with him; I am grieved when it goes ill with him. If he do Evil to me, I durst not so much as wish Evil to him.* And able to say, *It is my Delight and Study to do Good; and I labour to be a faithful Steward of the Talents wherewith my Saviour has betrusted me.* If thou canst not yett say such Things, give no Sleep to thine Eyes, nor Slumber to thine Eylids, until thou canst.

And then, what wouldst thou do, if the Summons were certainly brought unto thee, hearing thyself summoned within one Month to appear before God the Judge of all? Surely thou wouldest without **any** Delay, sett apart some Time to go through a Process of Repentance and lay hold on eternal Life. Instructed from the Gospel, in these Moments of Agony for Eternity, thou wouldest cry to God, that with Displays of Sovereign Grace He would quicken thee to do what thy Hand finds to do, that thou mayest be saved. Thou wouldest poenitently confess the Things, in which canst, upon Examination find, that thou hast offended Him. Thou wouldest carefully with Tears beg it of the compassionate God, that He would pardon all thy Offences, for the Sake of the Sacrifice which His beloved Jesus has offered up to the Divine Justice for thee. Thou wouldest plead that Sacrifice for thy Atonement, with Cries that would pierce the Heavens. And then thou wouldest give thyself up unto God, with Dispositions and Resolutions of all possible Obedience unto Him; with a Respect unto all His Commandments. All this wouldest thou do. Then do it; even all this. Do it just now. Lett it be done without any more adoe.

Finally, be inquisitive, what hast thou left undone, that if the Pulls of thy last Hour were now upon thee, thou wouldest wish that it had been done? My Friend, suppose thyself within a few Minutes of thy Expiration; suppose thyself in all the awful Solemnities of a Death-bed; suppose thy Life just agoing, and thy Soul presently to appear before the tremendous Tribunal of God. Now under the Illuminations of such a Supposal, ask thyself, *what should I wish to have done before I come to this?* Go do it out of Hand. Lett it be done with all the Dispatch, with all the Concern imaginable.

There is an Epitaph upon one laid in West-Minister-Abby, which has in it such Terms as these: *One who thro' the spotted Vail of the Small-Pox; rendered a pure and unspotted Soul to God.* Shouldest thou dy of the Small-Pox, after such a Conversion to God, this may be thy happy Epitaph. And as it is expressed on the Grave-Stone of another there, who dy'd of the like Distemper, thy Happiness will be, *ex Igne ac Tunica molesta evolasse ad Coelos;* to fly away for Heaven, out of as burning a Coat, as what Nero putt upon the ancient Martyrs.

But I may now suppose the Person thus praepar'd, become a Patient.

Being visited with the Small-Pox, there are many Exercises of Piety, which there will be a Call unto. Among which there will be none more pertinent than that of the deepest Self-Abhorrence, and Self-Abasement, from a Sense of the original Sin which will oblige us to cry out, *Unclean! Unclean!* and confess, *Lord, I am a filthy Creature!*

My Friend, what a loathsome Creature art thou! Loathsome even to thy self as well as to all that are about thee. Thy Sin has rendred thee so unto the Glorious God, who is of purer Eyes than to behold Evil, and cannot look upon Iniquity. It should render thee so unto thyself; loathing thyself in thy own Sight, for thy Iniquities, and for thy Abominations.

There is a Poison within thee, the Poison of an evil Heart which departs from the Living God. By Temptation as by a Contagion, the Poison makes horrible Eruptions. All the nasty Pustules which now fill thy Skin, are but little Emblems of the Errors which thy Life has been filled withal. Make thy Lamentation, *Lord, from the Sole of the Foot, even to the Head, there is no Soundness in me; Nothing but putrifying Sores.*

In the wearisome Nights that are appointed for thee, thy Complaint is, *my Skin is broken and become lothesome.* Thy Bed comforts thee not; thy Couch does not ease thy Complaint; perhaps thou art scared with Visions, and Things of a frightful Aspect appear before thy closed Eyes. Now lett Repentance have its perfect Work. And lett thy Condition lead thee to a repenting Sense of the Sin which has provoked and procured this Calamity for thee, and is livelily resembled in it. Poenitently say, *Lord my Wounds do stink and are corrupt, because of my Foolishness!*

Lett this Apprehension of thy loathsome Sin, drive thee to the Blood of thy Saviour, for the Pardon of it; that thou mayst be cleansed from all Sin. At the same Time, importunately sollicit for the Spirit of thy Saviour, to expell the Malignity of Sin that is lodged in thee, and send up thy Groans unto Him, for His purifying Influences.

While some are very sorely handled by this noisome and painful Distemper, others are favoured with a more gentle Visitation. If this be thy Case, be very thankful to a compassionate God. Thankfully own, *it is of the Lords Mercies that I am not consumed, because His Compassions fall not.*

There is one Circumstance of this Disease (which an acute and famous Anatomist, methinks, yett gives but a very weak Reason for;) It has hardly ever been seen, that any after having suffered it once, comes to suffer it a second Time. There are several other Fevers, it may be six or seven Sorts of them, that may have the same Observation made upon them: *no Man undergoes them twice.* It is to be hoped, O Man, that this Observation will be verified in thy moral Experience; and that the grosser Sins, which thou hast once repented of, thou wilt never again fall into them.

But thus having sought first what is most of all to be sought for, and serv'd the Kingdome of God and His Righteousness, from the Calamity that is come upon us, we may the more hopefully proceed unto the Work of encountring and conquering the Adversary.

An Adversary, which wilt thou play with him as with a Bird? No, he will fill thy Skin as with barbed Irons. And shall not one be cast down at the Sight of him? Who can come to him with his double Bridle? Sparks of Fire leap out of his Mouth. His Breath kindles Coals. When he raises up himself the Mighty are afraid. He spreadeth sharp pointed Things upon our Clay. He makes our Blood to boil as a Pott: he makes our Humours like a Pott of Ointment.

Yett lett us be of good Courage; yea, be very courageous. There is a way to manage him:

Unknown is the Number of Lives which the Glorious God has made our Sydenham, the Instrument of Saving, by teaching us a new and a right Method of treating the Small-Pox, and reclaiming People from the Madness of killing one another with Kindness, and praeposterous Proceedings.

I am willing to treat my Friends with what I know of the Sydenhamian Method. But at the same Time I must advise them, that from a Difference of Seasons and of Climates, there may happen some Circumstances that may require Proceedings wherein this incomparable Method must not be strictly in all Points adher'd unto. The Malady call'd *Variolae* is not without its Varieties: yea, I have myself seen Anomalies in the Small-Pox wherein a Sydenham himself might not be entirely relied upon. There is now then an Irregular Small-Pox, in which it may not be easy to fix Rules for an unchangeable Regimen. A skilful and thoughtful Physician must be always near the Patient, (my Friend, make sure, and then make much, of such an one!) And this Physician will take his Measures from the Indications as he finds them. Nevertheless, for the most Part, they will both of them find their Account in receiving and remembring such Things as I will deliver in the ensuing Aphorisms.

I. The Distemper we call the Small-Pox, is usually distributed into two Sorts: the distinct Sort; and the confluent Sort; the Symptoms whereof have some difference, and the Way of Managing must be also a little different.

By not being aware of this, what mortal Errors have been often run into!

II. By how much sooner the Pocks come out before the fourth Day of the Illness, ordinarily so much the more they will prove of the confluent Sort; however, sometimes there are Accidents that may keep a Restraint upon them.

III. If the Face be very full, tho' the Body should not be so, yett the Sick is in as much Danger as if every Member of the Body were crouded with them. And tho' the Body be full, yett if there be few in the Face, the Danger is not so great.

IV. Very violent Symptoms at the first Arrest of the Disease, and particularly, Convulsions in Children, you must not be always frighted at them. They very commonly introduce very moderate Effects, and the most comfortable Issue that can be look'd for.

V. I am going to mention the Enemy, of which I may say, *Thou shalt fight neither against small nor great, so much as this!* All possible Care must be used that the Ebullition of the Blood may not rise too high.

Either by hastening the Patients too soon unto their Beds, or by confining them too much there:

Or, by heaping on too many Cloathes, (which ought not to be more than what they are in their Health us'd unto:)

Or, by keeping the Air of the Chamber too close and too hott: (which in Summer may allow of a little Ventilation:)

Or, by giving of pretended Cordials, and Expellers: (vile Expellers, which have Millions of Times driven the poor Souls out of their fired Mansions.)

Too hasty an Assimulation of the variolous Matter has most certainly slain its Ten Thousands, yea, the most of the Multitudes, Multitudes that ly slain by the Hand of this Destroyer in the Valley of Death.

VI. On the other Side, unseasonable Vomits, and Purges, and Blood-Letting, may happen too much to diminish the necessary Ebullition. However, if there be a just Suspicion, that the Small-Pox coming out will prove of the confluent Sort, an Emetic may be useful; yea, a Phlebotomy may be needful.

O Wisdome, how profitable art thou to direct! and how requisite art thou to the Physician! how often to be exercised.

VII. Yett the Patients must not be exposed unto Injuries from the Cold. And if the Pustules happen to strike in, or the Swelling of the Hands and Face to fall, from such an Accident, (and a Return to the Warmth of the Bed be not enough to do it) there may be some Recourse to the otherwise exploded Cordials and Expellers. However still have a Care of being too lavish in them. Repeted Ebullitions of the Blood are very dangerous Things!

VIII. When the Distemper appears, lett the Patients forbear the Use of Wine and Flesh; and I again say, of Cordials and Expellers, and all Inflamers. Don't lett 'em swallow Fire-brands. Leave Nature undisturbed. It is hardly known that Nature fails of doing its Part for thrusting out the Small-Pox. Forcing it, is the most likely Way of Hindring it.

Lett their ordinary Drink be small Beer, gently warm'd with a Toast. And lett them drink their Bellyful.

Their Diet, lett it be Oat-meal gruel, or Barley-gruel, or Milk-porridge (one third, Milk, two thirds, Water.)

Roasted Apples are no forbidden Fruit.

Nay, roasted Apples with Milk, may now and then be allow'd of.

But Nothing too hott; Nothing too cold; Nothing too hard of Digestion.

IX. Tho' I said, what I said; yett, at the Time of Maturation, when the purulent Particles flowing back on the Blood threaten to poison it, three or four Spoonfuls of generous Wine, Morning and Evening, may, (if your Physician see no feavourish Prohibitions,) be allowed of.

X. Lett not the Patients be (as I have said once already) too soon, or too much, confined unto their Beds.

Lett them keep up as long as ever they can.

If the Small-Pox be of the distinct Sort (in which Case there usually needs little to be done,) I know not why they should ly stiffling and baking and roasting in their Beds, for whole Days together, if there be so much of Summer as will permit them to rise with Safety.

Be it how it will, if they should be taken out of their Beds, once or twice every Day, all the Time of their Illness, they might on many Accounts fare the better for it. (Only, be sure the Inconveniencies of taking any Cold, must be carefully watch'd against.)

And when they are abed, lett them change their Place ever now and then, to curb any Sweat they may fall into. The less they sweat, the better.

Some at the very Point of Death, yea, thought actually dead, have been saved by Nothing but being taken out of Bed.

Young Persons are sometimes afflicted with a total Suppression of Urine. Lett them only be taken out of Bed, and led once or twice cross the Room, they are help'd immediately!

XI. Anon, if the Small-Pox don't come out well, the Medicines called Paregoricks, have a Success to be wondred at. Your Liquid Laudanum (fourteen Drops for a grown Person; Children will not want it) or, Diascordium; and the like, mixed in a small Quantity, with some agreeable distilled Water, will check the boiling Blood, and Nature will freely then cast out the morbific Matter.

XII. Strong young Men, and such as have inflamed their Blood by free Drinking, may have Occasion to bleed in the Arm, when Things are hereabouts. Lett the Doctor see how it is.

XIII. In the confluent Sort of the Small-Pox, there comes on a Salivation, just upon or soon after their first coming out. This having preserved the Lives of the Patients, uses to cease about the eleventh Day. But a swelling of the Face and Hands must then supply the Place of it, without which they must go to their long Home. Tho' the Swelling of the Face also should a little abate, yett if the Swelling of the Hands continues and increases, there can be no surer Sign of Recovery. The Way to keep this Discharge of Nature, in an orderly Condition, is, to drink freely what was formerly allow'd; and be sure, such Drink as will provoke no Sweat upon them: and therewithal to take what shall presently be mentioned. I will only first observe, what has been in Part already observed, and what cannot be too often inculcated: that as a temperate Regimen is generally the All in All for the Management of the Small-Pox in all the Kinds of it; (Certainly, the Way to bring a great Company of People handsomely and quietly out of a Room, will not be to throw in Fire-works among them.) So, to prevent the too exorbitant Ebullition of the Blood, there can be Nothing more adviseable than the free Use of some innocent Liquor, which will allay the Heat that scorches and wearies the Patients. Besides the small Beer aforesaid; a Decoction of Bread, and a small Quantity of calcined Hartshorn, in a large Quantity of Water, sweetened with Sugar, may be very soberly advised unto. And so may a convenient Mixture of Milk and Water, if the Stomach be not overcooled with it.

XIV. What was just now promised shall now be mentioned. The Benefit of Narcoticks in this Case, is inconceiveable. Tho' my Sydenham a long while commended Liquid Laudanum, yett anon he came to praefer Diacodium: (only, where this might happen to be nauseated; and then to the Liquid Laudanum:) I say Diacodium: an Ounce of this, in cowslip Water, or some other such distill'd Water. It should be given about five or six in the Evening, before the restless Fitt usually comes upon the Patients. Give this, every Day after there appears Occasion for it; yea, it may be done from the very Sixth Day after the first Invasion. To some young Men, of what we call a very sanguine Complexion,

an Ounce and half will be requisite for a Dose. Yea, when the
Small-Pox do flux very much, this Anodyne may be given every
eighth Hour. The Efficacy of this Remedy surpasses Imagination.

We now come to this Leviathan, with a double Bridle!

XV. Besides the Intention of Bridling the Ebullition of the
Blood, there may be something also necessary to conquer the
Putrifaction. And for this Purpose we scarce know of Anything
better than that on the fifth or sixth Day, the Patients come to
have the Spirit of Vitriol dropt into their small Beer, so as to make
it a little acid. Lett this be the ordinary Drink; and lett them
drink freely, I say, drink largely of it. If they drink not enough of
it, (which it would be strange if they should not!) then mix that
Spirit of Vitriol with a proper Syrup, or some distilled Water and
Syrup; and give them now and then of that. It has done wonderful Things. When the Blood of young People, and such as have
been too much acquainted with the Bottel, has raged with such
Violence that it has broke out of the Arteries into the Bladder,
and they have made bloody Urine, which is as desperate a Symptom as the Small-Pox can be attended with; yett even then, this
Course has brought all to rights. My Sydenham seems almost in
the Transport of an Archimedes at this Discovery.

XVI. When Children have the Small-Pox of the confluent Sort,
a Looseness usually follows them, as a Salivation does People of
riper Years. But it must not be stopt. Thousands have been
kill'd, by stopping this Provision of Nature, for the Evacuation
of the morbific Matter.

XVII. If in the confluent Sort of the Small-Pox, the Spittle
be baked so tough by the preceding Heat that the Patients are
nigh strangled, use a Gargarism, (small Beer, or Barly-Water,
with Honey of Roses,) and syringe the Throat often with it.

If they are at the last Gasp of Choaking, a Vomit may be given
very seasonably.

XVIII. I have known an Instance that one taken with the
Small-Pox was thought siezed with only a Fever. They plied the
Soles of his Feet with Pigeons: and the Consequence of it was,

that he had no Small-Pox above his Waste, but enough below it. His Head and his Breast was kept also very easy all the Time of his Illness. Whether such Doings are adviseable, or may be ordinarily practised without Hazard,—*melius inquirendum.* However my Sydenham allows Epithems to the Soles of the Feet, in the Small-Pox of the confluent Sort. From the eighth Day, he allows to grown People, Garlick sliced and wrapped in a Cloath, to be repeted every Day.

XIX. *Experto credo:* after all the Methods and Medicines that our Sydenham and others rely upon, I can assure you there is Nothing found so sure and safe as this: procure for the Patient, as early as may be, by Epispasticks, a plentiful Discharge at the Hand-wrists, or Anckles, or both, and keep them running till all the Danger be over. When the Venom of the Small-Pox makes an evident and violent Invasion on the nobler Parts, this Discharge does wonderfully. If there be no such Danger, there is less Occasion for this or any other anxious Administration.

XX. When the Patients are on Recovery, and the Pustules are falling off, and they have begun to feed upon Flesh, (especially, if they have been violently handled) Bleeding in the Arm, will be seasonable, and may prevent very ill Effects of a depraved Blood. And a little Purging will now also come in Season. So all is concluded,—*si quid novisti rectius istis.*

¶But we will not content ourselves with one Doctors Opinion. Wherefore, tho' I will not oppress my Friends, with an ostentatious Heap of Collections, which it were easy to introduce on a Subject handled by so many Writers, I will call in two more, who may be enough with our Sydenham to constitute a Council of Doctors, on the present Occasion.

The ingenious Woodman observes that in the Assaults of the Small-pox, the Constitution of the Patients, is very much to be considered, whether it be what we call flegmatick, or cholerick. Bloodletting is fatal in the former; but in the latter it may be very expedient, yea, necessary, at the Beginning of the Distemper. Yett, if great Malignity attends it, Bloodletting must be omitted, whatever Symptoms may seem to demand it.

If the Stomach be clogg'd with gross Humours, a Vomit may be given at the Beginning, which may prevent a future Looseness.

A costive Belly is much praeferrible to a loose one. Yett there may be Occasion for a Clyster.

If a Looseness happens before the Eruption, it must be suppressed. But, if it happen after the Suppuration of the Pustules, and be not very violent, there needs little Notice to be taken of it. While it continues, or if it be fear'd approaching, lett the Drink be a Decoction of Hartshorn.

No Drinks whatsoever must be given actually cold. The small Beer may have a little Saffron infused in it.

Opiates are very good; not only to check a Looseness, but also to promote all Intentions.

If the Pocks retreat, because of a Looseness, take Venice-treacle one Dram; Oyl of Cinamon six Drops; Laudanum one Grain: mix: give it every two or three Hours.

If Choaking be fear'd, give a Vomit out of Hand.

If the Eyes do suffer very much, often drop into them white Rose-Water, wherein Saffron has been infused.

If a Cough be very troublesome, lett the Drink be a pectoral Decoction of Hysop, Colts-foot, Liquorice, and the like, sweetened with Syrup of Poppy-Heads.

If a Cold be taken after the Eruption, so that the Pustules retire, and Languors follow, the Party must be covered very warm, and Cordials be given, and Blisters be applied unto the Legs and the Feet; from whence if an Heat of Urine arises, it may be cured with Draughts of Whey, which has a few Grains of Gum Arabic dissolved in it.

He breaks off so, "More People are lost thro' a praeposterous Use of needless Remedies, which destroy the regular Ferment, and check the expulsive Efforts of Nature, than thro' the Vehemence of the Disease."

The celebrated Pitcairn, would have the Patient lett Blood, while the Fever does last; yea, tho' the Small-Pox do begin to come out. But I doubt he is too universal in this Direction. Do thou, O discreet Physician, determine when to bleed. However,

I must say I have seen an astonishing Success of Bleeding, when the second Fever has greatly threatened the Patient. And I have seen many a Life lost, in a Complement unto the Physicians who have earnestly forbidden it. If on the fifth, sixth, seventh or eighth Day after the Small-Pox be come out, it goes in again, this Gentleman sais, a Vein is to be again opened, and Cantharides in Powder must be laid unto the Neck.

When the first Fever is over, and the Small-Pox is come out, he would have the Patient often drink any of the simple, distilled, insipid Waters usually sold at the Apothecaries; in which lett Sheeps-Dung be infused for some Hours, and then add Syrup of white Poppy.

Besides Water-Gruel, he commends a Drink of Barly-Water, with Syrup of white-Poppy, which will mightily assist the important Salivation.

¶But have we no Praeservatives to defend us from the Invasion of this dreadful Distemper, or from the Violence of it when it has invaded us?

Our Sydenham thinks, that Purges duely used before the Infection be taken, do hopefully praepare the Body to fell fewer of the Small-Pox, and of the better Sort.

In a Time and Place of much Infection, perhaps there is, (give me Leave to say, after a due Improvement of the Ninety-first Psalm.) no Praeservative comparable to that of a Bit of Myrrh, carried in the Mouth of Persons who have already had the Small-Pox, and fear not the Return of it, yett if they visit many and nasty sick Chambers, may have their Spirits horribly poisoned with it. It may do well for them therefore to employ this Praeservative.

It has been thought that Infection commonly siezes first on the salival Juices. If so, the less we swallow our Spittle, the better, where we are in Danger of being infected.

Mantissa.

To the foregoing Entertainments, that there may be Nothing wanting, it is fitt that I should add at least a few Delibations

from what the valuable Dr. John Woodward has written, in his
Treatise about The State of Physic.

He observes, Dr Sydenham went a little too fast and too far,
into the Cooling Method, under the Small-Pox, and in his later
Time a little quitted it.

The Physicians chief Care in this Distemper, must be to steer
and rule the Passions, and keep up the Hopes of the Patient.
The Stomach is very much the Seat of the Passions; in which
Bowel also is found the Source of the Matter, that being sent from
thence into the Blood-Vessels with which it has a very notable
Communication, is the Cause of the Small-Pox: and a Disturbance
here, is quickly felt in the Blood, with pernicious Consequences.

If the Physician be consulted in the Beginning of the Distemper,
he has an Opportunity of superseding the Use of almost all other
Medicines, by casting out much of the morbid Matter with a
Vomit. This Operation being dexteriously managed and effectually pursued, the Patient is marvellously releeved. All the
Symptoms, not only of the Stomach, which indicate for this
Operation, but of the whole Body, remitt unto Admiration. Yea,
there have been Instances wherein the vitious Matter in the
Stomach happening to be little, and not over-boisterous, a Vomit
seasonably interposed, has discharged almost all the Matter, and
the Pustules that began to show themselves, have disappeared.
And in other Instances, where such an Evacuation has been made
in Season, the Pustules have not only proved very few, but also
begun to turn a Day or two sooner than even the most favourable
Sort use to do.

A putrid Phlegm, in Conjunction with a biliose Matter, seems
to be the Cause of the Small-Pox; which by the Luxury of the
later Times, is now more generated in us, than it was in our
Ancestors.

In this Distemper, the Diet must be plain, thin, light, exactly
temperate. Liquids must not be too plentifully taken. High
Cordials must not be given in great Quantity, and without great
Caution. If the Fever lower too much, then some small Drops of
such Things may be given.

The Acids commonly praescribed, are too much of the same Nature with the Salt, that constitutes the chief peccant Principle in this Disease. And absorbents don't answer Expectation.

In Case of a Diarrhaea, the main Care of the Physician must be, to support the Patient and remove Obstacles, that the Passage of the peccant Matter downwards, may not be hindred, and so stopped in the Intestines as to be turned back into the Blood; and appease the Tumults of the Stomach, so that it may cease any longer to send the Matter down.

To the Gentlemen who are for Purging in the Small-Pox, we may address the Words of Horace:

> *Periculosae plenum Opus aleae*
> *Tractas, et incedis per Ignes*
> *Suppositos cineri doloso.*

My Doctor finds, that of all the Remedies to encounter the Small-Pox, there are none comparable to the sweeter vegetable Oyls, especially the Oyl of sweet Almonds, and such unctuous Medicines, which may be mixed with Pulps, or Conserves, or Mucilages, for such as can't well take them alone. These wonderfully contribute unto the frustrating and subduing of that sharp and hott Matter which all the Mischiefs of the Small-Pox may be ascribed unto.

But all along, in the several Stadia of the Distemper, incredible would be the Benefit of seasonable Vomits. Only, they must be sufficient ones, and well-adapted. And among these, the Ipecacuanha appears one of the most manageable, and of the most easy Discipline.

In the End of the Disease, these will be of great Consequence, to prevent very grievous Consequences.

But I have now a further Story to tell you. What if we should find out a Way that the Contagion of the Small-Pox may not (by the salival Juices, as tis commonly thought,) enter the Stomach, and make a furious and fatal Combustion in the phlegmatic and biliose Matter there, nor enter the Lungs more immediately, as with many perhaps it may; but enter by the Outworks of the

Citadel, and carry off what it has to sieze with very gentle Symptoms, and when it reaches the Stomach in that Way yett be presently conquered with an easy Emetic there? This is the Story which I have now to tell you. And hundreds of thousands of Lives will be soon saved if my Story may be harken'd to.

Appendix

There has been a wonderful Practice lately used in several Parts of the World, which indeed is not yett become common in our Nation.

I was first instructed in it, by a Guramantee-servant of my own, long before I knew that any Europeans or Asiaticks had the least Acquaintance with it, and some Years before I was enriched with the Communications of the learned Foreigners, whose Accounts I found agreeing with what I received of my Servant, when he showed me the Scar of the Wound made for the Operation; and said, that no Person ever died of the Small-Pox, in their Countrey that had the Courage to use it.

I have since mett with a considerable Number of these Africans, who all agree in one Story; that in their Countrey grandy-many dy of the Small-Pox; but now they learn this Way: People take Juice of Small-Pox, and Cutty-Skin, and putt in a Drop; then by'nd by a little sicky, sicky; then very few little Things like Small-Pox; and no body dy of it; and no body have Small-Pox any more. Thus in Africa, where the poor Creatures dy of the Small-Pox like rotten Sheep, a Merciful God has taught them an infallible Praeservative. Tis a common Practice, and is attended with a constant Success.

But our Advice of this Matter, as it comes from Superiour Persons in the Levant, is what may have most Attention given to it.

Our first Communication comes from Dr Emanuel Timonius R.S.S. who writes from Constantinople, in December, 1713. To this Effect.

The Practice of procuring the Small-Pox, by a Sort of Inoculation, has been introduced among the Constantinopolitans, by the Circassians and Georgians, and other Asiaticks; for about fourty Years.

At the first, People were cautious and afraid. But the happy Success on thousands of Persons for eight years now past, has putt it out of all Suspicion. The Operation has been performed on Persons of all Ages, both Sexes, differing Temperaments, and even in the worst Constitution of the Air; and none that have used it ever died of the Small-Pox; tho' at the same Time, it were so malignant, that at least half the People died, that were affected with it in the common Way.

They that have this Inoculation practised on them (he sais) are subject unto very sleight Symptoms, and hardly sensible of any Sickness; nor do what Small-Pox they have, ever leave any Scars or Pitts behind them.

They make Choice of as healthy a young Person as they can find, that has the Small-Pox of the best Sort upon him; on the twelfth or thirteenth Day of his Decumibiture. With a Needle they prick some of the larger Pustules and press out the Matter coming from them into some convenient Vessel of Glass (or the like) to receive it; which ought first of all to be washed very clean with warm Water. A convenient Quantity of this Matter being thus collected, is to be stop'd close, and kept warm, in the Bosom of the Person that carries it (who ought rather to be some other Person than what visited the sick Chamber for it, lest the Infection of the Small-Pox be convey'd in the Garment as well as in the Bottel, and the intended Operation be hurt by the Infection being first convey'd another Way,) and so it should be convey'd as soon as may be, to the Person that is waiting to be the Patient.

The Patient being in a warm Chamber, is to have several small Wounds made with a Surgeons three-edged Needle, or with a Lancett, in two or more Places of the Skin; (the best Places are in the Muscles of the Arm:) till some Drops of Blood follow: and immediately lett there be dropt out a Drop of the Matter in the Glass, on each of the Places; and mixed well with the Blood that is issuing out. The Wound should be covered with half a Walnutt-Shell, or any such concave Vessel, and bound over, that the Matter may not be rubbed off by the Garments, for a few Hours. And now, lett the Patient (having Fillets on the Wounds) keep House, and keep warm, and be careful of his Diet. The Custome at Constantinople is to abstain from Flesh and Broth, for twenty Days or more.

They chuse to perform the Operation, either in the Beginning of the Winter, or the Spring.

The Small-Pox begins to appear sooner in some than in others, and with lesser Symptoms in some than in others: but, with happy Success in all. Commonly ten or twenty Pustules break out: here and there one has no more than two or three; few have an Hundred. There are some in whom no Pustule rises, but in the Places where the Insition was made, and here the Tubercles will be purulent. Yett even these, have never had the Small-Pox afterwards, tho' they have cohabited with Persons having of it. No small Quantity of Matter will run for several Days, from the Places of the Incision. The Pocks arising from this Operation, are dried up in a short Time, and fall off; partly in thin skins, and partly vanishing by an insensible Wasting.

The Matter is hardly so thick a Pus, as in the common Small-Pox; but a thinner Kind of Sanies; whence it rarely Pitts; except at the Place of the Incision, where the Cicatrices are never worn out, and where the Matter is more of the common Sort.

If an Apostem should break out in any, (which is more frequent in Infants,) yett there is no Fear, for tis heal'd safely by Suppuration.

They scarce ever use the Matter of the insitious Small-Pox to serve the Designs of a new Insition.

The Inoculation being tried on such as have had the Small-Pox before, it had no Effect upon them.

Dr. Timonius affirms, that he never yett observed any bad Consequence of the Practice which now so many do come into.

But it is in the Mouth of two or three Witnesses, that the Thing must be established.

We shall again see this Leviathan is not so fierce, but that there are some who dare to stir him up.

Since this Communication from Dr Timonius, we have another from an eminent Person whose Name is Jacobus Pylarinus, the Venetian Consul at Smyrna. Tis entituled, *Nova et Tuta Variolas excitandi per Transplantationem Methodus.*

This Gentleman observes that this wonderful Invention was first a *plebeia rudique Gente in humani Generis adjumentum, in saevissimi morbi solamen detecta,* found out, not by the learned Sons of Erudition, but by a mean, coarse, rude Sort of People, for the Succour of Mankind under and against one of the most cruel Diseases in the World. He seems to look on it as a marvellous Gift of a good God, unto a miserable World. It was rarely, if ever, used among People of Quality, until after the Beginning of the present Century. A noble Graecian then in Distress for his four little Sons, lest the Small-Pox might bereave him of them, consulted with him, about using the Inoculation upon them. At first, his Ignorance of the Matter, made him decline giving him any Advice upon it. But a Graecian Woman who was a notable Inoculatrix happening to come in while they were discoursing of the Matter, told them so much about it, that the Experiment was resolved upon. The Woman managed, in her Way, upon all the four Sons. The three younger, all of which were under seven Years of Age, felt a very gentle Illness, had a very few Pustules, and in about a Week all Fever and Hazard was over with them. The eldest, about eight Years old, was taken with a malignant Fever: and (tho' he had not many Pustules) narrowly escaped with his Life. Pylarinus imputes this to an atrabiliarious and otherwise humourous and unhealthy Constitution of the Lad, and a Neglect of using such preparatory Expiation of his Body, as they had been advised unto. But upon this happy Success, *Mirum quam multas nobiliorum Familias, ad Imitationem traxit!* It was wonderful to see what a Multitude of People of Fashion presently followed the Example, so that at this Day every one does without any Haesitation, and with all the Security imaginable, practise the Transplantation, except here and there a few

Cowards that are afraid of their Shadows. Indeed, the Turks, whose Faith in Fate is as we know, and who are a more indocible Sort of Animals, do not yett much come into it.

Pylarinus, instructed by his Greek Operatrix, directs: to take a proper Season for the Insition. She would use it only in the Winter; but he thinks the Spring may do as well.

The fermenting Pus must be taken from the mature Pustules of a good Sort, in a young Person of a good Constitution, kept warm in a close Viol, and hastened unto the Application.

The Air of the Chamber must be kept very temperate.

The Greek Operatrix prick'd more Places, and less fleshy ones, than Pylarinus approved of: with an oblique Stroke pricking the Places with an iron or golden Needle; and with the same Needle dropping and thrusting the Pus into the Wound; and so binding all with Fillets. Her Way was thus to prick the Forehead, the Chin, both Cheeks, both Wrists, and both Insteps. This was doubtless over-doing. Pylarinus affirms, that some have done the Business, *unico duntaxat Vulnusculo ad Brachium inflicto;* with no more than one little Insition in the Arm, and it has done very well. (So it has been with such Africans as have shown me the Marks of their Inoculation.)

They must not keep their Beds more than is necessary.

Wine, Flesh, Broth must be laid aside.

The Ferment comes into Action sooner in some than in others. Usually the Small-Pox appears on the seventh Day; sometimes on the very first.

The Symptoms prove remiss or intense, according to the various Constitution of the Bodies.

The Small-Pox proves of the distinct Sort; and there will be but few of them; it may be ten or twenty; rarely an hundred.

In some few, the Insition has produced no Small-Pox at all; but the Persons have afterwards been, in the common Way, taken and handled with it, like other People.

The Wounds made for the Insition prove often very sore. And with some they degenerate into Apostems; yea, these do swell sometimes, and rise, and fall, and rise again. There has also happened on this Occasion, an Abscess with Suppuration, in some Emunctory of the Body; but this is a very rare Occurrence.

In fine: Pylarinus affirms it was hardly ever known that there was any ill Consequnce of this Transplantation. *Quinimo rite recteque tractata, et in corporibus per peritum medicum apte praeparatis, certissiman promittit salutem.* The Business being well and wisely managed, and the Body being by a skilful Physician well-prepared; you may depend upon it (he sais) in an ordinary Way, there can be Nothing but a good Issue of it.

But, I remember, I spoke of three Witnesses. I will therefore add: Kennedy says that in the little Time that he was at Constantinople, he was assured of two thousand that had lately undergone the Method of the Small-Pox Inoculated; and there were no more than two who died under it, and the Death of these was entirely owing to their own ill Conduct in exposing themselves.

Hitherto you have Nothing but History. But a little Philosophy and Speculation may be now asked for; and an Enquiry into Causes a little endeavoured. No Doubt, among the wise Men of Enquiry, there may be found, so many Men so many Minds. Every Gentleman may form his own Hypothesis; and some of the later and more modern Curiosity will try how far the vermicular Scheme will carry them thro' a Solution of these and all Appearances in this Distemper.

I have seen the Point after this pothecary Manner talk'd about. The venomous Miasms (Lett that Word serve at the present) of the Small-Pox, entering into the Body, in the Way of Inspiration, are immediately taken into the Blood of the Lungs: And, I pray, how many Pulses pass before the very Heart is pierced with them? And within how many more they are convey'd into all the Bowels, is easily apprehended by all that know Anything how the Circulation of the Blood is carried on. At the same Time, the Bowels themselves are enfeebled, and their Tone impaired, by the Venom that is thus insinuated. Behold, the Enemy at once gott into the very Center of the Citadel. And the invaded Party must be very strong indeed, if it can struggle with him, and after all entirely expel and conquer him. Whereas, the Miasms of the

Small-Pox being admitted in the Way of Inoculation, their Approaches are made only by the Outworks of the Citadel, and at a considerable Distance from the Center of it. The Enemy, tis true, getts in so far as to make some Spoil, yea, so much as to satisfy him, and leave no Prey in the Body of the Patient for him ever afterwards to sieze upon. But the vital Powers are kept so clear from his Assaults, that they can manage the Combats bravely and, tho' not without a Surrender of those Humours in the Blood which the Invader makes a Siezure on, they oblige him to march out the same Way he came in, and are sure of never being troubled with him any more. But perhaps the few Words that I wrote in my introducing of the Story, may be as much to the Purpose as all of this Jargon. I'l have done with it.

I durst not engage that the Success of the Trial here will be the same that has been in all the other Countreys where it has been tried hitherto, tho' we have seen it succeed well in very different climates. Nor am I sure that if it should be made upon a Body, where the Blood is already nigh upon the Point of some unhappy Fever, this may not help to sett Fire to such a Thing. But I am very confident no Person would miscarry in it, but what would most certainly have miscarried upon taking the Contagion in the common Way. Wherefore, if it be made at all, (and all the Scruples that some have about the Tempting of Providence be also gott over) I advise, that it be never made but under the Management of a Physician, whose Conduct may be much relied upon, and who will wisely praepare the Body for it before he perform the Operation. I have done.[1]

I am now able, as an Eywitness, (and more than so) to give a more full Account of the Practice, which until now I could only propose as a Matter at a greater Distance.

About the Month of May, 1721, the Small-Pox being admitted into the City of Boston, I proposed unto the Physicians of the Town, the unfailing Method of preventing Death, and many other grievous Miseries, from a tremendous Distemper, by re-

---

[1] This paragraph is crossed out in the original ms.

ceiving and managing the Small-Pox, in the Way of Inoculation. One of the Physicians had the Courage to begin the Practice upon his own Children and Servants; and another expressed his Good Will unto it. But the Rest of the Practitioners treated the Proposal with an Incivility and an Inhumanity not well to be accounted for. Fresh Occasion I saw for the Complaint of a great Physician, *"Heus, quanto Dolore auger, dum video Naturae ministrum medicum, hostem ejus devenisse."* The vilest Arts were used, and with such an Efficacy, that not only the Physician, but also the Patients under the Small-Pox inocluated were in Hazard of their very Lives from an infuriated People. But I myself had thrown into my House in the dead of the Night, a fired Granado, charged with combustible Matter, and in such a Manner, that upon its going off, it must probably have killed them that were near it, and would have certainly fired the Chamber and speedily have laid the House in Ashes. But the merciful Providence of God our Saviour so ordered it, that the Granado passing thro' the Window, had by the Iron in the Middle of the Casement such a Turn given to it, that in falling on the Floor, the fired Wild-fire in the Fuse, was violently shaken out some Distance from the Shell, and burnt out upon the Floor, without firing off the Granado.[2]

The Opposition was carried on with a Folly, and Falsehood, and Malice, hardly ever known to be paralled'd on any Occasion. And in the Progress of the Distemper many hundreds of Lives were lost, which might have been saved, if the People had not been Satanically filled with Prejudices against this *Method of Safety.* However, the Practice went on, and tho' the Physician was under extreme Disadvantages on more Accounts than one, yett he was attended with vast[3] Success. The Experiment has now been made on several hundreds of Persons; and upon both Male and Female, both old and young, both strong and weak, both white and black, at all Seasons, of Summer and Autumn and Winter: And they have generally professed, *they had rather under-*

[2] Some lines thoroughly obliterated follow.

[3] "Constant" first written here and crossed out.

go the Small-Pox inoculated once every Year, than undergo the Small-
Pox once in their Lives after the common Way, tho' sure to live.

I shall now communicate our Way of Proceeding, in the
Practice.

I. We make usually a couple of Incisions in the Arms, where
we usually make our Issues; but somewhat larger than for them,
(sometimes in an Arm and in a Leg.)

II. Into these we putt Bitts of Lint, (the Patient at the same
Time turning his Face another Way and guarding his Nostrils,)
which have been dipt in some of the variolous Matter, taken in a
Vial, from the Pustules of one (if we can find such an one) that
has the Small-Pox of the more laudable Sort now turning upon
him; and so we cover them with a Plaister of Diachylon.

III. Yett we find the variolous Matter fetched from those that
have the inoculated Small-Pox, as agreeable and effectual as any
other. Yea, and so we do what is taken from them that have the
confluent Sort.

IV. In four and twenty Hours, we throw away the Lint; and
the Sores are dressed once or twice every four and twenty Hours,
with warmed Cabbage-Leaves.

V. The Patient continues to do Things as at other Times, only
he does not expose himself to the Injuries of the Weather, if
that be at all tempestuous. But we find the warmer he keeps
himself, he afterwards finds himself no Loser by it.

VI. About the seventh Day, the Patient feels the usual Symptoms of the Small-Pox coming upon him; and he is now managed
as in an ordinary putrid Feaver. If he can't hold up, he goes to
Bed. If his Head ake too much, we putt a common Poultis to his
Feet. If he be very Qualmish at the Stomach, we give him a gentle
Vomit, yea, we commonly do these Things almost of course,
(especially give the Vomit) whether we find the Patient want them
or no. If the Fever be too high, in some Constitutions, we bleed a
little. And, finally, to hasten the Eruption, if it come on too
slowly, we putt on an Epispastic.

VII. Upon or about the third Day from the Decumbiture, the
Eruption begins. The Number of Pustules is not alike in all.

In some, they are very few. In others, they amount unto an hundred. Yea, in many they amount unto several hundreds. Frequently, unto more than what the Accounts from the Levant say is usual there. But in some, there is not what may be fairly called a Decumbiture: the Eruption is made without their suffering one Minute of any sensible Sickness for it. Young Children, even such as are dandled on the knee, and hanging on the Breast, seem to fare the best of any under this Operation.

VIII. The Eruption being made, all Illness vanishes. There's an End on't; except there should be Something of the Vapours in those that are troubled with them. There is Nothing more to do, but keep warm; drink proper Tea's; eat Gruel, and Milk-Porridge, and Panada, and Bread and Butter, and almost any Thing equally simple and innocent.

IX. Ordinarily the Patient sitts up every Day, and entertains his Friends; yea, ventures upon a Glass of Wine with them. If he be too intense upon hard Reading and Study, we take him off.

X. Sometimes, tho' the Patient be on other Accounts easy enough, yett he can't sleep for diverse Nights together. In this Case, we don't give them Opiates or Anodynes; because we find that they who have taken these in the Small-Pox are generally pestered with miserable Boyls after their being recovered. So, we lett 'em alone; their Sleep will come of itself, as their Strength is coming on.

XI. On the seventh Day, the Pustules are all usually come to their maturity; (some, on the fifth); and soon after this, they go away, as those of the Small-Pox in the distinct Sort use to do.

XII. The Patient getts abroad quickly and is most sensibly stronger, and in better Health, than he was before. The Transplantation has been given to a Woman in Childbed, eight or nine Days after their Delivery and they have gott rather earlier out of their Childbed, and in better Circumstances than ever in their Lives. Those that have had ugly Ulcers long running upon them, have had them healed on and by the Transplantation. Some very feeble, crazy, consumptive People, have upon the Transplantation grown hearty, and gott rid of their former Maladies.

XIII. The Sores of the Incisions do seem to dry a little in the three or four Days of the feavourish Praeparation for the Eruption. After this, there is a plentiful Discharge at them. The Discharge continues for some Days after the Patient is quite well on other Accounts. But the Sores dry up soon enough of themselves; we count the later, the better. If they happen to be inflamed, or otherwise troublesome, we presently help them in the Way we do any ordinary Sores.

XIV. The Transplantation has been tried on such as have gone through the Small-Pox formerly in the common Way; and it has had no Effect upon them; except perhaps an Hour or two of harmless Indisposition, about the Time when the Irruption should otherwise have been made upon them.

It has been unhappily given to some few, that have already newly received the Infection in the common Way. The Eruption has then been presently made in two or three Days after the Incision, and they have undergone the Small-Pox in the common Way; hardly escaping with their Lives; tho' some have thought, the Running of the Sores in these has been some Advantage to them.

Two or three have died under or soon after the Inoculation, from a Complication of other mortal Distempers. [An Indian Servant getting a violent Cold, fell into a pleuretic Fever, that killed her. Another Person that had long been under a crazy Melancholy and Consumption, utterly refused all Sustenance and starved herself to Death.]⁴

But of all the Hundreds that have been under a regular Management, we know not of one but what rejoices in their having undergone the Operation.

---

⁴ The section in brackets is crossed out in the original.

Cap. XXI. *Kibroth Hattaavah,*

or, some clean Thoughts, on,
The Foul Disease.

The Sins of Unchastity are such Violations of the good Order, which the God of Nature has praescribed unto the Children of Men, wisely to govern the Appetites of Generation; such Trespasses on the Rules to be observed for the Comfort and Beauty of humane Society; such Pollutions of a Body, the Maker whereof has desired it for an holy Temple to Himself; that we have no Cause to wonder at what the Divine Oracles have told us: *The unjust shall be punished; but Chiefly they that walk after the Flesh in the Lust of Uncleanness.*

A great King once had a New Testament presented unto him, fairly bound and guilt, with that Sentence of it, inscribed in golden Letters on the Cover: WHOREMONGERS AND ADULTERERS GOD SHALL JUDGE.

The Threatenings and Fulminations against these Crimes, uttered by the Voice of the Glorious God, in the Book which He spread as a Firmament over His Church, are very terrible.

And how terribly do we see them executed.

Among other Judgments which even in this World overtake the Vicious, who being past all Feeling, have given themselves over unto Lasciviousness, to work all Uncleanness with Greediness; there is of later Time, inflicted a foul Disease, the Description whereof, and of the Symptoms that attend it, would be such a nasty Discourse, that Civility to the Readers will supersede it; and the Sheets of the Treatise now before him, shall not be stained with so much Conspurcation.

The common Tradition is, that America first convey'd this great Pox to Europe, in requital whereof, Europe has transmitted the Small Pox to America.

Doubtless a Mistake! Dr Patin has written a curious Dissertation to prove that this foul Disease is of greater Antiquity.

[187]

And Mr. Becket having with much Curiosity enquired after it, finds, that in the English Nation more than six Hundred Years ago, it went under the Name of Brenning, or Burning, which signified what is now called a Clap, and was not left off till this Appellation came in the Room of it. There were then in the Stews, *Muliores habentes Nephandam infirmitatem*. And the Stews, whereof the most famous was under the Government of the Bishop of Winchester, (a Bishop of a Church, you may well say that is the Mother of Harlotts!) were forbidden on certain Penalties to keep any such dangerous Creatures. However, the Plague is not of such an early Date as they imagine who fancy that they find Something like it in Hippocrates; or they who fancy that it is mentioned even in the sacred Scriptures; and who therefore have provided even from the Old Testament a Saint, unto whose Protection, or Compassion the *brent Bruits* may betake themselves. The nearest Resemblance of it in Antiquity, seems to be in the Condition of the Adulteress in the Holy Land, who, upon drinking the Water of Jealousy, had the Parts of Generation (called the Thigh) siezed with a Rottenness; and she became a Curse among the People. But this was an Infliction extraordinary and miraculous. What we now call the French Pox, Tis a new Scourge, which the Vengeance of a Righteous God has not until the later Ages inflicted on the growing Wickedness of the World: and was no more known in the former Ages, before the sixth Chiliad, than the Leprosy of the House is in ours. But a sore Scourge it is, unto the unhappy Criminals, who bring it on themselves, and list themselves among the Fools in Israel: yea, and unto those more innocent ones, who have the Unhappiness to be yoked in the married State with the Beasts which bring it unto them, and never can make you a Reparation. Lett us adore the Justice of the Glorious God in the Matter!

An eminent Italian published an Advertisement that he could furnish People with an infallible Praeservative, the Use of which would keep them from ever being infected with the foul Disease. People applying to him for his infallible Praeservative, he furnished them with a Picture of a miserable Transgressor languishing under the Effects of the destestable Distemper, his Flesh wasted, his Visage wan and lean, his Eyes hollow, the Bridge of his Nose eaten away, ugly Ulcers running upon him; all horrible! And he said with it, *When you are under Temptation to go into a baudy House, take out this Picture, and look attentively with some Deliberation upon it; and if after this, you can go in!—who shall I say has the Driving of you?*

But, alas, this infallible Praeservative has not proved so. The rueful Spectacles of People, not in Picture, but in Person, perishing under the foul Disease, have not effectually restrained Multitudes from venturing upon the Fireships, and going on as an Oxe unto the Slaughter. Tis astonishing to read what vast Multitudes one single Practitioner in the most public Manner pretends to have had under his Cure, for this secret Disease, as they call it: besides the huge Numbers that stand in the Bills of Mortality for it, either more openly in express Terms, or more covertly under the Term of a Consumption. How justly may our Saviour call ours also, an evil and an adulterous Generation! A famous Preacher in Switzerland said, *If the old Punishment of stoning Adulterers to Death were now in Fashion, it may be suspected the Stones of the neighbouring Mountain would not be enough to serve the Execution.* One would fear whether he who spoke at that rate in his Days, would change his Note, if he were to rise from the Dead, and preach in ours. How numerous are the Morsels of *Kibroth Hattaavah!* What Numbers are the insatiable Graves of Lust filled withal.

And now what shall be said unto the unhappy Creatures upon whom the *Lues Venerea* is fulfilling the Divine Menace to the Whoremonger, A Wound and a Dishonour shall he gett, when he so destroys his own Soul. Wretches, because you would not remove your Way far from the strange Woman, you are now mourning at the Last, when your Flesh and your Body are consuming.

Your foul Disease is too filthy and odious to have the nasty Symptoms of it mentioned. But a good Man, who had never been under your Defilement, and so was not under your Distemper, and who could appeal to Heaven for it, *My Heart has never been deceived by a Woman, and I have not laid wait by my Neighbours Door;* yett he had an Illness (Bartholinus thinks, the Ulcus Syriacum; somewhat like what we call the Yawes!) which produced Complaints that your Case is more uncomfortably filled withal. *My Flesh is clothed with Worms,* (Worms without a Metaphor; your abominable Ulcers are by Glasses found swarming with 'em!) *my Skin is broken and become lothsome, yea, my Leanness rising up in me bears Witness to my Face; my Bones are pierced in the Night Season, and my Sinews take no Rest.*

Having thus been in the Ditch, which none but the abhorred of the Lord fall into, and feeling the nasty Pickle in which you are come from thence, with what inexpressible Regret and Remorse must you abhor yourselves, and cry out, *I have sinned, and I have done very foolishly.*

Shut up with the Leper, cry out, *Unclean! Unclean!*

Every Pain and Smart that you feel in the Progress of the cursed Contagion that you have taken, speaks to you, with so many Lashes, in such Words as those; and, methinks, they should sting like Scorpions! *Thy Way and thy Doings have procured these Things unto thee. This is thy Wickedness. Lett it reach to thy Heart, and break thy impure Heart within thee.*

Thou Fool, call thyself by thy proper Name, and humble thyself exceedingly; lett no Humiliation appear too low for thee.

It may look almost like a Prostitution and Profanation to cloathe such an impure Case as thine, in the holy Style used by and for the Servants of God. Yett, for once, I will say: when thy Sore is running in the Night, and ceases not; now remember God. Remember how wickedly thou hast rebelled against the Commandments of God. Remember how agreeably and reasonably and righteously God is now chastening of thee. Remember what Warnings God has given thee, that these are but the Beginning of Sorrows—except thou repent! And so, Be Troubled.

Think: *What have I brought myself unto. But, my Soul, my Soul, my impure Soul, is in much more woful Circumstances than my Body. Oh! The Turpitude of what I have been guilty of!*

Lett thy Sin be now repented of, and not only with the Attrition of a Sorrow for thy having injured thyself, but with the Contrition of a Sorrow for thy having displeased the Great God—thoroughly repented of.

But, what a wonderful Display of Sovereign Grace will there be in it, if thy Repenting of this Iniquity may prove an Occasion of thy coming to a perfect Work of Repentance for all thy Evil-doings!

Wherefore, as the Motto on the Hospital for the forlorn Invalids under this Vengeance is, *Post voluptatem misericordia,* we will say, However despair not; there is yett Mercy for thee. Become a true Poenitent and there is a Reserve of Mercy for thee. *Tho' thou hast gone a whoring, yett return to me, saith the Lord; For I am merciful, saith the Lord. Only acknowledge thine Iniquity,* and earnestly plead the Sacrifice of thy Saviour for a Pardon: and lett the stolen Waters of Sin, be no longer sweet, but more bitter than Death unto thee!

As for any Remedies under this foul Disease—you are so offensive to me, I'l do Nothing for you. You shall pay for your Cure. Lett Poscinummius practice upon you for all me. And I shall not care, if he take the Italian Cortegiana's Way for your Cure, (a Quarter of an Ounce of Coloquinesda infused in a Quart of proper Wine) which will keep you in Torment for three Days together. Gett ye gone to the Cheirurgeon. And when he has made a thorough Cure—then, sin no more. Don't return to Folly any more. If you do, Fools bray'd in a Mortar, I have no more to say to ye.

Cap. XXII. *Malum ab Aquilone,*

or

The Scurvy, discoursed on.

The Northern Parts of Europe, and the Parts of America derived from them, have been of late Years, grievously infested with a Disease called, the Scurvy: wherein the Blood and other Juices have a fix'd and sharp Salt grievously depraving of them; and the Effects thereof are very deplorable.

I will not enter into the Dispute, whether this Disease were known unto the Ancients. While some imagine that Hippocrates means it, when he speaks of the swell'd Spleen, and of the Ειλεος ημαφητης, or, *Volvulus sanguineus,* and that Galen means it when he speaks of the *Vitiligo nigra;* yett others will by no means allow that those two Gentlemen have given us any tolerable Account of the proper Scurvy. Pliny may seem to have had more Knowledge of this Disease, when he mentions the *Stomacace,* and *Scalotyrhae,* found in the Army of Germanicus near the Sea. And he that gave the Name of *Gingipedium* to the Scurvy, did well enough consider the Condition of the Teeth and of the Feet in this Distemper. But so far as we are informed, the Scurvy had its Origin in the Northern Parts of Europe, and was for a long while peculiar to the People near the Baltic Sea, who gave unto it, the Name of *Schoerbuck,* or, *Scorbute,* by which it is now distinguished.

The Glorious Lord who has all Diseases at His Command, saying to one, Go, and it goes; to another, Come, and it comes; has ordered this Executioner of His Wrath upon the sinful Nations, to pass the ancient Limits; and particularly to visit the English Nation at such a Rate, that it is thought there are few English People, especially of them who fare well, but what are ill of it, and more or less tainted with it.

Among all our Maladies, there cannot be found such another Proteus. It appears in a vast Variety of Shapes; and sometimes the Symptoms [are] very distressing and calamitous. A Gentleman who wears the Name of Eugalenus, pretends to enumerate the Maladies which may go under the Denomination of the Scurvy, or are Attendents and Consequents upon it; and the Number arises to seven Times seven with him.

The infected Person has many humbling Things to think upon.

One of the first Circumstances, wherein the Distemper appears, is, a spontaneous Lassitude. The invaded Mortal grows weary, heavy, listless; tho' he does Nothing to tire himself, nor is he willing to do Anything, if he could help it. But lett the weary Patient think: *Lord, how naturally, how criminally, am I weary of Well-doing! How little Heart have I to the Work which thou hast given me! How little do I stir myself up to do the Work, which a dying Man ought to do with all his Might!*

My Friend, lett thy Head-ache bring into thy Head such Thoughts as these: *Lord, my Head has been too Destitute of those Thoughts, which are proper to be lodged in a Temple of God! But, oh, what vain Thoughts have been lodged there!*

Lett thy perishing Teeth cause thee to think, *how much have I err'd in my Feeding!*

Lett thy odious Breath cause thee to think, *in speaking, how much has my Throat been like an open Sepulchre!*

Lett thy pained and cramped Limbs, cause thee to think, *how irregular have I been in my Motions! How indisposed for moving as and where I should have done!*

Lett thy broken Sleep cause thee to think: *what a drowsy Creature have I been in the Service of my God, and of my Soul!*

Lett thy bad Stomach putt thee in Mind of thy Neglecting to digest that Word, that should be more to thee, than thy necessary Food.

Lett thy hideous Ulcers, cause thee to reflect on the Ebullitions and Prosecutions of thy Lusts, which have rendred thee full of putrifying Sores.

Idleness is often the Cause of the Scurvy. Repent of it, O Man, if thine have been so to thee.

Be sure, the Scurvy [is] a lively Emblem and Image of that Vice. Idleness is a scorbutic Affect of the Mind. It will be attended with as pernicious Consequences as any Scurvy. Tis as much to be dreaded, as much to be deprecated. *Awake, O Sluggard, and sett about thy Business!*

The learned Wedelius has written a Dissertation to show that the Malady wherein Lazarus lies an Invalid at the rich Mans Gate in the Gospel, must be the Scurvy. O Invalid, lett thy Scurvy provoke thee in the Methods of Piety to prepare for Paradise; and it will not be long before thou shalt be comforted.

Monsr. D'Ube in his *Poor Mans Physician*, writing about the Scurvy, has these religious Passages, which are not unworthy to be transcribed

There are divine Causes (of Diseases) by which we understand God Himself, as the Absolute and Principal Cause; or the Angels and the Daemons, as instrumental Causes; being made Use of by Almighty God, to afflict us Mortals with Diseases. These divine Causes have so ample a Share in this new Distemper, that we may justly, with Hippocrates, admonish our Physicians, that after they have enquired into the Nature of Distempers, they ought to have a special Regard unto the Divinum, or Supernatural, in them; the Interpretation of which has not a little puzzled some of our Physicians. The Scurvy, some Time a Foreigner to our Climate, has been since introduced by God Himself, altering the Constitution of our Air, to chastise us.

The Nature of this monstrous Distemper, together with its various Symptoms, are evident Signs, that the same is sent among us by God, as a Scourge for our Sins; there being scarce any Part of our Body on which this Disease does not leave very evident Marks, and convincing Proofs, of our Iniquities. Thus, our Ey-sight is corrupted, and our Eyes are inflamed; which have so often been the Idols of our Love and Flatteries. Our Gums are full of Ulcers, and the Teeth ready to fall out of the Head, which have so frequently served as Instruments to revile God and our Neighbours. Our Mouth and Breath, even from the Bottom of our Lungs, emitts such a nauseous Stench, as is scarce supportable. The Legs are full of Ulcers, and scarce able to support the Weight of the Body; to putt us in Mind, how often they have been accessary in promoting our luxurious Debaucheries. The same Application may be made, of the Ulcers and Gangrenes (attending this Distemper) in the inferiour Region of our Bodies; as well as the Palseys, Pains, fainting Fitts, and other Symptoms, which are the common Attendents of the Scurvy.

If then, this Chastisement is owing to our Sins, what have we to do else, than to have Recourse unto the Mercy of God; which we are most likely to obtain, by acknowledging the Heinousness of our Trespasses, and endeavouring to correct them by following as well the Doctrine as the Footsteps of our Saviour.

Dr Cheyne observes, There is no chronical Distemper more universal, or more obstinate, or more destructive to our Nation, than the Scurvy. Scarce any one chronical Distemper, but owes its Origin to it; or has a Degree of this Evil in it. Yea, scarce any single Individual of the better Sort is altogether free from it. The same Gentleman observes, that he scarce ever saw it wholly extirpated, in such as have had it in any Degree. Because it requires a Conduct so intirely contrary to the Habits and Customs, and Appetites of our People, who will surfeit on an animal Diet, and on strong fermented Liquors, tho' they dy for it. The bare Laying of those aside, has even fastened the Teeth when dropping out, and marvellously recovered the languishing.

The Scurvy is a chronical Disease. The Patient must have Patience. The Enemy is not presently to be conquered. It requires Time and Patience.

One sais, that *Sobriety is the Bane of the Scurvy; and Intemperance is the Mother that brings it into the World.*

The Scurvy is by the Italians and the Venetians called, Mal de Terra, or, the Earth-Disease; because, tis their common Practice to cure it by digging an Hole in the Earth, into which the Patient is putt, and all but his Head covered over with Earth.

Salt-Meats must not be liv'd upon.

The Belly must be always kept open. Laxative Things must be given; but not violent ones. Bleeding is generally hurtful, except a strong Pain of the Side, or an Asthma, do call for it. Vomiting must not be much used; but it may be needful, if the Stomach much heave that Way; however the Strength must be considered.

Spirit of Sal Armoniac, now and then taken in a Glass of Wine, is an excellent Thing for the Scurvy.

And so is Whey, with the Juice of Orange or Lemon in it.

Limons do Wonders, for the Releef of the Scurvy.

In the Scurvy, Mustard is reckoned a Specific.

Every Body knows many Specificks for the Scurvy, found in the vegetable Kingdome.

It may be none superiour to Sorrel. The French do wisely to cultivate it very much. Tea's and other Drinks made of it, are noble Anti-scorbuticks.

But Scurvy-grass does not well in some hott Sorts of Scurvies. The Spirit of Scurvy-grass, cried up so much, has not answered Expectation.

Garden-cresses are of such vast Use in this Distemper, that the Parisian Physicians have ordered a great Quantity, to grow near their General Hospital.

Take two handfuls of Water-trefoyl, and lett it work instead of Hops, in about eight Gallons of Wort. Lett the Patient use it for his ordinary Drink. Among the *Boylaean* Receits, this is called, *an excellent Drink for the Scurvy.*

Take the dried Leaves of Garden-cresses and Juniper-berries; equal Parts, each. After they are well-powdered, incorporate them with a sufficient Quantity of despumated Honey. Take the Quantity of the Bigness of a Walnut in a little Wine. D'Ube cries up this as a pretty Opiate.

As a Praeservative, (and so likewise a Restorative,) hear Master D'Ube. "I must recommend to you one Remedy more, which is easy to be had, costs little, and yett is of great Consequence against this Disease. Gather of Juniper-berries, when they are quite black, in the Beginning of September. These keep for your Use; and take five or six of them every Morning, fasting. This removes the scorbutical Obstructions; consumes the superfluous Humidity, and fortifies the Parts that are debilitated."

Woodman in his *Medicus Novissimus* tells you:

I recommend Cream of Tartar as the greatest Anti-scorbutick I ever mett with, in the whole Republic of Physick. By the Use of it, I have both seen and done Wonders; insomuch that in a Manner I have thrown by all other Anti-scorbuticks, except a very few, which are interlaced with the Use of the Cream of Tartar. Tis such a safe and cheap Remedy, that the meanest Persons may use it; for which Reason I make it here public; tho' I know, t'wil gett me Envy from those, who would not, if they could, do Good in their Generation. If you find no Alteration for the better in three or four Days Time, lett it not discourage you from a further use of the Cream of Tartar, but persist with Patience for some Time in the Use of it; and you will find (with Gods Blessing desired) Success, as I have often done. Lett me give you this only Caution in using it; that if by taking it four Times a Day (from half a Dram to a Dram) it should occasion above three Stools in twenty four Hours, either the Dose may be lessened, or you may omitt taking it once or twice a Day, as there is Occasion. It may be taken in any thing, as, Wine, Beer, Ale, Whey, Posset-drink. But the best Way of taking it, in the Morning and at Night, is in a Porringer of Water-gruel, sweetned with Sugar: which at once will be very pleasant, and serve for a Break-fast and Supper, as well as a Medicine for the Scurvy.

Willius writing, *De Morbis Castrensibus,* prescribes, as an excellent Remedy for the Scurvy: a Decoction of Trefolium Fibrinum in Beer, to be drunk largely and continually.

Scorbutic Ulcers, often washed with Lime-water, till the ill Habit of the Body be mended, have had some Releef.

Cap. XXV. *De Tristibus,*

or,

The Cure of Melancholy.

It has been a Maxim with some, *that a wise Man will be melancholy once a Day.* I suppose, they mean something more than, serious, and, thoughtful. Such a Frame as that, is to be advised for more than, once a Day. I must rather say, *My Son, be thou in it all the Day long.* I am sure, a dying Man, as thou art, has Reason to be so.

But, for a crasy Melancholy, or a froward Melancholy; for this, once a Day, is too much.

There is a Malady, which goes by the Name of Melancholy. Tis commonly called, the Hypocondriac Melancholy: (and for Brevity, and for Division, sake, often called, the Hypo':) because Flatulencies in the Region of the Hypocondria, often accompany it. And so, the poor Spleen frequently, but wrongfully enough, comes to be charged with it.

None are more subject unto it, than such as have had inveterate Headakes torturing of them; and Women who labour under Obstructions.

How the System of our Spirits, comes to be dulled, and sowred, in this Distemper, lett them, who know, declare; they who can only guess, will be modest and silent.

The Fancies and Whimsies of People over-run with Melancholy are so many, and so various, and so ridiculous, that the very Recital of them, one would think, might somewhat serve as a little Cure for Melancholy. The Stories might be, what the Title of some silly Books have been: *Pills to purge Melancholy.* Tho' truly unto a reasonable and religious Beholder of them, these Violations of Reason, are a Melancholy-Spectacle.

These Melancholicks, do sufficiently afflict themselves, and are enough their own Tormentors. As if this present evil World, would not really afford sad Things enough, they create a World of imaginary ones, and by meditating Terror, they make themselves as miserable, as they could be from the most real Miseries.

But this is not all. They afflict others as well as themselves, and often make themselves insupportable Burdens to all about them.

In this Case, we must bear one anothers Burdens, or, the Burdens which we make for one another.

Lett not the Friends of these poor Melancholicks, be too soon weary of the tiresome Things, which they must now bear with Patience. Their Nonsense and Folly must be born with Patience. We that are strong must bear the Infirmities of the weak; and with a patient, prudent, manly Generosity, pitty them, and humour them like Children, and give none but good Looks and good Words unto them. And if they utter Speeches that are very grievous (and like Daggers) to us, we must not resent them as uttered by these Persons. Tis not they that speak; tis their Distemper!

The Ministers of the Gospel, undergo a very particular Trial on this Occasion. These Melancholicks will go to, or send for, Ministers, and with long Impertinencies tell them how they seem unto themselves to be. And after the Ministers have spent many Hours in talking with them, they still are, just where they were before. Some diligent and vigilant Servants of God have observed something that has look'd like a sensible Energy of Satan operating in this Matter; inasmuch as the Time, which the Melancholicks often take, to pester them, has been, what the greatest Enemy of their more useful Studies, would have chosen, to give them an Interruption at.

If I may offer my Opinion, unto those who are to watch for Souls, I would say:

Syr, it will be easy for you to discover, whether your Patient be really under the Trouble of Mind, that calls for the Skill of one who shall be, *Insignis Animarum tractandarum artifex,* to be exercised upon it. If you do really discover, that the Patient is under Awakenings from the Spirit of God, and under Apprehensions of the Wrath reveled from Heaven against the Ungodliness and Unrighteousness of Men, God forbid, that you should make Light of the Matter. The profane, baneful, Epicurean Folly, of making such Trouble of Mind, nothing but a mechanical Business in our Animal Spirits, very ill becomes a Minister of the Gospel. The pastoral Care no better exercised than so, would become the Men that are sensual, not having the Spirit. No, all possible and exquisite Care must now, be taken, to carry the troubled Sinner thorough a Process of Repentance; and after a due Confession of his Guilt, and Impotency, and Unworthiness, lead him to the Rock: show him a Glorious Christ, able to save unto the uttermost, and willing to cast out none that come to Him. Having obtained his Consent, that a Glorious Christ should accomplish all the Offices of a mighty and Holy Redeemer for him, then gett him fixed in the Resolutions of Piety. And now, *comfort him, comfort him, speak thou comfortably to him.* Tell him what the very great and precious Promises in the Covenant of Grace do now assure him of; inculcate upon him, the Consolations of God.

But you may often see Cause to suspect, that the Spiritual Troubles of your Melancholicks are not of such an Original as is pretended for. If you trace them, you may perhaps find out, that some very intolerable Vexation, or some temporal Troubles, begun their Uneasiness, and first raised that Ulcer in their Minds, which now finds new Matter to work upon, and the old Matter is no longer spoken of. If this be the Case, Wisdome is profitable to direct, how the Patient is to be treated. A cheerful, courteous, obliging Behaviour to them, with Length of Time, and some notable Contrivance, if there be Opportunity, to mend what is amiss in their Condition, will do something towards the Cure.

If your Melancholicks are gott into a tedious Way, of complaining against themselves, why should not the best Way be, to allow that all their Complaints may be true. But then tell them, what is now to be done, that they may do better than they have done, and all may be well with them. Rebuke the pining, moaning, languid, and slothful Sort of Christians, and lett them know, that they must be rowsed out of their Inactivity, and abound more

in direct Acts, than in reflex ones. Grant, that they have never
yett repented, and beleeved, and laid Hold on the Covenant of
Life; but then, demand it of them that they do all of it Now;
and plainly describe to them the Acts of a Soul turning and living
unto God. Require them Now to make a Trial, whether they
can't, with the Aids of Heaven, do those Acts, and keep at the
Repetition of them, until they have some Satisfaction, that they
have heartily and sincerely done them.

It is not without a Cause, that Melancholy has been called,
Balneum Diaboli. Some Devil is often very busy with the poor
Melancholicks; yea, there is often a Degree of diabolical Possession in the Melancholy. King Saul is not the only Instance to
be produced for it. The diabolical Impression appears very sensible, either when Thoughts full of Atheism or Blasphemy are shott
like fiery Darts into their Minds, and so seriously infest them, that
they are even weary of their Lives; or, when their Minds are
violently impelled and hurried on to Self-murder, by Starving,
or Strangling, or Stabbing, and the like. In this Case, lett Prayer
with Fasting be employed; it may be the Kind will go out no
other Way. But the astonishing Experiments that I have seen, of
Beseeching the Lord Thrice, in this Way.—and of Prayer not prevailing, until the Number of Three Days could be reached unto!

As to Conferences with the Melancholicks, my Advice is, that
if you would not throw away much Time to little Purpose, you
would in short lett them know: that these are faithful Sayings,
and worthy of all Acceptation. First, a Glorious Christ, is willing
to make them righteous and holy, upon their cordial Consent
unto His doing so; and therefore invites them to look unto Him for
all the Blessings of His plenteous Redemption. Secondly, that
upon their looking up to Him, with a Soul consenting to be under
His gracious Influences, it is their Duty to entertain a Perswasion,
that He has made them righteous and will make them holy; and
so to resolve upon always chusing the Things that please Him.
Lett them know, that when you have said all that you can say, this
must be the Sum, and Scope of all. This is enough. With this,
bestow some suitable Book upon them; and so take your Leave.

Among melancholy Diseases, there is one which in Hippocrates goes by the Name, φροντις, or, Care; and he gives a very dismal Report of it. We must cure this as much as we can, and all the Ways we can, in our poor Melancholicks.

Curas tolle graves,—was a good Maxim, long before the *Schola Salerni* was in the World.

I will transcribe a Passage from a Treatise entituled, *The Curiosities of Common Water;* published by one John Smith C.M. (The learned may please to know the Difference between A.M. and C.M. to be this: that C.M. stands for Clock Maker!) And if the Passage only make the melancholy Reader to smile, even this may be a little Step towards his Cure. He says:

Being very hypocondriacal and of a melancholy Temper, I have often been strangely dejected in Mind, when under Grief for some Misfortunes, which sometimes have been so great, as to threaten Danger to Life. But I have now found a good Remedy: for upon drinking a Pint, or more, of cold Water, I find Ease in two or three Minutes, so that no Grief seems to afflict me. This Experience I discover for the Sake of others in the like Circumstances, being verily perswaded that the Stomach sympathizes with the Mind.

Borellus tells of a Lady, strangely overwhelmed with Melancholy, that was cured with wearing upon her Heart, a Bag of Saffron.

The Exercise of Riding, wisely managed and followed: by Degrees People have rid away Melancholy, that has been growing upon them. The wiser, and more pleasant the Company, the better.

Some have seen a strange Effect, of having their haemorrhoidal Veins drawn by Leeches applied unto them. Tis incredible, how lightsome and easy they have grown upon it, and for many Months free from the Melancholy that had besotted them.

Of singular Use in Melancholy, is, as Willis tells us; the Syrup of Steel, four Ounces; a Spoonful to be taken twice a Day in a convenient Vehicle.

He also mentions, a simple Medicine, used often with good Effect in Melancholy.

Tis this. Take Whey; infuse Epithymum in it; and of this drink plentifully for several Days. See Quincy's *Elixir Hypocondriacum.*

It is a very odd Observation of the famous Olaus Borrichius; in Bartholinus his *Acta Medica: sanatos melancholicos (convenit et hoc deliris aliis) medicum suum a quo gravi illo onere levari sunt, plerumque odisse:*—imagining it seems, that these their Friends retain a disadvantageous Remembrance of what pass'd in their Fitts; or that they have produced in the People a false Opinion of them, as having been whimsical, when they were not so. I hope, the Observation will not be always verified!

Cap. XXXIX. DESECTOR.

THE CONSUMPTION;
the Grand Mower felt by the Grass of the Field.

A dreadful Disease! But so incident unto us, that Foreigners call it, The English Disease.

What is the Spectacle that we have before us, when we see a Friend, with a Consumption upon him; and, *Ossa tegit macres, nec juvat ora cibus!* We see the Body wasting with a lingring Fever; and for the most Part a tedious Cough, proceeding from ill-figured Particles in the Blood, with which the Lungs are grievously corroded.

How instructive, how affecting, a Spectacle! How loudly preaching to the Spectator, upon the Venom and Mischief which our Taste of the forbidden Fruit has brought upon us; and enforcing that Confession, Lord, *When with Rebukes thou dost correct Man for Iniquity thou makest to waste, even as a Moth that which is his Desire.*

But then, surely the Patient himself, is under all possible Obligations, to hear the Voice of his own Malady. To Day if he will hear the Voice!

It is a very wholesome Advice, that Galen gives for them that are sick of a Consumption: *praedict their Danger to them; and forewarn them of their End.* Accordingly, the very first Thing whereto the Languishing are to be advised, is this. *Friend, suspect thy Danger, beleeve thy Danger, and putt not off thy Praeparation for thy End.* It is a Thing to be observed, that there is hardly any Distemper, wherein the Languishing are less aware of their Danger, than a Consumption. There seems an unaccountable Sleep upon them; a strange Inadvertency, Stupidity, and Security. Tho' they feel their hectic Fever every Day at or near a certain Hour coming on them; the red Spot in their Cheek proclaiming it unto the Standers-by: tho' their Appetite be gone, their Midriff puff'd up with Wind, their Stomach swol'n with a Mass of Ill-humours there, tho' their Pulse grow slow and weak; their Breathing difficult; their Cough so raging, so cruel, so violent, that it can't be long before their Lungs are lacerated and ulcerated, if they be not so already; tho' their Spittle stink; and their Urine be grown oily and fatty; and colliquative Sweats are spending of them; and their Feet and Legs are tumified; and they are so hoarse they can do little more than whisper to ye; and, in short, if a Looking-glass were called for, they could either not see their Face there or see such an Hippocratic one as might astonish them; yett they'l strangely flatter themselves. The little Revivals they have now and then, they improve into so many Flatteries: They may gett over yett! Alas, my Friend; be not so vain. Apprehend thyself under an Arrest, which there is very little Probability of thy escaping from.

Wherefore, the first Thing to be done, is to gett out of that unregenerate State, in which if a Man dy, it will be good for that Man that he had never been born. And in this, if thou linger, I must lay my Hand upon thee, as once the Angel upon Lot, escaping from eternal Burnings, and say, *Escape for thy Life; make Haste, and escape!*

A Process of Repentance will now be plainly and briefly sett before thee, and in going through it, it may be hoped, thy Conversion to God may be ascertained. Sett apart some Time, without Delay, and while thy Spirits may be most in Vigour for it. In this Time, first of all, cry to God, (even to the Holy Spirit of God,) with an unspeakable Agony, that He would quicken thee to turn unto Him; owning, that thou art of thy self able to do Nothing to Purpose without His Quickening, and that thou art as unable by any Thing to deserve His Quickening. Then, with much Contrition of Soul, confess before the Lord, thy sinful Violations of His Laws, enumerated in some Explanation of the Ten Commandments, and lay to Heart above all the Fountain of Sin in thy Heart, the Original, from which the vile Streams of thy actual Sins have issued. Now carefully with Tears beg it of the glorious God, that He would pardon all thy Offences, for the Sake of the Sacrifice which His beloved Jesus has offered up to the

Divine Justice for thee; the Sacrifice, which now plead for thy Atonement, with the Cries of a Soul in the Jaws of Death; Cries that will pierce the very Heavens. Hereupon give thyself up unto God, with Dispositions and Resolutions for His Holy Service, and be restless in thy Petitions to have thy Heart cleansed, filled, fired with His Love; and say, *What have I any more to do with Fools?* Consent unto the Covenant of Grace, unto all the Articles, unto all the Proposals of it; most heartily, earnestly, thankfully lay hold upon it; and so conclude, *O Lord, I am Thine; Save me. I desire to be Thine, and wait for thy Salvation.*

Having thus improved the Space of Repentance, which thou dost enjoy in the slow Progress of thy Distemper, and repeated this Action as often as thou canst, for the better assuring of it; now lett the several Symptoms of thy Malady, awaken in thee such Sentiments of Piety as may be suitable and savoury for one in thy Condition.

Think: "My outward Man is decaying day by day; oh! that my inward Man may be renewed! that as I grow weaker in Body, I may grow stronger in my Love to God and my Neighbour: stronger in my Faith on my Saviour; gain more Strength, to bear with a patient Submission, what it shall please Him to lay upon me, and overcome the Terrors of the Death which I am hastening to; encounter the King of Terrors which is now falling on me."

Think: "Tho' my Blood be soured and full of Acrimony; lett my Soul be sweetened with a Sense of the Divine Favour to me, and be full of Goodness."

Think: "Tho' I have a slow Fever, burning and melting of me, which at certain Hours rises into more sensible Paroxysms, yett lett the Passions with which my Soul is too ready to be fired, be all extinguished."

Think: "If I cough so vehemently, to cast up, what is amiss within me, lett me be as vehement in my Desires and Essays to cast out all that is amiss in my Soul; all that is provoking there."

Think: "Have I a Mass of ill Humours gathering in me? Lett not my Spirit have the ill Humours of a froward, peevish, or an envious, Mind, or any Impatience misbecoming a Child of God."

Think: "Is my Appetite gone? Oh! lett my Appetite unto all the Delights, and Riches, and Honours, of this World go with it! Have I the Aspect of a dead Man upon me, looking as if I were laid out already? Oh! lett me dy to Creatures as fast as I can; become as indifferent as a dead Man unto the Comforts and unto the Troubles, of this World. I must be dead, before I dy, or else I am not fitt to dy. My Life lies in such a Death as that; being dead with Christ, and feeling myself alive in conversing with Him alone."

Anon; as the Cough begins to abate, and the Flux comes upon thee, which is the immediate Harbinger of Death; Now, yeeld up thyself, O departing Spirit, unto thy Saviour, with all possible Resignation. Walk thro' the dark, Valley of the Shadow of Death, keeping a fast Hold on thy Saviour; Go up out of the Wilderness, leaning on thy Beloved.

Borellus has this Remark, on many Students falling into Consumptions; that is often proceeds, *a fumo candelarum hausto in musaeis undique clausis:* and he quotes the famous Placaeus, to confirm the Observation. The Admonition may be of some Use, by Way of Prevention: but not as an Encouragement unto Students to throw by their Lucubrations.

What is the Hectic Stone, they tell strange Things of? And of the Milk or Water, in which that Stone has been dipped [?] or quenched?

Among the Boylaean Receits, there is,

A very nourishing Aliment, that has recovered diverse in Consumptions.

Take eight or ten craw-fishes; and, after the blackest Gutt or String is taken out, boil them in Barley-water, till they become very red; then take them out, and beat them long, Shells and all, in a Stone or Glass Mortar, to a soft Mash; and strongly squeeze out the Juice. This may be given, either alone, or mixed with an equal Part of Chicken-broth, or some such convenient alimental Liquor.

A consumptive Cough has been thus releeved, when other Means have proved insignificant.

Take a dozen good Raisins of the Sun, and having taken out
the Kernels, then stuff them with the Tops, or small tender Leaves
of the Rue: take 'em in a Morning; and fast a little after 'em.

Tis incredible, how strangely and quickly even far-gone
Consumptions have been cured, by Nothing but this: lett a convenient Spott of Earth be opened, and lett the Patient stoup to
the Place, and there take the Smell of the fresh Earth, for a few
Minutes together. Why may not a Spadeful of the Fresh-earth,
be brought into the sick Chamber, and there smelt unto?

Our Indians cure Consumptions with a Mullein-Tea.

Red Nettle-seeds taken in Honey, a convenient Quantity, some
Time together. This has recovered those, who have been far-
gone in a Consumption, that has been look'd upon, as desperate.

Well-praepared Antimonials, are of great Efficacy to sweeten
the Blood, and keep off, if not gett off, a Consumption.

The Antihecticum of Poterius, in the common Praeparation,
often defeats the Expectations of them that use it. But rightly
praepared, it often does Wonders, in recovering People out of
desperate Consumptions.

The Use of Milk, is commended in a Consumption, especially,
Womens Milk. Next unto which, if I praefer that of Asses, I
should quote an Author for it. It shall be Avicen. But then, the
vicious Acids in the Stomach must be corrected by Absorbents;
else the Benefit of the Milk-diet will be defeated.

Milk-Thea, is a pretty Sweetener.

The Yolk of an Egg, in a Glass of good Wine, drunk in a Morning, has been sometimes of good Consequence.

But it is a just Caution Dolaeus gives, *Aqua vitae* is *aqua mortis*.

Pork boil'd in Milk, and the Broth drunk; this has been cried
up as a mighty Analeptic.

The Use of Snails has done Wonders in the speedy Cure of
Consumptions.

In a recent Phthisis, there is often praescribed, Syrup of Turnips.

Take Turnips sliced, and double refined Sugar, of each half a
Pound; putt them in a glaz'd Pott; setting a Lay of Turnips, and
a Lay of Sugar, till it is full. Cover the Pott with Paper, and putt

it into an Oven, to bake with Bread. When it is taken out, press out the Liquor, and keep it for Use. The Dose is, a Spoonful, Morning and Evening.

Raisins in Wine, baked; and a few of these Raisins taken every Day; have had a marvellous Efficacy.

And so, dried Figs.

Consumptions, from Obstructions within, wherein People sometimes unaccountably linger and languish, are sometimes helped by the Use of Millepedes.

An Issue may be of some Use. Advise about it.

Change of Air; what may be thought of that?

See what may be done, by sweetening the Blood, with Thea's, or Decoctions or Infusions, of Sassafras, of Sarsaparilla, of Guajacum, of China-roots, of Colts-foot, and the like.

A *Tea* of the Bark of Sassafras Roots, has marvellously cured Coughs, wherein a Consumption has been threatned, if not actually entred.

Take Myrrhe well powdered, two Drams; Saffron, half a Scruple; Nutmeg, half a Dram; Honey, two Ounces; mix. Th. Fuller sais, "It is readily admitted into the inmost Penetralia of the Lungs; and is a gallant Medicine for such a Consumption, as is not yett gone beyond the first Stade of one."

Physicians (especially Spaniards) tell of Ulcers in the Lungs cured, with a Decoction of Guajacum.

Here's a Receipt. Rx. Flowre of Sulphur, two Ounces; melt it in a large Iron Ladle; then add, by little and little the same Quantity of the best Salt of Tartar; stir them together continually, with an Iron Spatula, till they are well-mixed, and are of a dark red Colour. Then add, Olibanum, and Myrrh, of each in Powder, two scruples; and Saffron, half a Dram; stir them together for near a quarter of an Hour more; when tis cold, lett this Mass be dissolved in Canary Wine, two Pints; then add, of trebly-refined Sugar, three Pound. Boil this to the Consistency of a Syrup. Of this, give one or two Spoonfuls, four Times a Day, in a Draught of some pectoral Decoction warmed, or in a Glass of White-wine.

Woodman sais, "By this only Medicine, I have known People recovered from this Disease, when they have been thought by others, past Recovery. Tis to be used for a considerable Time. Tis a noble Medicine in hectic Fevers, if administred in Time."

Several have had the Heate of an hectic Fever not only allayd, but extinguish'd, by the Use of Succory Tea.

I knew a young Man recovered from an Hectic by using Whey as his constant Drink.[5]

Here's another, (that is mentioned among Dr Lowers Receits),

Take the Yolk of a new-laid Egg; Beat it with three Spoonfuls of Red-rose-water; putt to it half a Pint of the Strokings of Red-cows Milk; sweetened with a sufficient Quantity of Sugar of Roses; add to it a little Nutmeg scraped. Take this every Morning for a Month, fasting two Hours after it.

It is added: this alone restored a Gentleman, that was given over by the Physicians.

Here's another. Take two young Cocks, hatched in the Spring, and kill them with Strangling, not shedding any of their Blood; pick 'em, and gutt 'em. Don't wash 'em. While they are warm, now bruise them to a Mash, breaking all their Bones. Putt them into a clean earthen Pipkin; adding two Quarts of water, and one Pint of sweet rich Wine, wherein boil the Cocks to Rags. Then strain it hard thro' a clean Cloth; and into the strained Liquor putt one Pound and a half of stoned Raisins; two Drams of Saffron; one Ounce of Harts-horn; one Ounce of Ivory; one Handful of Maiden-hair; two Ounces of the Roots of Colts-foot sliced; and again lett it be well-boiled. Then strain it. So, give to the Patient, half a Pint, or a Gill, or less, as his Weakness is more or less, and his Stomach will bear it, every Morning. You may sweeten it with a Spoonful of Syrup of Gilly-flowres, or Maiden-hair; until you find the Cough departed. Every full Moon purge a little with Pill. Ruffi.

The Account added is: "An excellent Remedy for those that are inclining to a Consumption, or any inward Weaknesses, attended with a Cough. Proved by many Experiments."

[5] The last two paragraphs are not in the handwriting of Cotton Mather.

Strong Wort boil'd unto the Consistence of a Cataplasm, with a little Venice-turpentine added; this laid unto the Breast, will strangely nourish and strengthen the Vitals; and prevent a Consumption coming on.

Dr Morgan observes, "He who shall go about to cure an Hectic, without a primary and chief Regard unto the Scurvy, of which it is a Symptom, will find himself unhappily mistaken." For this he cries up certain mercurial and antimonial Praeparations; as, the Ethiops, Cinnabar, Diaphoretic Antimony; and the Antihecticum Poterii.

Take Vervain, a convenient Quantity. Make a strong Decoction. Then add unto the Decoction an aequal Quantity of Honcy; and boil them together into the Consistency of a Syrup. Of this, take now and then a Spoonful.

Tis a very remarkable, and often experimented, Cure for Consumptions.

Cap. XL.

A Pause made upon,

The Uncertainties of the

PHYSICIANS.

When we are upon a Consumption, it may be as proper a Time and Place as any to make a Remark upon, The Uncertainties of the Physicians, on whose Advice the Patients depend so much for their Lives, and the Comfort of them. Their Uncertainties appear notoriously and sufficiently in their Contradictions to one another; which indeed are very conspicuous in this Distemper (as Dr Marten in his, *New Theory*, has with a just Ingenuity observed,) but also to be found in all other Diseases. How rarely does, a Council of Doctors, do the Patient so much good, as a single one happens to do! A famous Physician, who shall be nameless, died of a Disease, which at that very Time, he had a Book in the Press, to teach the Cure of. We will single out, the Consumption, for our Experiment; because it is one of those Maladies, which have the greatest Share in the Depraedations of Mortality; and on which more has been written than upon many others. And here, we will not concern ourselves with the Differences among the Physicians, about the Cause of this Distemper; (whereupon, who can read the Collection made by Dolaeus, and not cry out, The Diviners are mad!) but only see, how they differ about the Cure of it.

Some Physicians are violent in it, that the Cure of a Consumption must be accomplished only by Alcali's. Others with as much Violence urge, that it must be only by Acids. I will spare the Names of the Gentlemen on both Sides.

Many hold, that no Good is to be done in a Consumption, without Opiates. It is held by others, that they are pernicious Things, and no better than an Halter. I still spare the Names of my Gentlemen.

But, I will do that no longer.

We know, what Shelves of Medicines are prepared with Sugar, for a Consumption. But Harvey exclaims against Pectorals prepared with Sugar. Helmont sais, that Syrups and Lohochs have not benefited one in a Thousand: Heurnius, and Wedelius, and Capivaccius, are against all sweet Lambatives. Dolaeus affirms, they rather increase the Disease than releeve it.

Conserve of Roses, has been in high Esteem for many Ages; and an Army of Advocates, besides the great Names of Platerus, and Forestus, and Riverius, might be mustered for the Defending of it. But Sylvius decries it as an useless Thing, and Harvey asserts the Patients to be rather the worse than the better for it.

Balsam of Sulphur is cried up to the Skies: and particularly by Sylvius tis valued above all Medicines. But Hoffman and Walschmid, as vehemently disrelish it: and say, it rather increases than extirpates the Distemper. Deckers reports, that some have been brought into the Distemper by using of it. And Michael, quoted by Dolaeus, will confirm the Report.

The Decoctions of Guajacum, and some other such Things, much in Vogue, for a Consumption: have had the like Reputation; prais'd by some, and scoff'd by others.

Have not Snails, gott as early as any Remedies, into general Esteem and Practice? Cardan sais, he has made a Cure of desperate Consumptions with them. Harvey despises them. Salins reproaches them.

The Milk-diet is recommended by Dolaeus, and a Thousand more. Harvey sais, Tis useless; and in many Cases, hurtful. And in how many Cases does Morton forbid it?

Lett Weikard and Harvey engage one another upon the Juice of Turnips; the former with Panegyricks, the latter with Invectives.

Ground-Ivy has mett with the like Reception.

They warn us against Aloeticks in a Consumption. And yett, my Friends, how much do you rely on your Elixir proprietatis? whereof yett some will tell you, the frequent Use of it has brought a Consumption.

Helmont, and Ettmuller, and Borellus, and Dolaeus, condemn the Letting of Blood in a Consumption: and Capivaccius thinks, there will be seldome, if ever, any Need of it. Yett Galen, and Mercatus, and Spigelius, and Sylvius, and Willis, and many others, approve it; especially on the Beginning of the Disease. Hippocrates would have us bleed in Distempers of the Lungs, as most as long as there is any Blood in the Body. Yea, our Sydenham does allow Bleeding on some Invitations; and our Morton does advise it, as often as a new Peripneumonick Feaver happens in this Distemper.

For emetic and cathartic Medicines; Hippocrates condemns Vomits; and Helmont as much condemns Purges, in this Malady. Dolaeus tells us, Vomits are ever suspected; and Purges are seldom safe. Whereas Morton is not against both gentle Vomits and Purges, in that which they call, the first State of the Distemper. Prosper Martianus is very zealous for Vomits. Hartman favours them. Ettmuller sais, there is no Remedy that aequals them. Crato and Baglivi are against Purges, in this and all Diseases of the Breast. But Galen, and Avicen, and most of the Ancients, purged plentifully in this Malady. And Mercatus urges it, as almost the only Way to cure a Phthisis. Willis also, and Barbette, and Deckers, are for sleight Purgations.

Morton speaks but suspiciously of Diaphoreticks in this Distemper. But what say others?

Galen condemns Diureticks. But Montanus and Crucius, and Willis, and Sylvius, and Dolaeus direct them. They are approved by Morton, and admired by Baglivi.

Authors disagree about all the Methods of Evacuation. And there is as much Disagreement among them about Issues, and Blisters, and external Applications. Alas, what a Blindmans Buffet carried on among them!

Of how great Consequence is the Doctrine of animal Spirits, in Physic! And yett, Morgan derides it, as an Hypothesis only serving to explain those Diseases which the Physicians have been ignorant of, or surprised at: like the common Refuge of Witchcraft among the Vulgar!

Oh! the Darkness that we find sett in our Pathes!

"But from this Darkness tis as clear as the Light, That our Dependence must be no longer on our Physicians for the Cure of our Diseases. T'wil be a very foolish and faulty Thing, to fall into the Distemper of him, concerning whom it is left upon Record: *In his Disease he sought not unto the Lord, but unto the Physicians.* Relying upon them, we may feel that Word fulfilled upon us, *Thou shalt use many Medicines, and thou shalt not be cured.* Yea, we may be like the Woman, of whom the Beloved Physician honestly relates, *she spent all her Living on Physicians, neither could be healed of any.*

"O thou afflicted, and under Distemper, go to Physicians, in Obedience to God, who has commanded the Use of Means. But place thy Dependence on God alone to direct and prosper them. And know, that they are all Physicians of no Value, if He do not so. Consult with Physicians; but in a full Perswasion, that if God leave them to their own Counsels, thou shalt only suffer many Things from them; they will do thee more Hurt than Good. Be sensible, tis from God, and not from the Physician, that my Cure is to be looked for."

Tis a sad Story told by Huartus, that when the Arabick Medicine flourished in Italy, there was a Physician so celebrated for his learned Writing, Reasoning, Disputing, Distinguishing, and making of Conclusions, that his Auditors expected, he would not only cure Diseases, but even raise the Dead. But after all, when he came to Practice, hardly any of his Patients escaped with their Lives. They did by their Death so generally expiate the empty Knowledge of the Professor, that with Confusion he bid adieu to the World, and ended his Days in a Convent.

What an Oracle has Hippocrates been to our Physicians, who profanely enough use to putt the Title of Divine upon him! How extravagantly, is he revered, by those, with whom after Macrobius he is blasphemously esteemed as, *Tam fallere quam falli nescius!* How hyperbolically extolled by those who like Heurnius assert of him, *cujus tanta fuit benignitas, ut nihil sciverit quod nos nescire voluerit; tanta autem solertia et sapientia, ut nemo post eum sciverit, quod ipse ignoraverit!* And yett; what are the Aphorisms of Hippocrates; many of which are trivial enough, and known to our very Barbers; and those that are more important, many of them found false in very many Cases; many full of Uncertainty? Sanctorius has done enough to demonstrate, that they are not so infallible as they have been commonly taken to be. Even Celsus himself, that great Plagiary of Hippocrates, is compelled from Experience to make that Confession upon them, *Vix ulla perpetua praecepta ars medicinalis recipit.* There are *no Rules in Physick to be relied upon!* What are his Prognosticks? Those that are true of them, are such as fall under the Observation of our poorest Nurses, and the Meanest who tend upon the Sick! An ingenious Gentleman, who has written a Treatise entituled *Medela Medicinae,* has made sufficient Remarks upon them. And indeed our incomparable Boyl could not forbear saying, that he *might venture to say, that some of those rigid Laws of Draco, the Severity whereof made Men say, they were written in Blood, cost fewer Persons their lives, than* one Passage which he mentions, of Hippocrates.

As for Galen, the learned Man who writes, *De Vitandis Erroribus,* hath reckoned up above Thirty of his Notable Errors. And whereas Galen seems most of all to triumph in his Book, *De Usu Partrum;* the acute Anatomist Vesalius derides his Ignorance of Anatomy, and showes that he never performed one Dissection, and proves him to have erred in one hundred and sixteen Particulars.

It is a sad Story, which one of the greatest Physicians that ever France could boast of, has confess'd unto the World. *Certum est, numerum aegrorum a medicis curatorum, non attingere, illum eorum, quos ad orcum pomposa cum latinitate deducunt.* Yea, the Story goes on; *Ars divina medicinae, metuo ne ad illud deveniat ut juxta merita crimina, obque perpetua homicidia, in exilium, sicut antiquitus a Romanis, arceatur.*

It was thought, that Argenterius far surpassed Galen, in reducing, the Art of Physic, to a yett more perfect Method; and yett it is reported of him, that most of his Patients dyed under his Hands; or fell into incureable Distempers; insomuch that his affrighted Countreymen gave over employing of him.

The Result of this Discourse is, to take off our Dependence on an Arm of Flesh, and show what Cause we have to depend on the glorious God alone, for the Cure of our Diseases. What should be the Motto on the Curtains of every sick Bed, but this: *My Help cometh from the Lord who made Heaven and Earth!*

All this, without the least Intention to depreciate the skilful and faithful Physician.

The Words in the thirty eighth Chapter of Ecclesiasticus, deserve as good a Reception with us, as the most oraculous that ever fell from the Pen of an Hippocrates.

Honour a Physician with the Honour due to him, for the Uses you may have of him. Inasmuch as the Lord hath created him; for of the Most High cometh Healing; and the Skill of the Physician shall lift up his Head.

Give Place to the Physician for the Lord hath created him; lett him not go from thee for thou hast Need of him. There is a Time when in their Hands there is good Success.

Cap. LXI. *Medicamenta sine quibus,*

or, certain Remedies, that People of any Condition,
may always have ready at Hand, for themselves
and their Neighbors.

A Family-Plaister.

There is a certain Plaister of such extensive Benefit, that it is
Pitty any Family should be without it. It very little differs from
what has gone under some other Names; but, for the Cause I have
mention'd, I am willing to have it called, The Family Plaister.

Take two Pound of the best Oil Olive; of good Red Lead, one
Pound; White Lead, one Pound; well beaten to Powder: twelve
Ounces of Castile-sope: (good old Mrs Eliot, from whom Hundreds of People had it, and had good by it, under the Name of her
Spleen-plaister, added a little Oyl of Bayberries:) Incorporate all
these together, in an earthen Pott well-glazed. After they are
well incorporated, and the Sope comes upwards then putt it upon
a small Fire of Coals, and keep stirring it there with some convenient Instrument, for about an Hour and half; then increase the
Fire, till what was red grow gray, and then also leave not off till
it grow a little dark. Drop it then upon a woodden Trencher,
and if it cleave not unto your Fingers, tis done enough. So make
it up into rolls. It will keep twenty Years: the older the better.

A World of People are labouring under Disorders, which they
commonly ascribe to, the Spleen, few are entirely free from them.
To remove or suppress these Disorders, would restore the Comforts
of Life, to thousands of People, that are overwhelmed with
Vapours, and with the splenetic Maladies, which may say, *Our
Name is Legion,* as well for the Number of them, as for much of the
Devil often in them. This Plaister is peculiarly calculated for
these vexatious Maladies; and a vast Multitude of People far
and near have with notable Success found it serviceable to them
on these Accounts. I have already mentioned one in this Countrey, who charitably dispensed it unto hundreds of People, that

gave Thanks unto Heaven for the Advantage they received from it. Apply the Plaister to the Region of the Spleen; and renew it, as there may be Occasion.

This Plaister laid unto the Stomach, is very good for a weak Stomach; will notably assist and excite the Appetite. And every Body knows, that all the Wheels of Nature, are kept in the better Trim, when this great one is well provided for.

This Plaister laid unto the Belly gives Ease in the Cholic. I knew a Practitioner, who used it as a Secret with such Success in cholical Affects, that People sent from very distant Parts unto him for it.

This Plaister laid unto the Region of the Kidneys, it stops the Bloody Flux, and the Running of the Reins, and praeternatural Heats in the Kidneys.

It is an admirable Plaister for Sores, and Swellings, and Aches, and Bruises, and Chilblains, and Kibes, and Corns.

It breaks Boils, and Felons, and Impostumes; and it heals them when it has broken them.

If the Skin be rubb'd off the Legs, our Plaister commonly cures. It will also draw out running Humours in the Legs, without breaking the Skin.

And they that have Issues, can't easily dress them with a better Thing. Take a little square Peece of brown Paper; on the middle of which you may rub a little of this Plaister, holding the End of the Roll to a Candle for that Purpose. You may prepare an Hundred of them in a few Minutes; and as often as you dress your Issue renew them.

There are many other Uses of this Plaister. But here is enough to recommend it.

Since I wrote this, I find this Plaister among the Chymical Receits of Sir Kenelm Digby; who cries it up, for all the Virtues aforesaid; and adds: Being applied unto the Head, it strengthens the Ey-sight.

I am well aware, what sharp Satyrs have been written against Women pretending to practice Physick: "The *Hae Galeni* (say, Master Whitlock!)—*Nam Genus variant.*—The quacking Hermophrodites; the Physician and Physic, both Simples, compounding the

Destruction of the Patient: applying their Medicines (as the Athenians their Altar, unto an unknown God) unto an unknown Disease. In the Bills of Mortality (quoth my Satyrist,), we may justle
in She-physicians among the S's for a Disease, as surely killing as
Stone or Surfeit. A practising Rib shall kill more than the Jaw-
bone of an Ass, and a quacking Dalilah than a valiant Sampson."

It was reckoned a sad Story; and, *O miserae Leges!* was cried
out upon it.

> *Fingit se Medicum quivis idiota, profanus,*
> *et Distillator, histrio, Tonsor, Anus.*

But yett after all, in the most ancient Writers, we find Women
celebrated as eminent in the Art of Healing. Homer in his eleventh
Iliad, mentions Agamede, in Terms almost like what we read of
Solomon:

> *She that all Simples healing Vertues knew,*
> *And every Herb that drinks the Morning Dew.*

And in his Odysses, he mentions Polydamne as excelling in this
Way of Usefulness.

I call to mind also Mr George Herberts Advice, that the Wife
of the Countrey-Minister, should have some Skill and Will to
help the Sick. More particularly, he adds what I shall not judge
it amiss to transcribe. "Accordingly for Salves, his Wife seeks
not the City, but prefers her Garden and Fields, before all out-
landish Gums. And surely, Hyssop, Valerian, Mercury, Adders-
tongue, Yarrow, Melilot, and St Johns Wort, made into a Salve;
and Eldar, Camomil, Mallows, Comfry and Smallage, made into
a Poultis; have done great and rare Cures." Tis true, there was a
Law among the Athenians, which forbad Women to meddle with
Medicine. The young Lady Agnodice, to gratify her Inclination
that Way, disguised herself in a masculine Habit. The Court of
Areopagus upon the Discovery would have punished her upon
the Law of Athens. But the Dames of the City made an Uproar,
and procured an Abrogation of the Law.

We will then venture to proceed, and say, it would be a laudable Thing for our Gentlewomen to have their Closetts furnished

with several harmless, and useful, (and especially external)
Remedies, for the Help of their poor Neighbours on several
Occasions continually calling for them.

Such more particularly would be,

Ointment of Tobacco,—for Sores,

Ointment of Marsh-mallows, for Pains,

And several of the Remedies, mention'd in several of the former
Capsula's. Take your Choice, Ladies!

But, be sure, don't forgett the *Amarum salubre* in the Capsula
of, *Help for the Stomach depraved*

An Appendix

What is your Occupation?
or, The Trades-mans Praeservative.

At the Bottom of this Capsula, the Reader must find lodged, a
short Advertisement about the Maladies, which the several
Trades, that People subsist upon, do most meet withal and most
lead unto.

I will in the first Place, readily acknowledge, that one of the
worst Maladies, which a Man in any Trade, or Way of Living,
ever can fall into, is, for a Man to be sick of his Trade. If a Man
have a Disaffection to the Business, that he has been brought
up to, and must live upon, tis what will expose him to many and
grievous Temptations, and hold him in a Sort of perpetual Im-
prisonment. Man, beg of God, an Heart reconciled unto thy
Business. And if He has bestow'd such an Heart upon thee, as to
take Delight in thy daily Labour, be very thankful for such a
Mercy! There is much of the divine Favour in it.

But then, there are more special Maladies, which the various
Employments of Men, do more peculiarly expose them to. And,
they that are wise, will consider how to guard against them.

Some learned and wholesome Things have been written *De
Morbis Artificum*. What Ramazzini has done upon this Head,
is well worthy to be more known among Artificers.

Yett more particularly. Seeing how liable Mariners are to the Scurvy, one cannot but encourage them to their Pease-Diet, and the Use of Limons, and the drinking of the best fair Water they can come at, and feeding on as much fresh Provisions as tis possible.

Seeing how liable the Blacksmiths are, to Impairments of their Eyes, one cannot but recommend much Use of Ey-bright for them. And since they are so prone to be very costive; one would invite them to Suppers of Barley-gruel, with Raisins and Corints.

When we see how the caustic Powder of the Lime they deal in, brings Consumptions upon Masons, one would exhort them to drink much Water, and eat Abundance of Almonds.

When we see, how Millers and Bakers, contract Asthma's by the Flowre entring into their Breasts, one would wish them, some ingenious Contrivances, that the Air may be inspired without it.

The poor Potters, and Plumbers, and Painters, who are poisoned with mineral Fumes; and the People, whose Work is much about Quicksilver; what shall be done for these, that they may not find their Death in their Way of Living? Proper and early Antidotes must be thought upon.

Scriveners, Tailors, and others that sitt still, with little Motion of their Bodies, in the Work of their Hands, must think on frequent Exercise, to stir their Limbs.

Be sure, Students, and Men that lead sedentary Lives, will do well to be on Horse-back, as much as they can.

For [the] rest,—consult a wise Physician.

Since we are proposing Remedies to be always ready at Hand, a Collection of easy Emeticks, and of easy Catharticks to be had always ready at Hand, may be neither unserviceable nor unacceptable.

Data Tempore prosunt.

I. For easy Vomits.

Take lukewarm Water, one Pint; Oil (of Olives, or of Almonds,) four Ounces. Mix for a Draught.

Green Tea, half an Ounce: boil it in Water, (or, Ale) from one Pint to half a Pint; for a Draught.

Oxymel of Squills, three Ounces; drink it in a Draught of Posset.

Emetic Tartar, from one Grain, to five or six. Of this, I can scarce forbear saying, there is none like it.

Salt of Vitriol, from one to two or three Scruples; given in a Draught of Posset.

Syrup of Peach-blossoms. There is hardly a better or safer. It may be given to Infants; yea, as soon as they are born.

Powdered Root of Ipecacohana; from half a Scruple (for a Child:) to half a Dram, or two Scruples, (for a Man.) Sir John Colbatch says, *Tis the safest, and perhaps the best Vomit, that ever was made known to the World, barely as a Vomit, to cleanse the Stomach.* This is now in its Reign; the most fashionable Vomit.

Penetrate the Throat with a Feather: Borellus writes, that his Father (and some other Gentlemen) lived unto a great Age, by vomiting once a Month, no other Way.

You'l pardon me, that I don't recommend another famous Vomit; but rather transcribe the Words of an eminent Physician. "It is well known (he says,) that a pretended Chymist, who calls himself Lockyer, hath gained by a Pill many thousand Pounds, which is one of the vilest and most contemptible, among all the mineral Praeparations I ever yett knew tried in Medicine."

I am not sorry that Antimonial Emeticks begin to be disused.

Instead thereof, I will recite the Words of honest John Smith, in his Essay upon common Water.

By Means of Water, all Sickness at the Stomach may be cured. It is done thus. Take four Quarts of Water; make it as hott over the Fire as you can drink it: of which Water lett a Quart be taken down at several Draughts. Then wrap a Rag round a small Piece of a Stick, till it is about the Bigness of a Mans Thumb; ty it fast with some Thread; and with this, by endeavouring gently to putt it a little Way down your Throat, provoke yourself to vomit up again most of the Water. Then drink another Quart, and vomit up that; and repeat the same, the third and fourth Time. You may also provoke vomiting, by tickling your Throat with your Finger, or the Feather-end of a Goose-quill. By this

Way of vomiting, which will be all performed in an Hours Time, that viscous and roapy Flegm, which causes the Sickness, will be cast up, so that the Party in that Time will be free from all that inward Disturbance, if you use the Remedy at first. But, if the Sickness hath continued for a Time, it will require the same Course, once or twice more; which may be done in three or four Hours, one after another. This Remedy by forty Years Experience, I look upon to be infallible, in all Sickness at the Stomach, from what Cause soever, and for all Pains in the Belly, that seem to be above the Navel; which Pains are generally counted the Cholic, but they are not so. By this Means I have eased very great Pains, caused by eating Mussels that were poisonous. And it is also a certain Cure for all Surfeits, or Disorders that follow after much eating; so that the Lives of Multitudes might be saved by this Means, who, for Want of expelling what offends, do often dy in Misery: for by this cleansing of the Stomach at the first, the Root of Diseases proceeding from surfeiting, or unwholesome Food, or any viscous Humours from a bad Digestion, are prevented: the Stomach being the Place in which all Distempers do at first begin. Tis not a nauseous Remedy; it does not make the Patient sick; as the best of all Vomits do. And then, tis a Vomit which is at our own Command; since we can leave it off when we please. As for People who are troubled with *Shortness of Breath*, tis certain from Experience, that Vomiting with warm water three or four Times will afford certain Relief. Dr *Cook*, in his *Observations on English Bodies*, does praescribe for the *Cure of Fevers*, first a *Vomit*, and afterwards as much *cold water* as the Patient can drink. *Rest, Fasting*, and *Drinking much Water*, after a *Vomit* or two, is a Course that hath never failed to cure *Fevers;* by clearing the Stomach of that sordid Filthiness, which causes the Distemper.

II. For easy *Purges*.

Take a little Manna. From two Drams to an Ounce, for Children. An Ounce or two, or more, for grown Persons. It must be remembred, that old Manna sometimes has proved as bad as Poison.

A little Senna.

Syrup of Roses.

An Infusion of Senna, Liquorice, Anniseed, of each half an Ounce; with Salt of Tartar, a Dram; in a Pint of Water scalding hott, for half an Hour. Take four Spoonfuls of this every Hour, until it begin to work.

Fresh Damask-Rose Buds, one Ounce. Putt them into a Quart of Whey over Night. Strain it, and drink it, the next Morning.

Slice Liquorice; beat Anniseeds; shred Hysop; and boil these in white-Wine. Strain it. Take from half an Ounce to an Ounce, or more. Tis a Purge for tender Children.

Syrup of Violets. Infants may take this gentle Purger. And indeed it is most proper for them.

Two Ounces of Rhubarb; four Ounces of Gentian; a Quart of good Anniseed Water. Infuse the Roots in this Water. Two Spoonfuls is a Dose.

Pillulae Ruffi. Especially, when chalybeated with adding about a third Part, Sal martis.

An Ounce of choice Rhubarb, finely powdered; eight Ounces of good Currants; pick'd and wash'd; and rubb'd dry. Beat these together in a Glass, or stone Mortar, for near two Hours. Take about the Bigness of a Chestnut in a Morning. Tis a pretty purging Electuary; especially for Children.

Or, keep in the House a Bottel of Anniseed Water, with a convenient Quantity (a Dram or two) of Rhubarb steeped in it. It is an excellent and ungriping Purge; useful on a thousand Occasions. Especially to stop Fevers, and cure Fluxes. It has been thought by some, it can't be cried up too much.

It is a general Caution for Purges; that they be very sparingly used in the Decline of the Year; especially after an hott Summer.

Super-purgation is presently cured with a Scruple of Venice-Treacle.

Cap. LXII. *Fuga Daemonum,*

or, Cures by Charms
considered,
And, a Seventh-Son examined.

The Wicked Spirits, which are the Power or Army of the Air, under the Command of a Prince that headed them in their Apostasy from God, are doubtless very many. No Man alive can tell how many. They come down upon us, as Grasshoppers for Multitude, and the Frogs or Flies in the Plagues of Egypt swarmed not in such inexpressible Numbers. They and their Hosts, are much People even as the Sand that is on the Sea-shore for Multitude. A Daemon who comes to possess and molest one poor Man, may have a Legion attending on him. These evil Spirits, are poisoned with, and confirmed in, a Disposition to affect the Honours, which are due to none but the Infinite God: and among those Honours, there may be none that their Affectation may be sett more upon, than to have paid unto them the Regards which belong to, the Lord our Healer. Yea, they may apprehend, that if the poor Children of Men apply unto them for their Health, it may not only gratify them in their Usurpation, but we shall thereby provoke the God of Heaven to deliver us further up unto the Power of those to whom we have so impiously resigned ourselves, and permitt them to inflict some greater Mischief on us, after they have done what seem'd a Kindness. Now, as the Kingdome of Heaven, so the Kingdome of Darkness, has the Sacraments, in the Observation whereof, we declare our Subjection thereunto; and subscribe ourselves, the Children of the Kingdome. And the Sacraments of Hell are particularly observed, in the Sorceries, wherewith many ungodly and unhappy People seek the Cure of their Diseases. Upon the Practice of certain Sorceries, People often find a strange Releef [of] their Maladies: and upon Use of odd and mad Charms, the Spirits of the Invisible World, some or other of which are always at Hand, and are, no

[226]

Doubt, very skilful Physicians, help them to some Ease of their Distempers. It is doubtless a Mistake in a great Philosopher, *Diaboli potestas eo se non extendit, ut claudum pediculum restituet.* By the Charms, of Words and Marks, and the like, which tis plain can be of no natural Efficacy for the Cure of Diseases, People in short plainly go to the Devil for a Cure; and how tremendous must be the Consequences!

But this Impiety, how commonly is it practised: even among those who have been baptised for God, and in their Baptism have renounced all Dependence on the Devil!

The learned Borellus who has collected many Exemples of such Things, passes this Judgment upon them; *Latet ut opinor, aliquid Diabolici in his Curis, seu pacti impliciti cum Daemone, ut fere ab omnibus notatum fuit.* In short, theres the Devil in them; yea, an implicit Covenant with the Devil.

In what Fernelius has written, *De abditis rerum causis*, the Curious may read more of these Things. But I would not have quoted these Authors, if I thought our common Fools could come at them. The learned will not be such Fools, as to try the cursed Experiments.

Indeed I am lothe to describe any of these Charms, lest I should unawares instruct some vicious Minds, and furnish them, for a criminal Employment of them; as the excellent Hemingius relates, that he pleasantly reciting to his Pupils, a Distich of unintelligible Terms, which being written and eaten, by one at a Time, on a Peece of Bread, would cure an Ague, by the Time that all the Terms had been so swallowed; a silly, but an honest Youth, taking him in Earnest, made the Experiment, with such Success, that he quickly cured a notable Number of Patients.

I know very well, that Austin reports, that Charms are no longer efficacious, after they come to be divulged. But yett I think, the Divulgation of such Things, as for Instance I find foisted I guess, by the bold whimsical, maggoty Bookseller, into a Book of, *Remarkable Providences*, to have been a very indiscreet and pernicious Action.[6]

---

[6] If this paragraph relates to printer Samuel Green and Increase Mather's *Essay for the Recording of Illustrious Providences* it throws new light on an old controversy.

The wise Reader will but smile at the old Cure for a Quartan Ague, which yett was very seriously praescribed by Serenus Sammonicus, a Physician, and Praeceptor to the younger Gordian, the Roman Emperour.

Maeoniae Iliados quartum suppone timenti.

However, I may venture to complain of such Things, as the nefandous Abuses, which many Jews putt upon the Psalms in our Psalter, when they employ these and those Passages in them, as Charms for the Cure of Diseases, in such Ways, as have been related by Amama, in his *Antibarbarus Biblicus.*

Even the Plant called, *Fuga Daemonium*, has been so employd by People, that the Power and Service of Daemons has been therewith brought into Operation.

How frequently is Bleeding stancht, by writing of Something, with some Ceremonies, on the Forehead!

How frequently is a Toothache eas'd, and an Ulcer stop'd, and an Ague check'd, by Papers, with some Terms and Scrawls in them, sealed up and worn about the Neck.

Famous is the Operation of Abracadabra: a Word wherein some learned Men suppose a Reference to the Chaldee Names for the three Persons in the eternal Godhead: tho' our Selden supposes it may refer to Abraxas, a certain Deity about which he, and Beyerus and Saubertus and others have entertained us with some Strokes of Erudition.

Others besides Lagneus, have done strange Cures, with a magical Staff, made with foolish Regards to the Aspects of the Stars.

The Sigils of Paracelsus being worn, have been follow'd with strange Cures, on some that have been too willing by wearing them to list themselves among the Votaries of the Devil: and become sealed for Perdition.

The *Curatio morborum per mensurationem*, reported by the most learned Pen of the North, is one of these Transgressions wherein the Wicked say, There is no Fear of God before their Eyes.

But that which has been wicked in this Kind, cannot be numbred.

It is not for my Purpose, to make any Delibations here from the *Scrutinium Amuletorum*, published by Jacob Wolff, which has in it a vast Amassment of Things, that occurr in the Writings of the learned, about the many Sorts of superstitious Amulets, wherewith Millions of unadvised People, have surrendred themselves unto Satan, and confessed themselves the Children of the wicked one.

I will only exhibit a Couple of Relations, wherein I think, I may venture to mention the Charms; I need not fear, that any will venture to repeat them.

The one shall be, what Gotschalcus has given us, as what he himself knew to be true. A Woman grievously troubled with sore Eyes, engaged a liberal Reward unto any one that would help her. A Scholar, who was altogether unskilful in Medicine, yett undertook to do it. He gave her a folded Bitt of Paper, which he wrap'd up in a Bag, and order'd her to wear it about her Neck. She did so, and found upon it, a marvellous Releef of the Infirmity. After a Year or two, her Curiosity led her to pry into this wonderworking Paper. Opening of it, she found some Characters of no regular or intended Shape, and this filthy Sentence under-written, *Diabolus eruat tibi Oculos, et foramina stercoribus impleat.* She threw it away with Indignation. But, which is very surprizing; her Infirmity immediately returned upon her. My Author adds; *Unde efficacia, nisi a Daemone, qui ista fraude delectabatur?*

The other, shall be of a late sorrowful Exemple. A gentle Woman in the City of London, that shall be nameless; being troubled and much tired, with an Ague, at Length, came to the Remedy of wearing a folded Bitt of Paper about her Neck. She found her Sickness releeved and removed upon it. But after some Time, she must needs enquire into the Contents of the feverfrighting Paper. Opening of it, she found that fearful Sentence written in it: *Ague, farewell, till thee and I meet in Hell.* It struck her with horrible Consternation. She fell into Horror of Conscience. Her Soul was fill'd with the Terrors of God. She never saw good Hour more in the World. She died in a Despair, that was very lamentable.

My Friend, be warned against such Impiety! Rather undergo any Miseries, as long as an Holy God may please to lay them, and keep them on thee, than repair unto Devils to take them off. They may have Leave to gratify and encourage thy Impiety, with a present Show of Success; but it will be only that they may afterwards exercise a more dreadful Tyranny over thee, and have thee fall as a more certain and woful Prey unto them.

It is old and sage Advice, that we find in the thirty eighth Chapter of Ecclesiasticus: *The Lord has created Medicines out of the Earth, and he that is wise will not abhor them.* Certainly, far from wise, are they that will go to Hell for Medicines: if we are wise we [end of sentence worn off].

Mantissa.

We have a Fancy among our common People, that a Seventh Son among Brethren that have not had a Sister born between them, is endued with I know not what, Power of Healing various Distempers, with a Touch of his Hand upon the Part affected. But may we not be afraid lest some unlawful Fellowship with the Invisible World may ly at the Bottom of it? If we suppose the Matter of Fact, I would enquire:

First; can any reasonable Man imagine, that a Seventh Son should be distinguished naturally, with such a sanative and balsamic Vertue in his Constitution, that he should be like the miraculous Pool, when an Angel made his Descent into it? Why should the intervening of a Sister deprive him of this distinguishing Praerogative? Why should the seventh have it any more than the first-born, to whom there belongs *the Excellency of Dignity and the Excellency of Power?* Yea, is not the first-born as really the seventh as the last? Or, is it requisite, that all the seven have the same Father and Mother: Or, may the Father have the seven sons by different Wives? or, the Mother of these Maccabees, by different Husbands? or, how?

Or, secondly; is it possible to resolve the Matter into any other than a sacramental Original?

Either we must suppose, that the glorious God, before whom we are as the Clay before the Potter, has endued the seventh Son with a Gift of Healing, like that which in the primitive Times of Christianity, recommended some Favourites of Heaven among the first Preachers of the Gospel unto the World; or at least, like that which the famous Greatreats, the Stroker in Ireland, was for a While an unaccountable Instance of. But where have we been taught of God any Thing of this Importance? or, what if the seventh Son should be a vile Person; a Child of Belial; a Devil incarnate? and one belonging to the Tribes that are the abhorred of the Lord?

Or, we must suppose, (what is most likely) that in the Kingdome of Darkness, there is a surprizing Imitation of many Things that occur in the Kingdome of God. And as the Number Seven, has been strangely considered in the Affairs of the Heavenly World, (as well as the Number, Twelve,) so, in the Kingdome of Darkness, it is affected, for the Number Seven to be brought into a peculiar Consideration, (as well as the Number, twenty-five!) And more particularly, an Application to a seventh Son for a Cure, shall be a Sacrament, wherein the Daemons that attend him, shall reckon themselves acknowledged, as the Dispensers of the Cure, that is here looked for!

That the Daemons are very officious to convey Cures, unto the Patients, that with Caeremonies approved by them, do seek unto them, is notorious from the Experience of all Ages, and of all Places, as well as from the Dreams of old obtained in the Temple of Esculapius.

If the healing Vertue be not in the natural Constitution of the seventh Son, must it not needs be in the Operation of some assisting Daemons? And the Homage, or the Regard, that is paid unto the Number Seven in this Way, is the Sacrament that brings the Patient under the Efficacy of it.

But what an enchanted Field are we now brought into: and what a Door is opened unto ten thousand Sorceries! If Numbers are to be esteemed for the Healing of Diseases, why should not Figures be so too? And from Figures let us pass to Letters, yea,

to all the Ephesian ones.   And why should not the seventh Son
pronounce Words, and use his *Lip* as well as his Hand, for a Cure?
And why not also manage the Motions of his Hand, in the Way
of magical Caeremonies?   And would not a Cure be wrought as
effectually, if he should only pronounce Words, and make no Use
of his Hand at all?   Would not a Spell from him do as well as a
Touch?   I doubt it not!

Indeed, I have read concerning the seven Sons of one Sceva a
Jew, among certain Exorcists and Vagabonds, who did some
notable Things.   But among these, all the seven, for ought we
see, were as potent Knaves as the seventh.   And I make no Doubt,
that if People would once take up the Fashion of applying to a
sixth Son, they would find him do as notable Things as now they
think the seventh can do for his ill-advised Patient.

I pray, lett us not foolishly leave the ordinary Ways of Cure,
and run into impertinent, yea, very unwarrantable Superstitions.

In my Opinion; one setting up for, an Healer, no otherwise
qualified and empowered for it, than as being, a seventh Son,
deserves little better Usage than a Quack was wont formerly at
Montpelier to meet withal.   *Is apprehensus Asino imponitur,
et urbe pellitur, ovis putridis et alijs sordibus, sit venia dicto, quae
in ipsum conjiciunt, donec per urbem magno dedecore deductus sit,
alium locum petiturus.*

An Appendix.

Popery ridiculed.

Protestants, be ye thankful that a gracious God has rescued
you from the strong Delusions of Popery, and that you are no
longer under the Fascinations, which the Man of Sin had laid
upon a woful World.   How ridiculously foolish is the revived
Paganism in the popish Idolatries and Superstitions, applying to
such and such particular Saints, for the Cure of these and those
Diseases!   One can hardly recount the Follies of the miserable
Papists in this one Article, without some Thought on St Medard,
the Saint which they say, helps to smiling or laughing.   Most cer-

tainly, if Saint Maturin, whom they make the Physician for
Fools; or Saint Acaire, who cures the Furious, or Saint Avertin
who cures the Lunatic, would exert their pretended Energies, these
Follies would soon be cured in their Votaries. Doubtless the
Saints of such Names were stumbled on for such Cures, because
of some Signification in the Names leading thereunto: as Maturin,
the Saint for *Sotts;* (But, if, to all such, how large his Diocese!)
from the Italian Matto, which comes from the Greek Μὸταιθ .
But how blundred were they, when they made Saint Eutropius
the Physician for a Dropsy, if they confounded Eutropius with
Hydropicus? There is more of Homonymie, in making Saint
Mammard the Physician for Distempers of the Paps: and Saint
Main for those of the Hands; and Saint Phiacre for the (Phy, or)
Emrods; and Saint Genou for the Gout, which is often in the
Knee. There was a grievous Trespass on Chronology, in making
Job, the Physician for the foul Disease. It seems, the heavenly
Physicians in this differ from our terrestrial ones: they don't
profess the Cure of all Diseases as ours do; but Saint John and
Saint Valentine cure only the falling Sickness, (which is called
Saint Johns Evil:) Saint Sebastian cures only the Plague: (and
worthy to be a Saint, could he do that!) Saint Roch cures only
the Scab; (no doubt making People sound as a Roche:) Saint
Petronelle (Saint Peters Daughter) cures Fevers. Saint Romain
dispossesses Devils. But Saint Cosmas and Saint Damia are
only Cheirurgeons. If Saint Claire a woman-Saint cure sore
Eyes, here again there was doubtless an Eye to the Etymology of
the Name; for they tell us, there is no better Way to cure the
Eyes, than to make them see clearly. But sometimes there are
several Saints, that stand Competitors for the Office of curing one
Disease. And Saint Quintin can't peaceably alone enjoy the
Office of curing a Cough. And some have pleaded, that Saint
Christopher may come in with Saint Apollonia for the Cure of
the Toothache, considering the Size of his Tooth, which they
show among their adored Reliques.

But I will stop; not for the Reason given by the witty Henry
Stephens, lest I should purchase the Displeasure of the Colledge

of Physicians; in the Peoples leaving them, and going to the Saints, and I be accused of marring their Market. Nor need we be afraid, that the Saints who may be overlooked, will take the Vengeance of a Saint Antony upon us.

We are by our happy Instruction in the Protestant Religion emancipated from these Fooleries; and instead thereof, we have so learned Christ as to understand, that we have an admirable Saviour, in whom alone we shall truly find All the scattered Powers and Favours, for which the deluded Gentiles have look'd unto their several Idols. And He is a God who will hear them that call upon Him.

Yea, and by hearkening to the Maxims of this Religion, and following and obliging the Holy Author of it, a Man will himself become a Saint, by which there will be greater Cures wrought on him, and Things done for him, than could be expected from all the Saints that are the Inhabitants of the Heavens.

But that we may yett further depreciate the healing Vertues of the Saints; I have been told, that when a languid Pretender to the Crown of Spain to whom the Queen of England lent her Assistances, expressed his Hopes in the blessed Virgin for his obtaining of what he desired, an English General freely and wisely told him, that if his Royal Mistress did him not more Service than Saint Mary, he would have no great Harvest of it. This I will say; a skilful and faithful Physician will do more for a poor Patient than all the Saints in the Romish Kalender.

I will take leave to add this one Thing more. The assigning of particular Plants to particular Planets, or to say, as your Culpepper continually does, that such an Herb is governed by Saturn, and such an one is under the Dominion of Jupiter, and the Rest; it is a Folly akin to the Idolatry and the Superstition of the Roman-Catholicks, in looking to Saints, for their Influences on our several Diseases. Tis amazing to see Mankind so planet-struck; and Men that can handle the Pen of the Writer become so very impertinent and ridiculous.

Index